Basic Computer Engineering

Basic Computer Engineering

Prashant Lakkadwala

M.E. Computer Engg(Automation), B.E. Computer Sci. & Engg.
Diploma Electrical Engg., P.G.C. Cyber Law,
LM-CSI (Secretary- CSI Indore Chapter), LM-ISTE

Asst. Professor and Head,
Computer Science & Engineering and Information Technology Dept.,
Chameli Devi Group of Institutions,
Indore

Swati Lakkadwala
M.C.M, M.C.A

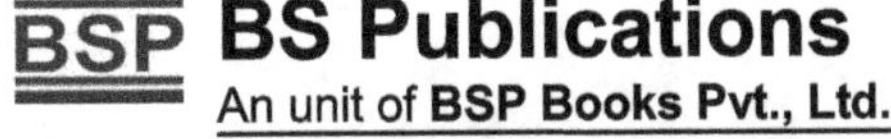

BS Publications
An unit of **BSP Books Pvt., Ltd.**

4-4-309, Giriraj Lane, Sultan Bazar,
Hyderabad - 500 095 - A.P.
Phone : 040 - 23445605, 23445688

Published by :

 **BS Publications**
An unit of **BSP Books Pvt., Ltd.**

4-4-309, Giriraj Lane, Sultan Bazar,
Hyderabad - 500 095 - A.P.
Phone : 040 - 23445605, 23445688
e-mail : info@bspbooks.net
www.bspublications.net

ISBN : 978-93-89974-55-3

Dedicated to

My Grandmother and Grandfather

Preface

The textbook of "Basic Computer Engineering" has been written according to the syllabus prescribed by RGPV, Bhopal for the first year students.

This book is written keeping in mind the needs of B.E. First year all branch students and all other computer courses also. Starting from the very basic of computer concepts with programming knowledge in C++, Operating System, DBMS and Networking concepts, it is presented in such a technical manner, simple and lucid language with neat and self explanatory diagrams, which could be easily understood by average students. It is designed into five chapters;

Chapter 1 Basic concepts of Computer with classification and Application

Chapter 2 Fundamental of Operating system and programming generation and approach

Chapter 3 Basics of C++ and object oriented approach

Chapter 4 Introduction to Database Management System

Chapter 5 Concepts of Networking with Internet and Network Security, E-Commerce.

Also included some programs in C++.

In spite of our best efforts, some errors might have crept in the book. Report of any such errors and all suggestions for improving the future editions of the book are welcome and will be gratefully acknowledged.

Prashant Lakkadwala

Acknowledgement

I strongly believe that the Almighty God alone plans every thing that happens in the world. So, i sincerely thank the Almighty God for showering his blessing upon me and using me to write this book.

I express my profound thanks to my Mother **Smt. Lata Lakkadwala**, Father **Mr. Ashok Lakkadwala**, Brother **Mr. Sushant Lakkadwala** and **Modi family**, who have cultivated devotion and determination in me and have been a deep source of wisdom and inspiration for such initiatives.

I wish to express my deep sense of gratitude to **Mr. Vinod Agrawal** Chairman, **Dr. S. Rajashekharaiah** Director, **Dr. CNS Murthy** Dean, ChameliDevi Group of Institutions, Indore and **Dr. M. Chandwani**, **Dr.Durgesh Kumar Mishra** for their kind co-operation and motivation for writing this book.

I express my gratefulness and appreciation to all my academic colleagues who gave me valuable suggestion during the course of preparation of this book.

I would like to express my affection appreciation to my wife **Mrs. Swati Lakkadwala** and loving little son **Aayushyamaan** whose precious and cheerful time i pilfered time to time to fulfill the task in time.

In the end, I am highly obliged to production teams of BS Publication for their encouraging interactions with me throughout the production process of the book in its present form in record time.

Any suggestion for improving the contents would be warmly appreciated.

Prashant Lakkadwala

Contents

Basic Concepts of Computer with Classification and Application

Objectives

At the end of this session, the learner will be able to:

Define computer and it's classification.

Write the element of CPU.

Summaries the Instruction set and Bus architecture.

Define the computer Ethics.

Discuss computer application in various field.

Illustrate multimedia and animation.

Introduction

Computers have an important impact on our daily life and are a necessary tool which help better living of mankind. Today's highly developed and sophisticated world, the food processing and marketing, water management for various crops on a piece of saline land, and many others like this are computer analyzed and computer aided solutions of complicated problems. In an increasing number of situations, the computer is a visible component of scientific, manufacturing, engineering, business, marketing, and other activities.

The impact of industrialization on the life style of mankind can be visualised by means of increasing needs and complexity of life style. Various driving forces and their counterparts forced to think for information technology that can be utilised through database for decision making and managerial solutions. Collection of data and their processing is a big, tedious and cumbersome task. Today's modern life style does not permit even a single day to be wasted. The management of huge amount of data for efficient decisions can be achieved by Electronic Data Processing Systems which handle data storage, retrieval and produce meaningful outputs in a comparatively very less time period.

A question may arise in your mind as to what is computer? Computer is an electronic device that can perform substantial computations of repeated, complicated and cumbersome calculations, may be arithmetical or logical, with high precision of accuracy practically in very short time. Technically, a computer is a programmable machine. This means it can execute a programmed list of instructions and respond to new instructions that it is given. Today, however, the term is most often used to refer to the desktop and laptop computers that most people use. When referring to a desktop model, the term "computer" technically only refers to the computer itself -- not the monitor, keyboard, and mouse. Still, it is acceptable to refer to everything together as the computer. If you want to be really technical, the box that holds the computer is called the "system unit."

Some of the major parts of a personal computer (or PC) include the motherboard, CPU, memory (or RAM), hard drive, and video card. While personal computers are by far the most common type of computers today, there are several other types of computers. For example, a "minicomputer" is a powerful computer that can support many users at once. A "mainframe" is a large, high-powered computer that can perform billions of calculations from multiple sources at one time. Finally, a "supercomputer" is a machine that can process billions of instructions a second and is used to calculate extremely complex calculations.

Generations of Computer

A generation refers to the state of improvement in the development of a product. This term is also used in the different advancements of computer technology. With each new generation, the circuitry has gotten smaller and more advanced than the previous generation before it. As a result of the miniaturization, speed, power, and memory of computers have proportionally increased. New discoveries are constantly being developed that affect the way we live, work and play.

The First Generation: 1946-1958 (The Vacuum Tube)

The first generation computers were huge, slow, expensive, and often undependable. In 1946two Americans, Presper Eckert, and John Mauchly built the ENIAC electronic computer which used vacuum tubes instead of the mechanical switches of the Mark I. The ENIAC used thousands of vacuum tubes, which took up a lot of space and gave off a great deal of heat just like light bulbs do. The ENIAC led to other vacuum tube type computers like the EDVAC (Electronic Discrete Variable Automatic Computer) and the UNIVAC I (UNIVersal Automatic Computer).

The vacuum tube was an extremely important step in the advancement of computers. Vacuum tubes were invented the same time the light bulb was invented by Thomas Edison and worked very similar to light bulbs. It's purpose was to act like an amplifier and a switch. Without any moving parts, vacuum tubes could take very weak signals and make the signal stronger (amplify it). Vacuum tubes could also stop and start the flow of electricity instantly (switch). These two properties made the ENIAC computer possible.

The ENIAC gave off so much heat that they had to be cooled by gigantic air conditioners. However even with these huge coolers, vacuum tubes still overheated regularly. It was time for something new. First generation computers relied on machine language, the lowest-level programming language understood by computers, to perform operations and they could only solve one problem at a time. Input was based on punched cards and paper tape, and output was displayed on printouts.

The Second Generation: 1959-1964 (The Era of the Transistor)

The transistor computer did not last as long as the vacuum tube computer lasted, but it was no less important in the advancement of computer technology. In 1947 three scientists, John Bardeen, William Shockley, and Walter Brattain working at AT&T's Bell Labs invented what would replace the vacuum tube forever. This invention was the transistor which functions like a vacuum tube in that it can be used to relay and switch electronic signals.

There were obvious differences between the transistor and the vacuum tube. The transistor was faster, more reliable, smaller, and much cheaper to build than a vacuum tube. One transistor replaced the equivalent of 40 vacuum tubes. These transistors were made of solid material, some of which is silicon, an abundant element (second only to oxygen) found in beach sand and glass. Therefore they were very cheap to produce. Transistors were found to conduct electricity faster and better than vacuum tubes. They were also much smaller and gave off virtually no heat compared to vacuum tubes. Their use marked a new beginning for the computer. Without this invention, space travel in the 1960's would not have been possible. However, a new invention would even further advance our ability to use computers.

Second-generation computers moved from cryptic binary machine language to symbolic, or assembly, languages, which allowed programmers to specify instructions in words. High-level programming languages were also being developed at this time, such as early versions of COBOL and FORTRAN. These were also the first computers that stored their instructions in their memory, which moved from a magnetic drum to magnetic core technology. The first computers of this generation were developed for the atomic energy industry.

The Third Generation: 1965-1970 (Integrated Circuits - Miniaturizing the Computer)

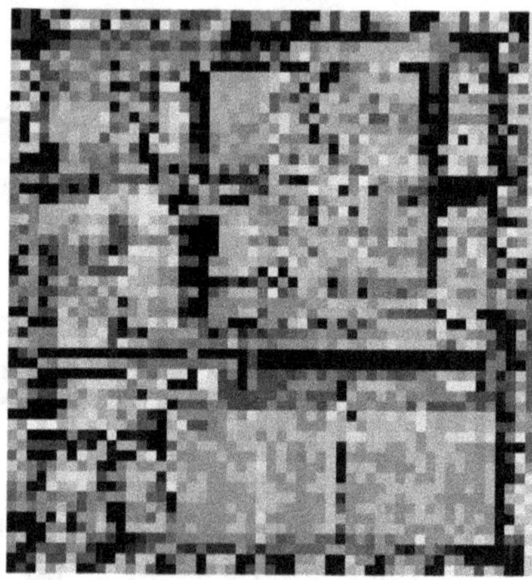

Transistors were a tremendous breakthrough in advancing the computer. However no one could predict that thousands even now millions of transistors (circuits) could be compacted in such a small space. The integrated circuit, or as it is sometimes referred to as semiconductor chip, packs a huge number of transistors onto a single wafer of silicon. Robert Noyce of Fairchild Corporation and Jack Kilby of Texas Instruments independently discovered the amazing attributes of integrated circuits. Placing such large numbers of transistors on a single chip vastly increased the power of a single computer and lowered its cost considerably.

Since the invention of integrated circuits, the number of transistors that can be placed on a single chip has doubled every two years, shrinking both the size and cost of computers even further and further enhancing its power. Most electronic devices today use some form of integrated circuits placed on printed circuit boards-- thin pieces of bakelite or fiberglass that have electrical connections etched onto them -- sometimes called a mother board.

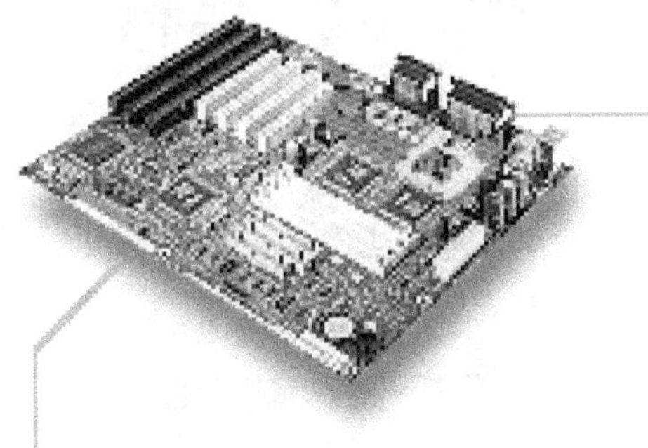

These third generation computers could carry out instructions in billionths of a second. The size of these machines dropped to the size of small file cabinets. Yet, the single biggest advancement in the computer era was yet to be discovered.

Instead of punched cards and printouts, users interacted with third generation computers through keyboards and monitors and interfaced with an operating system, which allowed the device to run many different applications at one time with a central program that monitored the memory. Computers for the first time became accessible to a mass audience because they were smaller and cheaper than their predecessors.

The Fourth Generation: 1971-1995 (The Microprocessor)

This generation can be characterized by both the jump to monolithic integrated circuits (millions of transistors put onto one integrated circuit chip) and the invention of the microprocessor (a single chip that could do all the processing of a full-scale computer). By putting millions of transistors onto one single chip more calculation and faster speeds could be reached by computers. Because electricity travels about a foot in a billionth of a second, the smaller the distance the greater the speed of computers.

However what really triggered the tremendous growth of computers and its significant impact on our lives is the invention of the microprocessor. Ted Hoff, employed by Intel (Robert Noyce's new company) invented a chip the size of a pencil eraser that could do all the computing and logic work of a computer. The microprocessor was made to be used in calculators, not computers. It led, however, to the invention of personal computers, or microcomputers.

It wasn't until the 1970's that people began buying computer for personal use. One of the earliest personal computers was the Altair 8800 computer kit. In 1975 you could purchase this kit and put it together to make your own personal computer. In 1977 the Apple II was sold to the public and in 1981 IBM entered the PC (personal computer) market. Today we have all heard of Intel and its Pentium® Processors and now we know how it all got started. The computers of the next generation will have millions upon millions of transistors on one chip and will perform over a billion calculations in a single second. There is no end in sight for the computer movement.

The Fifth Generation (Present and Beyond) Artificial Intelligence

Fifth generation computing devices, based on artificial intelligence, are still in development, though there are some applications, such as voice recognition, that are being used today. The use of parallel processing and superconductors is helping to make artificial intelligence a reality. Quantum computation and molecular and nanotechnology will radically change the face of computers in years to come. The goal of fifth-generation computing is to develop devices that respond to natural language input and are capable of learning and self-organization.

Quick view of Generations of computer

Generations	Period	Electronic component	Introduced Computers
First	1946-1958	Vacuum Tube	ENIAC, EDSAC, EDVAC
Second	1959-1964	Transistor	IBM 7070, UNIVAC 490
Third	1965-1970	Integrated Circuits	UNIVAC 1100 & 9000
Fourth	1971-1995	Large Scale Integrated Circuits	STAR 1000, DEC 1090
Fifth	1995 onwards	Very Large Scale Integrated Circuits	INTEL, IBM 370

Characteristics of Computer

Now-a-days computer is playing a main role in everyday life it has become the need of people just like television, telephone or other electronic devices at home. It solves the human problems very quickly as well as accurately. The important characteristics of a computer are described below:

1. *Speed*: The computer is a very high speed electronic device. The operations on the data inside the computer are performed through electronic circuits according to the given instructions. The data and instructions flow along these circuits with high speed that is close to the speed of light. Computer can perform million of billion of operations on the data in one second. The computer generates

signals during the operation process therefore the speed of computer is usually measure in mega hertz (MHz) or gega hertz (GHz). It means million cycles units of frequency is hertz per second. Different computers have different speed.

2. ***Arithmetical and Logical Operations***: A computer can perform arithmetical and logical operations. In arithmetic operations, it performs the addition, subtraction, multiplication and division on the numeric data. In logical operation it compares the numerical data as well as alphabetical data.

3. ***Accuracy***: In addition to being very fast, computer is also very accurate device. it gives accurate output result provided that the correct input data and set of instructions are given to the computer. It means that output is totally depended on the given instructions and input data. If input data is in-correct then the resulting output will be in-correct. In computer terminology it is known as garbage-in garbage-out.

4. ***Reliability***: The electronic components in modern computer have very low failure rate. The modern computer can perform very complicated calculations without creating any problem and produces consistent (reliable) results. In general, computers are very reliable. Many personal computers have never needed a service call. Communications are also very reliable and generally available whenever needed.

5. ***Storage***: A computer has internal storage (memory) as well as external or secondary storage. In secondary storage, a large amount of data and programs (set of instructions) can be stored for future use. The stored data and programs are available any time for processing. Similarly information downloaded from the internet can be saved on the storage media.

6. ***Retrieving data and programs***: The data and program stored on the storage media can be retrieved very quickly for further processing. It is also very important feature of a computer.

7. **Automation:** A computer can automatically perform operations without interfering the user during the operations. It controls automatically different devices attached with the computer. It executes automatically the program instructions one by one.

8. ***Versatility***: Versatile means flexible. Modern computer can perform different kind of tasks one by one of simultaneously. It is

the most important feature of computer. At one moment your are playing game on computer, the next moment you are composing and sending emails etc. In colleges and universities computers are use to deliver lectures to the students. The talent of computer is dependent on the software.

9. *Communications*: Today computer is mostly used to exchange messages or data through computer networks all over the world. For example the information can be received or send throug the internet with the help of computer. It is most important feature of the modern information technology.

10. *Diligence*: A computer can continually work for hours without creating any error. It does not get tired while working after hours of work it performs the operations with the same accuracy as well as speed as the first one.

11. *No Feelings*: Computer is an electronic machine. It has no feelings. It detects objects on the basis of instructions given to it. Based on our feelings, taste, knowledge and experience: we can make certain decisions and judgments in our daily life. On the other hand, computer can not make such judgments on their own. Their judgments are totally based on instructions given to them.

12. *Consistency*: People often have difficulty to repeat their instructions again and again. For example, a lecturer feels difficulty to repeat a same lecture in a class room again and again. Computer can repeat actions consistently (again and again) without loosing its concentration:

To run a spell checker (built into a word processor) for checking spellings in a document.

To play multimedia animations for training purposes.

To deliver a lecture through computer in a class room etc.

A computer will carry out the activity with the same way every time. You can listen a lecture or perform any action again and again.

13. *Precision*: Computers are not only fast and consistent but they also perform operations very accurately and precisely. For example, in manual calculations and rounding fractional values (That is value with decimal point can change the actual result). In computer however, you can keep the accuracy and precision up to the level, you desire. The length calculations remain always accurate.

Classification of Computers

Computers are classified according to their data processing speed, amount of data that they can hold and price. Generally, a computer with high processing speed and large internal storage is called a big computer. Due to rapidly improving technology, we are always confused among the categories of computers.

Depending upon their speed and memory size, computers are classified into following four main groups.

1. Supercomputer
2. Mainframe computer
3. Mini computer
4. Microcomputer

1. **Super Computer:** Supercomputer is the most powerful and fastest, and also very expensive. It was developed in 1980s. It is used to process large amount of data and to solve the complicated scientific problems. It can perform more than one trillions calculations per second. It has large number of processors connected parallel. So parallel processing is done in this computer. In a single supercomputer thousands of users can be connected at the same time and the supercomputer handles the work of each user separately. Supercomputer are mainly used for:

   Weather forecasting.

   Nuclear energy research.

   Aircraft design.

   Automotive design.

   Online banking.

   To control industrial units.

   The supercomputers are used in large organizations, research laboratories, aerospace centers, large industrial units etc. Nuclear scientists use supercomputers to create and analyze models of nuclear fission and fusions, predicting the actions and reactions of millions of atoms as they interact. The examples of supercomputers are CRAY-1, CRAY-2, Control Data CYBER 205 and ETA A-10 etc.

2. **Mainframe Computers:** Mainframe computers are also large-scale computers but supercomputers are larger than mainframe. These are also very expensive. The mainframe computer specially

requires a very large clean room with air-conditioner. This makes it very expensive to buy and operate. It can support a large number of various equipment. It also has multiple processors. Large mainframe systems can handle the input and output requirements of several thousand of users. For example, IBM, S/390 mainframe can support 50,000 users simultaneously. The users often access then mainframe with terminals or personal computers. There are basically two types of terminals used with mainframe systems. These are:

(i)   *Dumb Terminal*: Dumb terminal does not have its own CPU and storage devices. This type of terminal uses the CPU and storage devices of mainframe system. Typically, a dumb terminal consists of monitor and a keyboard (or mouse).

(ii) *Intelligent Terminal*: Intelligent terminal has its own processor and can perform some processing operations. Usually, this type of terminal does not have its own storage. Typically, personal computrers are used as intelligent terminals. A personal computer as an intelligent terminal gives facility to access data and other services from mainframe system. It also enables to store and process data locally. The mainframe computers are specially used as servers on the World Wide Web. The mainframe computers are used in large organizations such as Banks, Airlines and Universities etc. where many people (users) need frequent access to the same data, which is usually organized into one or more huge databases. IBM is the major manufacturer of mainframe computers. The examples of mainframes are IBM S/390, Control Data CYBER 176 and Amdahl 580 etc.

3. **Minicomputers:** These are smaller in size, have lower processing speed and also have lower cost than mainframe. These computers are known as minicomputers because of their small size as compared to other computers at that time. The capabilities of a minicomputer are between mainframe and personal computer. These computers are also known as midrange computers.

The minicomputers are used in business, education and many other government departments. Although some minicomputers are designed for a single user but most are designed to handle multiple terminals. Minicomputers are commonly used as servers in network environment and hundreds of personal computers can be connected to the network with a minicomputer acting as server like mainframes, minicomputers are used as web servers. Single user minicomputers are used for sophisticated design tasks.

The first minicomputer was introduced in the mid-1960s by Digital Equipment Corporation (DEC). After this IBM Corporation (AS/400 computers) Data General Corporation and Prime Computer also designed the mini computers.

4. **Microcomputer:** The microcomputers are also known as personal computers or simply PCs. Microprocessor is used in this type of computer. These are very small in size and cost. The IBM's first microcomputer was designed in 1981 and was named as IBM-PC. After this many computer hardware companies copied the design of IBM-PC. The term "PC-compatible" refers any personal computer based on the original IBM personal computer design.

The most popular types of personal computers are the PC and the Apple. PC and PC-compatible computers have processors with different architectures than processors in Apple computers. These two types of computers also use different operating systems. PC and PC-compatible computers use the Windows operating system while Apple computers use the Macintosh operating system (MacOS). The majority of microcomputers sold today are part of IBM-compatible. However the Apple computer is neither an IBM nor a compatible. It is another family of computers made by Apple computer.

Personal computers are available in two models. These are:

1. Desktop PCs

2. Tower PCs

A desktop personal computer is most popular model of personal computer. The system unit of the desktop personal computer can lie flat on the desk or table. In desktop personal computer, the monitor is usually placed on the system unit.

Another model of the personal computer is known as tower personal computer. The system unit of the tower PC is vertically placed on the desk of table. Usually the system unit of the tower model is placed on the floor to make desk space free and user can place other devices such as printer, scanner etc. on the desktop. Today computer tables are available which are specially designed for this purpose. The tower models are mostly used at homes and offices.

Microcomputer are further divided into following categories.

1. Laptop computer
2. Workstation
3. Network computer
4. Hand-held computer

1. **Laptop computer:** Laptop computer is also known as notebook computer. It is small size (85-by-11 inch notebook computer and can fit inside a briefcase. The laptop computer is operated on a special battery and it does not have to be plugged in like desktop computer. The laptop computer is portable and fully functional microcomputer. It is mostly used during journey. It can be used on your lap in an airplane. It is because it is referred to as laptop computer.

   The memory and storage capacity of laptop computer is almost equivalent to the PC or desktop computer. It also has the hard dist, floppy disk drive, Zip disk drive, CD-ROM drive, CD-writer etc. it has built-in keyboard and built-in trackball as pointing device. Laptop computer is also available with the same processing speed as the most powerful personal computer. It means that laptop computer has same features as personal computer. Laptop computers are more expensive than desktop computers. Normally these computers are frequently used in business travelers.

2. **Workstations:** Workstations are special single user computers having the same features as personal computer but have the processing speed equivalent to minicomputer or mainframe computer. A workstation computer can be fitted on a desktop. Scientists, engineers, architects and graphic designers mostly use these computers.

   Workstation computers are expensive and powerful computers. These have advanced processors, more RAM and storage capacity than personal computers. These are usually used as single-user applications but these are used as servers on computer network and web servers as well.

3. **Network computers:** Network computers are also version of personal computers having less processing power, memory and storage. These are specially designed as terminals for network environment. Some types of network computers have no storage. The network computers are designed for network, Internet or Intranet for data entry or to access data on the network. The

network computers depend upon the network's server for data storage and to use software. These computers also use the network's server to perform some processing tasks.

In the mid-1990s the concept of network computers became popular among some PC manufacturers. As a result several variations of the network computers quickly became available. In business, variations of the network computer are Windows terminals, NetPCs and diskless workstations. Some network computers are designed to access only the Internet or to an Intranet. These devices are sometimes called Internet PCs, Internet boxes etc. In home some network computers do not include monitor. These are connected to home television, which serves as the output devices. A popular example of a home-based network computer is Web TV, which enables the user to connect a television to the Internet. The Web TV has a special set-top box used to connect to the Internet and also provides a set of simple controls which enable the user to navigate the Internet, send and receive e-mails and to perform other tasks on the network while watching television.

Network computers are cheaper to purchase and to maintain than personal computers.

4. **Hand held computer:** In the mid 1990s, many new types of small personal computing devices have been introduced and these are referred to as hand held computers. These computers are also referred to as Palmtop Computers. The hand held computers sometimes called Mini-Notebook Computers. The type of computer is named as hand held computer because it can fit in one hand while you can operate it with the other hand. Because of its reduced size, the screen of hand-held computer is quite small. Similarly it also has small keyboard. The hand held computers are preferred by business traveler. Some hand-held computers have a specialized keyboard. These computers are used by mobile employees, such as meter readers and parcel delivery people, whose jobs require them to move from place to place.

The examples of hand-held computers are:

1. Personal Digital Assistance

2. Cellular telephones

3. H/PC Pro devices

1. **Personal Digital Assistance (PDAs):** The PDA is one of the more popular lightweight mobile devices in use today. A PDA provides special functions such as taking notes, organizing telephone numbers and addresses. Most PDAs also offer a variety of other application software such as word processing, spreadsheet and games etc. Some PDAs include electronic books that enable users to read a book on the PDA's screen.

   Many PDAs are web-based and users can send/receive e-mails and access the Internet. Similarly, some PDAs also provide telephone capabilities.

   The primary input device of a PDA is the stylus. A stylus is an electronic pen and looks like a small ballpoint pen. This input device is used to write notes and store in the PDA by touching the screen. Some PDAs also support voice input.

2. **Cellular Phones:** A cellular phone is a web-based telephone having features of analog and digital devices. It is also referred to as Smart Phone. In addition to basic phone capabilities, a cellular phone also provides the functions to receive and send e-mails & faxes and to access the Internet.

3. **H/PC Pro Devices:** H/PC Pro dive is new development in hand-held technology. These systems are larger than PDAs but they are not quite as large as typical notebook PCs. These devices have features between PDAs and notebook PCs. The H/PC Pro device includes a full-size keyboard but it does not include disk. These systems also have RAM with very low storage capacity and slow speed of processor.

Organization of Computer: Organization of computer means how different parts of a computer are organized and how various operations are performed between different parts to do a specific task. the internal architecture of computer may differ from system to system, but the basic organization remains the same for all computer systems.

Basic Computer Operations

A computer as shown in Fig. performs basically five major operations or functions irrespective of their size and make. These are 1. it accepts data or instructions by way of input, 2. it stores data, 3. it can process data as required by the user, 4. it gives results in the form of output, and 5. it controls all operations inside a computer. We discuss below each of these operations.

1. **Input:** This is the process of entering data and programs in to the computer system. You should know that computer is an electronic machine like any other machine which takes as inputs raw data and performs some processing giving out processed data. Therefore, the input unit takes data from us to the computer in an organized manner for processing.

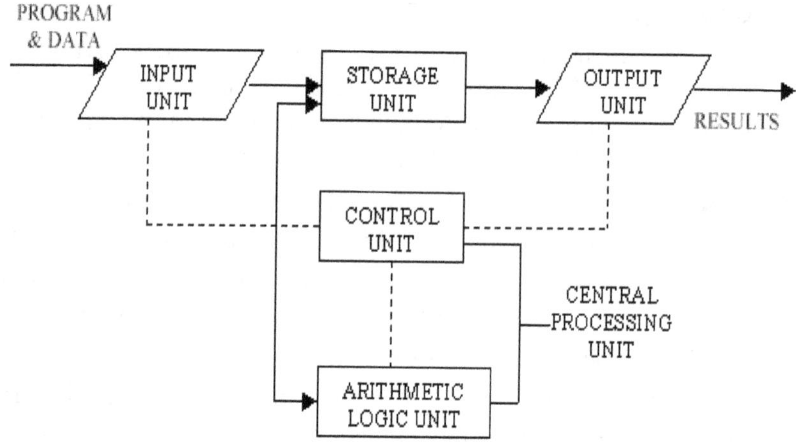

Fig.1.1 Basic computer Operations.

2. **Storage:** The process of saving data and instructions permanently is known as storage. Data has to be fed into the system before the actual processing starts. It is because the processing speed of Central Processing Unit (CPU) is so fast that the data has to be provided to CPU with the same speed. Therefore the data is first stored in the storage unit for faster access and processing. This storage unit or the primary storage of the computer system is designed to do the above functionality. It provides space for storing data and instructions.

The storage unit performs the following major functions:

All data and instructions are stored here before and after processing.

Intermediate results of processing are also stored here.

3. **Processing**: The task of performing operations like arithmetic and logical operations is called processing. The Central Processing Unit (CPU) takes data and instructions from the storage unit and makes all sorts of calculations based on the instructions given and the type of data provided. It is then sent back to the storage unit.

4. **Output:** This is the process of producing results from the data for getting useful information. Similarly the output produced by the computer after processing must also be kept somewhere inside the computer before being given to you in human readable form. Again the output is also stored inside the computer for further processing.

5. **Control:** The manner how instructions are executed and the above operations are performed. Controlling of all operations like input, processing and output are performed by control unit. It takes care of step by step processing of all operations in side the computer.

Functional Units

In order to carry out the operations mentioned in the previous section the computer allocates the task between its various functional units. The computer system is divided into three separate units for its operation. They are 1. arithmetic logical unit, 2. control unit, and 3. central processing unit.

1. **Arithmetic Logical Unit (ALU):** After you enter data through the input device it is stored in the primary storage unit. The actual processing of the data and instruction are performed by Arithmetic Logical Unit. The major operations performed by the ALU are addition, subtraction, multiplication, division, logic and comparison. Data is transferred to ALU from storage unit when required. After processing the output is returned back to storage unit for further processing or getting stored.

2. **Control Unit (CU):** The next component of computer is the Control Unit, which acts like the supervisor seeing that things are done in proper fashion. The control unit determines the sequence in which computer programs and instructions are executed. Things like processing of programs stored in the main memory, interpretation of the instructions and issuing of signals for other units of the computer to execute them. It also acts as a switch board

operator when several users access the computer simultaneously. Thereby it coordinates the activities of computer's peripheral equipment as they perform the input and output. Therefore it is the manager of all operations mentioned in the previous section.

3. **Central Processing Unit (CPU):** The ALU and the CU of a computer system are jointly known as the central processing unit. You may call CPU as the brain of any computer system. It is just like brain that takes all major decisions, makes all sorts of calculations and directs different parts of the computer functions by activating and controlling the operations.

Personal Computer Configuration

Now let us identify the physical components that make the computer work. *These are*:

1. Central Processing Unit (CPU)
2. Computer Memory (RAM and ROM)
3. Data bus
4. Ports
5. Motherboard
6. Hard disk
7. Output Devices
8. Input Devices

All these components are inter-connected for the personal computer to work.

Registers

A special, high-speed storage area within the CPU. All data must be represented in a register before it can be processed. For example, if two numbers are to be multiplied, both numbers must be in registers, and the result is also placed in a register. (The register can contain the address of a memory location where data is stored rather than the actual data itself.)

The number of registers that a CPU has and the size of each (number of bits) help determine the power and speed of a CPU. For example a 32-bit CPU is one in which each register is 32 bits wide. Therefore, each CPU instruction can manipulate 32 bits of data.

Usually, the movement of data in and out of registers is completely transparent to users, and even to programmers. Only assembly language programs can manipulate registers. In high-level languages, the compiler is responsible for translating high-level operations into low-level operations that access registers.

Bus Architecture

Definition: A set of parallel conductors, which allow devices attached to it to communicate with the CPU.

The bus consists of three main parts:

1. Control lines
2. Address lines
3. Data lines

1. ***Control lines***: These allow the CPU to control which operations the devices attached should perform, I.E. read or write.

2. ***Address lines***: Allows the CPU to reference certain (Memory) locations within the device.

3. ***Data lines***: The meaningful data which is to be sent or retrieved from a device is placed on to these lines.

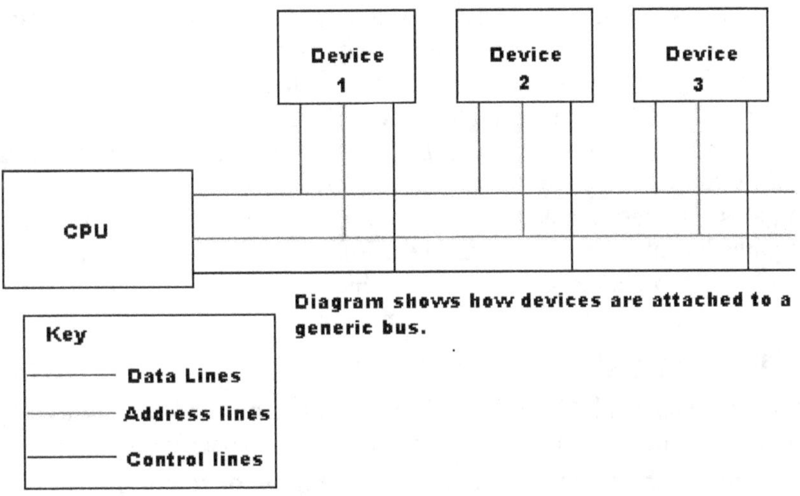

Diagram shows how devices are attached to a generic bus.

The Bus is set to run at a specified speed which is measured in MHz.

Instruction Set

An instruction set, or instruction set architecture (ISA), is the part of the computer architecture related to programming, including the native data types, instructions, registers, addressing modes, memory architecture, interrupt and exception handling, and external I/O. An ISA includes a specification of the set of opcodes (machine language), and the native commands implemented by a particular processor.

Instruction set architecture is distinguished from the microarchitecture, which is the set of processor design techniques used to implement the instruction set. Computers with different microarchitectures can share a common instruction set. For example, the Intel Pentium and the AMD Athlon implement nearly identical versions of the x86 instruction set, but have radically different internal designs.

This concept can be extended to unique ISAs like TIMI (Technology-Independent Machine Interface) present in the IBM System/38 and IBM AS/400. TIMI is an ISA that is implemented by low-level software translating TIMI code into "native" machine code, and functionally resembles what is now referred to as a virtual machine. It was designed to increase the longevity of the platform and applications written for it, allowing the entire platform to be moved to very different hardware without having to modify any software except that which translates TIMI into native machine code, and the code that implements services used by the resulting native code. This allowed IBM to move the AS/400 platform from an older CISC architecture to the newer POWER architecture without having to rewrite or recompile any parts of the OS or software associated with it other than the aforementioned low-level code. Some virtual machines that support bytecode for Smalltalk, the Java virtual machine, and Microsoft's Common Language Runtime virtual machine as their ISA implement it by translating the bytecode for commonly-used code paths into native machine code, and executing less-frequently-used code paths by interpretation; Transmeta implemented the x86 instruction set atop VLIW processors in the same fashion.

Machine Language

Machine language is built up from discrete statements or instructions. On the processing architecture, a given instruction may specify:

- Particular registers for arithmetic, addressing, or control functions
- Particular memory locations or offsets
- Particular addressing modes used to interpret the operands

More complex operations are built up by combining these simple instructions, which (in a von Neumann architecture) are executed sequentially, or as otherwise directed by control flow instructions.

Some operations available in most instruction sets include:

Data Handling and Memory Operations

Set a register (a temporary "scratchpad" location in the CPU itself) to a fixed constant value move data from a memory location to a register, or vice versa. This is done to obtain the data to perform a computation on it later, or to store the result of a computation. read and write data from hardware devices

Arithmetic and Logic

Add, subtract, multiply, or divide the values of two registers, placing the result in a register perform bitwise operations, taking the conjunction and disjunction of corresponding bits in a pair of registers, or the negation of each bit in a register compare two values in registers (for example, to see if one is less, or if they are equal).

Control Flow

Branch to another location in the program and execute instructions there conditionally branch to another location if a certain condition holds indirectly branch to another location, but save the location of the next instruction as a point to return to (a call)

Some computers include "complex" instructions in their instruction set. A single "complex" instruction does something that may take many instructions on other computers. Such instructions are typified by instructions that take multiple steps, control multiple functional units, or otherwise appear on a larger scale than the bulk of simple instructions implemented by the given processor. Some examples of "complex" instructions include:

- saving many registers on the stack at once
- moving large blocks of memory
- complex and/or floating-point arithmetic (sine, cosine, square root, etc.)
- performing an atomic test-and-set instruction
- instructions that combine ALU with an operand from memory rather than a register

A complex instruction type that has become particularly popular recently is the SIMD or Single-Instruction Stream Multiple-Data Stream operation or vector instruction, an operation that performs the same arithmetic operation on multiple pieces of data at the same time. SIMD have the ability of manipulating large vectors and matrices in minimal time. SIMD instructions allow easy parallelization of algorithms commonly involved in sound, image, and video processing. Various SIMD implementations have been brought to market under trade names such as MMX, 3DNow! and AltiVec.

The design of instruction sets is a complex issue. There were two stages in history for the microprocessor. The first was the CISC (Complex Instruction Set Computer) which had many different instructions. In the 1970s, however, places like IBM did research and found that many instructions in the set could be eliminated. The result was the RISC (Reduced Instruction Set Computer), an architecture which uses a smaller set of instructions. A simpler instruction set may offer the potential for higher speeds, reduced processor size, and reduced power consumption. However, a more complex set may optimize common operations, improve memory/cache efficiency, or simplify programming.

Memory and Storage Systems

Computer data storage, often called storage or memory, refers to computer components and recording media that retain digital data used for computing for some interval of time. Computer data storage provides one of the core functions of the modern computer, that of information retention. It is one of the fundamental components of all modern computers, and coupled with a central processing unit (CPU, a processor), implements the basic computer model used since the 1940s.

In contemporary usage, memory usually refers to a form of semiconductor storage known as random-access memory, typically DRAM (Dynamic-RAM) but many times other forms of fast but temporary storage. Similarly, storage today more commonly refers to storage devices and their media not directly accessible by the CPU (secondary or tertiary storage) — typically hard disk drives, optical disc drives, and other devices slower than RAM but more permanent. Historically, memory has been called main memory, real storage or internal memory while storage devices have been referred to as secondary storage, external memory or auxiliary/peripheral storage).

Primary Storage (or main memory or internal memory), often referred to simply as memory, is the only one directly accessible to the CPU. The CPU continuously reads instructions stored there and executes them as required. Any data actively operated on is also stored there in uniform manner.

Historically, early computers used delay lines, Williams tubes, or rotating magnetic drums as primary storage. By 1954, those unreliable methods were mostly replaced by magnetic core memory. Core memory remained dominant until the 1970s, when advances in integrated circuit technology allowed semiconductor memory to become economically competitive.

This led to modern random-access memory (RAM). It is small-sized, light, but quite expensive at the same time. (The particular types of RAM used for primary storage are also volatile, i.e. they lose the information when not powered).

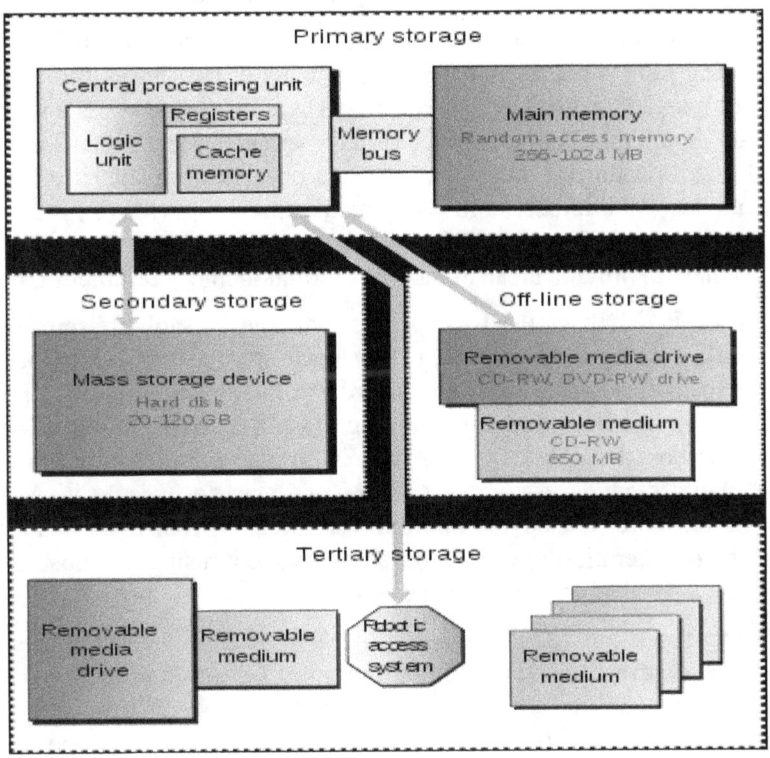

As shown in the diagram, traditionally there are two more sub-layers of the primary storage, besides main large-capacity RAM:

- Processor registers are located inside the processor. Each register typically holds a word of data (often 32 or 64 bits). CPU instructions instruct the arithmetic and logic unit to perform various calculations or other operations on this data (or with the help of it). Registers are technically among the fastest of all forms of computer data storage.

- Processor cache is an intermediate stage between ultra-fast registers and much slower main memory. It's introduced solely to increase performance of the computer. Most actively used information in the main memory is just duplicated in the cache memory, which is faster, but of much lesser capacity. On the other hand it is much slower, but much larger than processor registers. Multi-level hierarchical cache setup is also commonly used— primary cache being smallest, fastest and located inside the processor; secondary cache being somewhat larger and slower.

Main memory is directly or indirectly connected to the central processing unit via a memory bus. It is actually two buses (not on the diagram): an address bus and a data bus. The CPU firstly sends a number through an address bus, a number called memory address, that indicates the desired location of data. Then it reads or writes the data itself using the data bus. Additionally, a memory management unit (MMU) is a small device between CPU and RAM recalculating the actual memory address, for example to provide an abstraction of virtual memory or other tasks.

As the RAM types used for primary storage are volatile (cleared at start up), a computer containing only such storage would not have a source to read instructions from, in order to start the computer. Hence, non-volatile primary storage containing a small startup program (BIOS) is used to bootstrap the computer, that is, to read a larger program from non-volatile secondary storage to RAM and start to execute it. A non-volatile technology used for this purpose is called ROM, for read-only memory (the terminology may be somewhat confusing as most ROM types are also capable of random access).

Many types of "ROM" are not literally read only, as updates are possible; however it is slow and memory must be erased in large portions before it can be re-written. Some embedded systems run programs directly from ROM (or similar), because such programs are rarely changed. Standard computers do not store non-rudimentary programs in

ROM, rather use large capacities of secondary storage, which is non-volatile as well, and not as costly.

Secondary Storage (also known as external memory or auxiliary storage), differs from primary storage in that it is not directly accessible by the CPU. The computer usually uses its input/output channels to access secondary storage and transfers the desired data using intermediate area in primary storage. Secondary storage does not lose the data when the device is powered down, it is non-volatile. Per unit, it is typically also two orders of magnitude less expensive than primary storage. Consequently, modern computer systems typically have two orders of magnitude more secondary storage than primary storage and data is kept for a longer time there.

In modern computers, **hard disk drives** are usually used as secondary storage. The time taken to access a given byte of information stored on a hard disk is typically a few thousandths of a second, or milliseconds. By contrast, the time taken to access a given byte of information stored in random access memory is measured in billionths of a second, or nanoseconds. This illustrates the very significant access-time difference which distinguishes solid-state memory from rotating magnetic storage devices: hard disks are typically about a million times slower than memory. **Rotating optical storage devices, such as CD and DVD drives,** have even longer access times. With disk drives, once the disk read/write head reaches the proper placement and the data of interest rotates under it, subsequent data on the track are very fast to access. As a result, in order to hide the initial seek time and rotational latency, data are transferred to and from disks in large contiguous blocks.

When data reside on disk, block access to hide latency offers a ray of hope in designing efficient external memory algorithms. Sequential or block access on disks is orders of magnitude faster than random access, and many sophisticated paradigms have been developed to design efficient algorithms based upon sequential and block access . Another way to reduce the I/O bottleneck is to use multiple disks in parallel in order to increase the bandwidth between primary and secondary memory.[3]

Some other examples of secondary storage technologies are: flash memory (e.g. USB flash drives or keys), **floppy disks, magnetic tape, paper tape, punched cards, standalone RAM disks, and Iomega Zip drives.**

The secondary storage is often formatted according to a file system format, which provides the abstraction necessary to organize data into files and directories, providing also additional information (called metadata) describing the owner of a certain file, the access time, the access permissions, and other information.

Most computer operating systems use the concept of virtual memory, allowing utilization of more primary storage capacity than is physically available in the system. As the primary memory fills up, the system moves the least-used chunks (pages) to secondary storage devices (to a swap file or page file), retrieving them later when they are needed. As more of these retrievals from slower secondary storage are necessary, the more the overall system performance is degraded.

Tertiary storage *or **tertiary memory***: provides a third level of storage. Typically it involves a robotic mechanism which will mount (insert) and dismount removable mass storage media into a storage device according to the system's demands; this data is often copied to secondary storage before use. It is primarily used for archival of rarely accessed information since it is much slower than secondary storage (e.g. 5–60 seconds vs. 1-10 milliseconds). This is primarily useful for extraordinarily large data stores, accessed without human operators. Typical examples include **tape libraries** and **optical jukeboxes.**

When a computer needs to read information from the tertiary storage, it will first consult a catalog database to determine which tape or disc contains the information. Next, the computer will instruct a robotic arm to fetch the medium and place it in a drive. When the computer has finished reading the information, the robotic arm will return the medium to its place in the library.

Off-line storage is a computer data storage on a medium or a device that is not under the control of a processing unit. The medium is recorded, usually in a secondary or tertiary storage device, and then physically removed or disconnected. It must be inserted or connected by a human operator before a computer can access it again. Unlike tertiary storage, it cannot be accessed without human interaction.

Off-line storage is used to transfer information, since the detached medium can be easily physically transported. Additionally, in case a disaster, for example a fire, destroys the original data, a medium in a remote location will probably be unaffected, enabling disaster recovery. Off-line storage increases general information security, since it is physically inaccessible from a computer, and data confidentiality or integrity cannot be affected by computer-based attack techniques. Also, if the information stored for archival purposes is accessed seldom or never, off-line storage is less expensive than tertiary storage.

In modern personal computers, most secondary and tertiary storage media are also used for off-line storage. **Optical discs** and **flash memory devices** are most popular, and to much lesser extent removable **hard disk drives**. In enterprise uses, **magnetic tape** is predominant. Older examples are **floppy disks, Zip disks,** or **punched cards.**

Magnetic storage uses different patterns of magnetization on a magnetically coated surface to store information. Magnetic storage is non-volatile. The information is accessed using one or more read/write heads which may contain one or more recording transducers. A read/write head only covers a part of the surface so that the head or medium or both must be moved relative to another in order to access data.

In modern computers, magnetic storage will take these forms:

- Magnetic disk
- Floppy disk, used for off-line storage
- Hard disk drive, used for secondary storage
- Magnetic tape data storage, used for tertiary and off-line storage

In early computers, magnetic storage was also used for primary storage in a form of magnetic drum, or core memory, core rope memory, thin-film memory, twistor memory or bubble memory. Also unlike today, magnetic tape was often used for secondary storage.

Optical storage, the typical optical disc, stores information in deformities on the surface of a circular disc and reads this information by illuminating the surface with a laser diode and observing the reflection. Optical disc storage is non-volatile. The deformities may be permanent (read only media), formed once (write once media) or reversible (recordable or read/write media). The following forms are currently in common use:[12]

- **CD, CD-ROM, DVD, BD-ROM:** Read only storage, used for mass distribution of digital information (music, video, computer programs)
- **CD-R, DVD-R, DVD+R, BD-R:** Write once storage, used for tertiary and off-line storage
- **CD-RW, DVD-RW, DVD+RW, DVD-RAM, BD-RE:** Slow write, fast read storage, used for tertiary and off-line storage

- Ultra Density Optical or UDO is similar in capacity to BD-R or BD-RE and is slow write, fast read storage used for tertiary and off-line storage.

Magneto-optical disc storage is optical disc storage where the magnetic state on a ferromagnetic surface stores information. The information is read optically and written by combining magnetic and optical methods. Magneto-optical disc storage is non-volatile, sequential access, slow write, fast read storage used for tertiary and off-line storage.

3D optical data storage has also been proposed.

I/O Devices

The computer will be of no use unless it is able to communicate with the outside world. Input/Output devices are required for users to communicate with the computer. In simple terms, input devices bring information INTO the computer and output devices bring information OUT of a computer system. These input/output devices are also known as peripherals since they surround the CPU and memory of a computer system.

Some commonly used Input/Output devices are listed in table below.

Input Devices	Output Devices
Keyboard	Monitor
Mouse	LCD
Joystick	Printer
Scanner	Plotter
Light Pen	
Touch Screen	

Input Devices

(a) **Keyboard:** It is a text base input device that allows the user to input alphabets, numbers and other characters. It consists of a set of keys mounted on a board.

The Keyboard

Alphanumeric Keypad: It consists of keys for English alphabets, 0 to 9 numbers, and special characters like $+-/*$ ( ) etc.

Function Keys: There are twelve function keys labeled F1, F2, F3... F12. The functions assigned to these keys differ from one software package to another. These keys are also user programmable keys.

Special-Function Keys: These keys have special functions assigned to them and can be used only for those specific purposes. Functions of some of the important keys are defined below.

Enter: It is similar to the 'return' key of the typewriter and is used to execute a command or program.

Spacebar: It is used to enter a space at the current cursor location.

Backspace: This key is used to move the cursor one position to the left and also delete the character in that position.

Delete: It is used to delete the character at the cursor position.

Insert: Insert key is used to toggle between insert and overwrite mode during data entry.

Shift: This key is used to type capital letters when pressed along with an alphabet key. Also used to type the special characters located on the upper-side of a key that has two characters defined on the same key.

Caps Lock: Cap Lock is used to toggle between the capital lock features. When 'on', it locks the alphanumeric keypad for capital letters input only.

Tab: Tab is used to move the cursor to the next tab position defined in the document. Also, it is used to insert indentation into a document.

Ctrl: Control key is used in conjunction with other keys to provide additional functionality on the keyboard.

Alt: Also like the control key, Alt key is always used in combination with other keys to perform specific tasks.

Esc: This key is usually used to negate a command. Also used to cancel or abort executing programs.

Numeric Keypad: Numeric keypad is located on the right side of the keyboard and consists of keys having numbers (0 to 9) and mathematical operators (+ − * /) defined on them. This keypad is provided to support quick entry for numeric data.

Cursor Movement Keys: These are arrow keys and are used to move the cursor in the direction indicated by the arrow (up, down, left, right).

(b) **Mouse:** The mouse is a small device used to point to a particular place on the screen and select in order to perform one or more actions. It can be used to select menu commands, size windows, start programs etc.

The most conventional kind of mouse has two buttons on top: the left one being used most frequently.

The Mouse

Mouse Actions

- *Left Click:* Used to select an item.
- *Double Click:* Used to start a program or open a file.
- *Right Click:* Usually used to display a set of commands.
- *Drag and Drop:* It allows you to select and move an item from one location to another. To achieve this place the cursor over an item on the screen, click the left mouse button and while holding the button down move the cursor to where you want to place the item, and then release it.

(c) Joystick: The joystick is a vertical stick which moves the graphic cursor in a direction the stick is moved. It typically has a button on top that is used to select the option pointed by the cursor. Joystick is used as an input device primarily used with video games, training simulators and controlling robots

The Joystick

(d) Scanner: Scanner is an input device used for direct data entry from the source document into the computer system. It converts the document image into digital form so that it can be fed into the computer. Capturing information like this reduces the possibility of errors typically experienced during large data entry.

The Scanner

Hand-held scanners are commonly seen in big stores to scan codes and price information for each of the items. They are also termed the bar code readers.

(e) Bar codes: A bar code is a set of lines of different thicknesses that represent a number. Bar Code

Readers are used to input data from bar codes. Most products in shops have bar codes on them.Bar code readers work by shining a beam of light on the lines that make up the bar code and detecting the amount of light that is reflected back

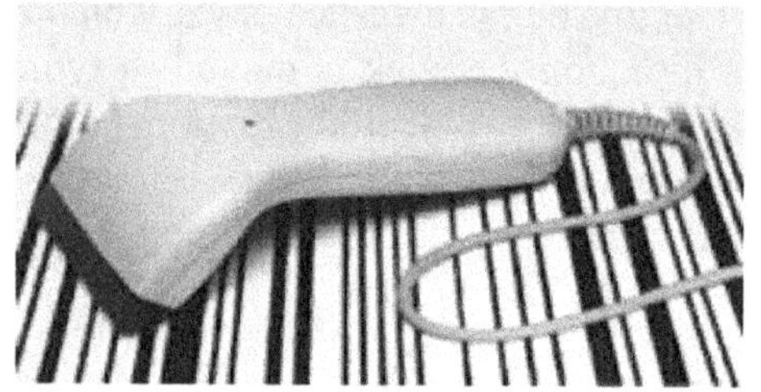

The Bar Code Reader

(f) Light Pen: It is a pen shaped device used to select objects on a display screen. It is quite like the mouse (in its functionality) but uses a light pen to move the pointer and select any object on the screen by pointing to the object.

Users of Computer Aided Design (CAD) applications commonly use the light pens to directly draw on screen.

(g) Touch Screen: It allows the user to operate/make selections by simply touching the display screen.

Common examples of touch screen include information kiosks, and bank ATMs.

(h) Digital camera: A digital camera can store many more pictures than an ordinary camera. Pictures taken using a digital camera are stored inside its memory and can be transferred to a computer by connecting the camera to it. A digital camera takes pictures by converting the light passing through the lens at the front into a digital image. It is an easy to connect low- resolution digital camera normally employed for transfer of images on the web-based conferencing.

The Digital camera

Web Camera

(i) **The Speech Input Device:** The "Microphones - Speech Recognition" is a speech Input device. To operate it we require using a microphone to talk to the computer. Also we need to add a sound card to the computer. The Sound card digitizes audio input into 0/1s .A speech recognition program can process the input and convert it into machine-recognized commands or input.

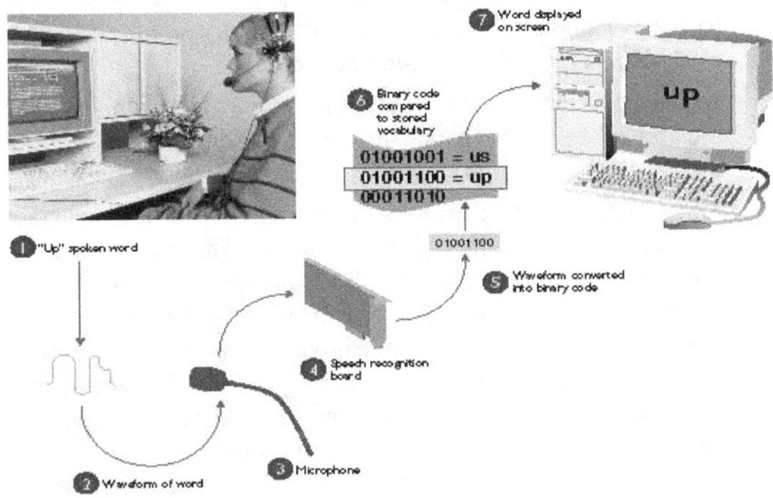

The Microphone

Output Devices

(a) **Monitor:** Monitor is an output device that resembles the television screen and uses a Cathode

Ray Tube (CRT) to display information. The monitor is associated with a keyboard for manual input of characters and displays the information as it is keyed in. It also displays the program or application output. Like the television, monitors are also available in different sizes.

(b) Liquid Crystal Display (LCD): LCD was introduced in the 1970s and is now applied to display terminals also. Its advantages like low energy consumption, smaller and lighter have paved its way for usage in portable computers (laptops).

The LCD

(c) Printer: Printers are used to produce paper (commonly known as hardcopy) output. Based on the technology used, they can be classified as Impact or Non-impact printers.

Impact printers use the typewriting printing mechanism wherein a hammer strikes the paper through a ribbon in order to produce output. Dot-matrix and Character printers fall under this category.

Dot Matrix Printer: Printers in this category print the characters / images using dots through inked ribbon. These printers are very economic and require very less maintenance cost. The print quality of the dot matrix printer is decided by the quantity of pins it has. The number of the pins can vary from nine to twenty four, depending on the kind of dot matrix printer. When compared to the other kind of printers, like the laser printers or the ink jet printer, the dot matrix printer is much more expensive. The dot matrix printer has a tendency to make a lot of noise when compared to the other kinds of printers. This is why the dot matrix printer is not very popular among customers. Quality of print in this category is not very high but is highly suitable for printing situations requiring multiple copies. These printers can print through hammering pattern of dots on the printing ribbon and can thus print multiple copies of document i multiple papers separated by carbon papers are inserted in it. Note that this feature is not available with any other category of printers.

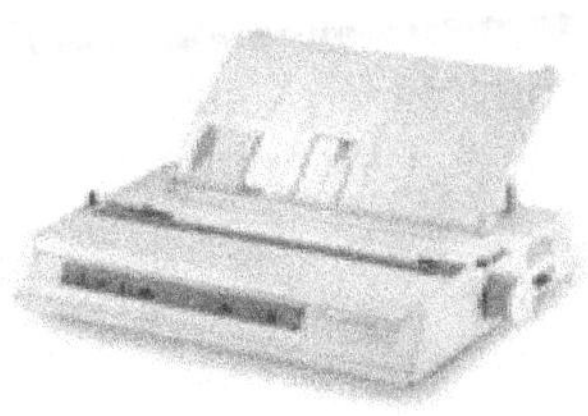

Non-impact printers do not touch the paper while printing. They use chemical, heat or electrical signals to etch the symbols on paper. Inkjet, Deskjet, Laser, Thermal printers fall under this category of printers.

Inkjet / Deskjet / Bubblejet Printer: Printers in this category are most popular. These printers are very low priced with high running/maintennce cost. These printers work on liquid ink technology and print the image using circuit-controlled jet of ink. An inkjet sprays the ink onto the paper in tiny droplets to form text and graphics. Printing speed of these printers is not very high compared to Laser Printers. These printers are suitable for people having less printing jobs with a desirable print quality. These printers are available in 'Coloured' and 'Black & White' options.

Different companies have branded their products using the same technology with different names e.g.

- Hewlett Packard (hp) manufactures DeskJet Printers
- Epson manufactures Inkjet Printers
- Canon manufactures Bubble Jet Printers

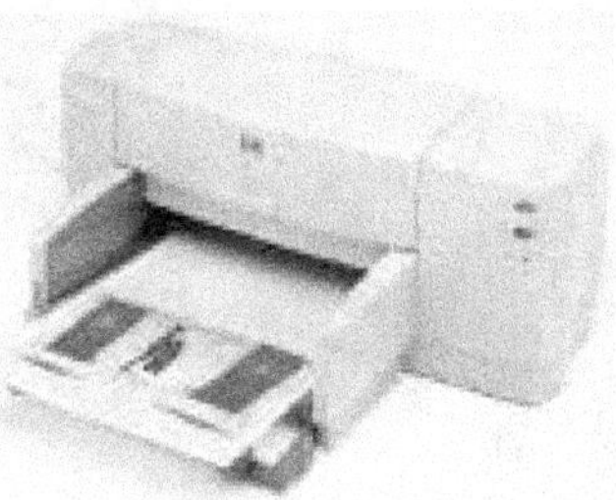

When we talk about printers we refer to two basic qualities associated with printers: resolution, and speed. Print resolution is measured in terms of number of dots per inch (dpi). Print speed is measured in terms of number of characters printed in a unit of time and is represented as characters-per-second (cps), lines-per-minute (lpm), or pages-per-minute (ppm).

Laser Printer

These printers use a technique, which is a combination of laser and Xerox technology. The technology involves dry powder based ink, which is adhered to a drum through magnetic force, and when a paper is passed through the drum it releases ink on that paper. These are the fastest available printers in category and are most suitable for uses involving high-speed quality prints.

(d) **Plotter:** Plotters are used to print graphical output on paper. It interprets computer commands and makes line drawings on paper using multicolored automated pens. It is capable of producing graphs, drawings, charts, maps etc. Computer Aided Engineering (CAE) applications like CAD (Computer Aide Design) and CAM (Computer Aided Manufacturing) are typical usage areas for plotters.

The Plotter

  (e) **Audio Output: Sound Cards and Speakers:** The Audio output is the ability of the computer to output sound. Two components are needed: Sound card – Plays contents of digitized recordings, Speakers – Attached to sound card

System and Application software

Hardware: Computer hardware refers to the physical parts of a computer and related devices. Internal hardware devices include motherboards, hard drives, and RAM. External hardware devices include monitors, keyboards, mice, printers, and scanners. The internal hardware parts of a computer are often referred to as components, while external hardware devices are usually called peripherals. Together, they all fall under the category of computer hardware.

Software: Computer software, or just software, is the collection of computer programs and related data that provide the instructions telling a computer what to do. We can also say software refers to one or more computer programs and data held in the storage of the computer for some purposes. Program software performs the function of the program it implements, either by directly providing instructions to the computer hardware or by serving as input to another piece of software. The term was coined to contrast to the old term hardware (meaning physical devices). In contrast to hardware, software is intangible, meaning it "cannot be touched". Software is also sometimes used in a more narrow sense, meaning application software only. Sometimes the term includes data that has not traditionally been associated with computers, such as film, tapes, and records.

Major Types of Software

Programming Software: This is one of the most commonly known and popularly used forms of computer software. These software come in forms of tools that assist a programmer in writing computer programs. Computer programs are sets of logical instructions that make a computer system perform certain tasks. The tools that help the programmers in instructing a computer system include text editors, compilers and interpreters.

System Software: It helps in running the computer hardware and the computer system. System software is a collection of operating systems; devise drivers, servers, windowing systems and utilities. System software helps an application programmer in abstracting away from hardware, memory and other internal complexities of a computer.

Application Software: It enables the end users to accomplish certain specific tasks. Business software, databases and educational software are some forms of application software. Different word processors, which are dedicated for specialized tasks to be performed by the user, are other examples of application software. Apart from these three basic types of software, there are some other well-known forms of computer software like inventory management software, ERP, utility software, accounting software and others. Take a look at some of them.

Inventory Management Software: This type of software helps an organization in tracking its goods and materials on the basis of quality as well as quantity. Warehouse inventory management functions encompass the internal warehouse movements and storage. Inventory software helps a company in organizing inventory and optimizing the flow of goods in the organization, thus leading to an improved customer service.

Utility Software: Also known as service routine, utility software helps in the management of computer hardware and application software. It performs a small range of tasks. Disk defragmenters, systems utilities and virus scanners are some of the typical examples of utility software.

Data Backup and Recovery Software: An ideal data backup and recovery software provides functionalities beyond simple copying of data files. This software often supports user needs of specifying what is to be backed up and when. Backup and recovery software preserve the original organization of files and allow an easy retrieval of the backed up data.

System software

The **operating system** and **utility programs** are the two major categories of system software. **Operating system:** Just as the processor is the nucleus of the computer system, the operating system is the nucleus of all software activity. The operating system is the most important program that runs on a computer. Every general-purpose computer must have an operating system to run other programs. Operating systems perform basic tasks, such as

- recognizing input from the keyboard
- sending output to the display screen
- keeping track of files and directories on the disk
- controlling peripheral devices such as disk drives and printers.

It is the first program loaded into memory when the computer is turned on and, in a sense, brings life to the computer hardware. Without it, you cannot use your word processing software, spreadsheet software, or any other applications. Without an operating system, you cannot communicate with your computer. When you give the computer a command, the operating system relays the instructions to the 'brain' of the computer, called the microprocessor or CPU. You cannot speak directly to the CPU because it only understands machine language. When you are working in an application software program, such as Microsoft Word, commands that you give the application are sent through the operating system to the CPU. Windows2000, Window95/98, Mac OS, Unix and DOS are all examples of operating systems.

Utility Programs

Utility programs help manage, maintain and control computer resources. These programs are available to help you with the day-to-day chores associated with personal computing and to keep your system running at peak performance.

Some examples of utility programs include:
- Virus scanning software
- Backup software
- Scandisk
- Disk defragmenter

Virus Scanning Software are utility programs designed to protect your computer from computer viruses. Virus scanning software is critical to uses, due to the number of computer viruses (small computer programs created to disrupt and destroy computer files and/or operating system software).

Virus scanning software scans your disk each time you insert it into a computer at Alverno. If you receive a warning that there is a virus suspected on your disk - contact the lab assistant to help you eliminate the virus. If you own your own computer, you should have a good virus scanning software package installed. Remember - virus scanning software needs to be updated on a regular basis (usually monthly). Updates insure that your virus scanning software will protect you from the most recent viruses. Virus scanning packages come with directions on how to receive updates to your software!

Backup software is software that assists you in backing up your files and even the entire computer hard drive. It is important for you to back up your files regularly (see the File Management Tutorial for more information). If you own your own computer, you should think about how to backup your valuable data on your hard drive. At Alverno, the server that houses your Home Folder is backed up regularly!

Scandisk is a utility provided with Windows computers. Scandisk scans your disks to see if there are any potential problems on the disk, such as bad disk areas. Since disks are magnetic media, all disks, including your hard drive can be corrupted.

Disk Defragmenter software assists you in keep reorganizing your disk drives. After files are saved, deleted and resaved again, the disk can become fragmented --- available space is in small blocks located throughout the disk. Disk defragmenters gather those free spots and put them together to enable you to continue to save your data in the most efficient manner.

Application Software

applications software (also called end-user programs) includes database programs, word processors, and spreadsheets. Applications software sits on top of systems software because it is unable to run without the operating system and system utilities. Application software utilizes the capacities of a computer directly to a dedicated task. Application software is able to manipulate text, numbers and graphics. It can be in the form of software focused on a certain single task like word processing, spreadsheet or playing of audio and video files.

Different Types of Application Software: There are several types of applications utilized to make the task of a user easy and smooth. A computer user can exercise a number of functions using these applications. A person can present and manage information competently and proficiently. Following are the main applications with different functions:

Database application: This kind of computer program enables a user to collect and organize the data or information. It equips a user to store and retrieve data at any time and for any purpose. For instance, this application is useful for archiving or storing information in online library.

Spreadsheet application: This program enables a user to perform mathematical calculations. These applications exhibit a grid containing multiple cells. A good example is Microsoft Excel that embeds various formula.

Multimedia application: This application equips a user to deploy multimedia elements like audio and video. You can use animation and other graphics to make your document attractive and professional.

Word Processing application: This application is able to edit and create documents in various formats. These formats are PDF, Word, Notepad and other text editors. They also have conversion ability with which you can convert a file from one format to another. For example, you can convert PDF to Word or back from Word to PDF.

These applications are used in commercial and non-commercial organizations to deliver high quality output. They are also deployed by educational or health care institutions. Individuals deploy the programs at homes for personal uses. The beneficial features of various types of applications make them flexible for any type of purpose.

Examples of Application Software Enterprise Software: It deals with the needs of organization processes and data flow. The customer relationship management or the financial processes in an organization are carried out by means of enterprise software.

Information Worker Software: Individual projects within a department and individual needs of creation and management of information are handled by information worker software. Documentation tools, resource management tools and personal management systems fall under the category of this form of application software.

Educational Software: It has the capabilities of running tests and tracking progress. It also has the capabilities of collaborative software. It is often used in teaching and self-learning.

Simulation Software: Used to simulate physical or abstract systems, simulation software finds applications in both, research and entertainment. Flight simulators and scientific simulators find a place in the list of simulation software.

Content Access Software: It is used to access content without editing. The common examples of content access software are web browsers and media players.

Firmware

Firmware is a combination of software and hardware. Computer chips that have data or programs recorded on them are firmware. These chips commonly include the following:

- ROMs (read-only memory)
- PROMs (programmable read-only memory)
- EPROMs (erasable programmable read-only memory)

Firmware in PROM or EPROM is designed to be updated if necessary through a software update. In electronics and computing, firmware is a term often used to denote the fixed, usually rather small, programs and/or data structures that internally control various electronic devices. Typical examples of devices containing firmware range from end-user products such as remote controls or calculators, through computer parts and devices like hard disks, keyboards, TFT screens or memory cards, all the way to scientific instrumentation and industrial robotics. Also more complex consumer devices, such as mobile phones, digital cameras, synthesizers, etc., contain firmware to enable the device's basic operation as well as implementing higher-level functions.

Computer Ethics

Ethics is the field of study that is concerned with questions of value, that is, judgments about what human behavior is "good" or "bad". Ethical judgments are no different in the area of computing from those in any other area. Computers raise problems of privacy, ownership, theft, and power, to name but a few.

Computer ethics can be grounded in one of four basic world-views: **Idealism, Realism, Pragmatism, or Existentialism.** Idealists believe that reality is basically ideas and that ethics therefore involves conforming to ideals. Realists believe that reality is basically nature and that ethics therefore involves acting according to what is natural. Pragmatists believe that reality is not fixed but is in process and that ethics therefore is practical (that is, concerned with what will produce socially-desired results). Existentialists believe reality is self-defined and that ethics therefore is individual (that is, concerned only with one's own conscience). Idealism and Realism can be considered ABSOLUTIST worldviews because they are based on something fixed (that is, ideas or nature, respectively). Pragmatism and Existentialism can be considered RELATIVIST worldviews because they are based or something relational (that is, society or the individual, respectively). Thus ethical judgments will vary, depending on the judge's world-view.

Some examples: First consider theft. Suppose a university's computer is used for sending an e-mail message to a friend or for conducting a full-blown private business (billing, payroll, inventory, etc.). The absolutist would say that both activities are unethical (while recognising a difference in the amount of wrong being done). A relativist might say that the latter activities were wrong because they tied up too much memory and slowed down the machine, but the e-mail message wasn't wrong because it had no significant effect on operations. Next consider privacy. An instructor uses her account to acquire the cumulative grade point average of a student who is in a class which she instructs. She obtained the password for this restricted information from someone in the Records Office who erroneously thought that she was the student's advisor. The absolutist would probably say that the instructor acted wrongly, since the only person who is entitled to this information is the student and his or her advisor. The relativist would probably ask why the instructor wanted the information. If she replied that she wanted it to be sure that her grading of the student was consistent with the student's overall academic performance record, the relativist might agree that such use was acceptable.

Finally, consider power. At a particular university, if a professor wants a computer account, all she or he need do is request one but a student must obtain faculty sponsorship in order to receive an account. An absolutist (because of a proclivity for hierarchical thinking) might not have a problem with this divergence in procedure. A relativist, on the other hand, might question what makes the two situations essentially different (e.g. are faculty assumed to have more need for computers than students? Are students more likely to cause problems than faculty? Is this a hold-over from the days of "in loco parentis"?).

Applications in e-business

eBusiness (e-Business), or Electronic Business, is the administration of conducting business via the Internet. This would include the buying and selling of goods and services, along with providing technical or customer support through the Internet. e-Business is a term often used in conjunction with e-commerce, but includes services in addition to the sale of goods.

Applications can be divided into three categories:

1. **Internal business systems**
   - customer relationship management
   - enterprise resource planning
   - document management systems
   - human resources management

2. **Enterprise communication and collaboration**
   - VoIP
   - content management system
   - e-mail
   - voice mail
   - Web conferencing
   - Digital work flows (or business process management)

3. **Electronic commerce - business-to-business electronic commerce (B2B) or business-to-consumer electronic commerce (B2C)**
   - internet shop
   - supply chain management
   - online marketing
   - offline marketing

BioInformatics

Bioinformatics is the analysis of biological information using computers and statistical techniques; the science of developing and utilizing computer databases and algorithms to accelerate and enhance biological research. Bioinformatics is more of a tool than a discipline, the tools for analysis of Biological Data. "Bioinformatics is the field of science in which biology, computer science, and information technology merge into a single discipline. There are three important sub-disciplines within bioinformatics: the development of new algorithms and statistics with which to assess relationships among members of large data sets; the analysis and interpretation of various types of data including nucleotide and amino acid sequences, protein domains, and protein structures; and the development and implementation of tools that enable efficient access and management of different types of information.".

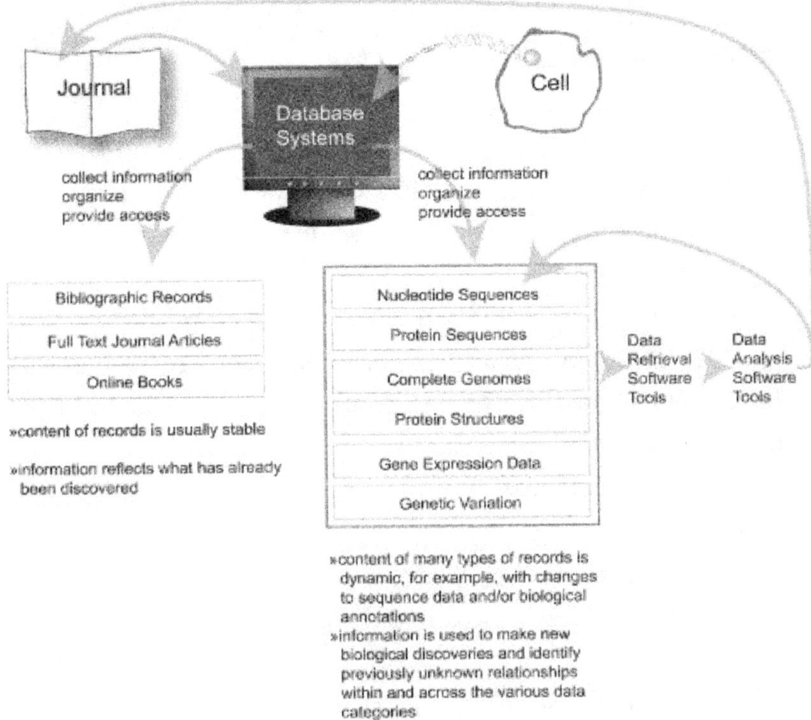

The three terms bioinformatics, computational biology and bioinformation infrastructure are often times used interchangeably. These three may be defined as follows:

1. bioinformatics refers to database-like activities, involving persistent sets of data that are maintained in a consistent state over essentially indefinite periods of time;

2. computational biology encompasses the use of algorithmic tools to facilitate biological analysis; while

3. bioinformation infrastructure comprises the entire collective of information management systems, analysis tools and communication networks supporting biology. Thus, the latter may be viewed as a computational scaffold of the former two.

Aims and Objectives

Bioinformatics is at the interface between two of the most influential scientific fields. An appreciation of computational and biological sciences, in particular the terminology employed in both fields, is essential for those working at such an interface. In this course, we aim to cover the following:

1. The concepts of computer science that relate to problems in biological sciences.

2. Commercial and academic perspectives on bioinformatics.

3. The impact of bioinformatics on the methodologies used in biological science.

4. The influence biological science has on computing science.

Real world applications of bioinformatics: The science of bioinformatics has many beneficial uses in the modern day world.

These include the following:

1. **Molecular medicine**
   - 1.1 More drug targets
   - 1.2 Personalised medicine
   - 1.3 Preventative medicine
   - 1.4 Gene therapy

2. **Microbial genome applications**
   - 2.1 Waste cleanup
   - 2.2 Climate change
   - 2.3 Alternative energy sources
   - 2.4 Biotechnology
   - 2.5 Antibiotic resistance
   - 2.6 Forensic analysis of microbes
   - 2.7 The reality of bioweapon creation
   - 2.8 Evolutionary studies

3. **Agriculture**
   - 3.1 Crops
   - 3.2 Insect resistance
   - 3.3 Improve nutritional quality
   - 3.4 Grow crops in poorer soils and that are drought resistant

4. **Animals**

5. **Comparative studies**

Application of Bioinformatics in various Fields

Molecular medicine: The human genome will have profound effects on the fields of biomedical research and clinical medicine. Every disease has a genetic component. This may be inherited (as is the case with an estimated 3000-4000 hereditary disease including Cystic Fibrosis and Huntingtons disease) or a result of the body's response to an environmental stress which causes alterations in the genome (eg. cancers, heart disease, diabetes.). The completion of the human genome means that we can search for the genes directly associated with different diseases and begin to understand the molecular basis of these diseases more clearly. This new knowledge of the molecular mechanisms of disease will enable better treatments, cures and even preventative tests to be developed.

Personalised medicine: Clinical medicine will become more personalised with the development of the field of pharmacogenomics. This is the study of how an individual's genetic inheritence affects the body's response to drugs. At present, some drugs fail to make it to the market because a small percentage of the clinical patient population show adverse affects to a drug due to sequence variants in their DNA. As a result, potentially life saving drugs never make it to the marketplace. Today, doctors have to use trial and error to find the best drug to treat a particular patient as those with the same clinical symptoms can show a wide range of responses to the same treatment. In the future, doctors will be able to analyse a patient's genetic profile and prescribe the best available drug therapy and dosage from the beginning.

Gene therapy: In the not too distant future, the potential for using genes themselves to treat disease may become a reality. Gene therapy is the approach used to treat, cure or even prevent disease by changing the expression of a persons genes. Currently, this field is in its infantile stage with clinical trials for many different types of cancer and other diseases ongoing.

Drug development: At present all drugs on the market target only about 500 proteins. With an improved understanding of disease mechanisms and using computational tools to identify and validate new drug targets, more specific medicines that act on the cause, not merely the symptoms, of the disease can be developed. These highly specific drugs promise to have fewer side effects than many of today's medicines.

Waste cleanup: Deinococcus radiodurans is known as the world's toughest bacteria and it is the most radiation resistant organism known.

Scientists are interested in this organism because of its potential usefulness in cleaning up waste sites that contain radiation and toxic chemicals.

Crop improvement: Comparative genetics of the plant genomes has shown that the organisation of their genes has remained more conserved over evolutionary time than was previously believed. These findings suggest that information obtained from the model crop systems can be used to suggest improvements to other food crops. At present the complete genomes of Arabidopsis thaliana (water cress) and Oryza sativa (rice) are available.

Climate change studies: Increasing levels of carbon dioxide emission, mainly through the expanding use of fossil fuels for energy, are thought to contribute to global climate change. Recently, the DOE (Department of Energy, USA) launched a program to decrease atmospheric carbon dioxide levels. One method of doing so is to study the genomes of microbes that use carbon dioxide as their sole carbon source.

Health Care

Computers play a key role in almost every sphere of life. They facilitate storage of huge amounts of data, they enable speedy processing of information and they possess an inbuilt intelligence. Owing to these unique capabilities, computers function on levels close to that of a human brain. Computers can hence be employed in a wide variety of fields like engineering, data processing and storage, planning and scheduling, networking, education as well as health and medicine.

Computer networking enables quicker communication. Computers and Internet have proved to be a boon in all the spheres of life. In the field of medicine, computers allow for faster communication between a patient and a doctor. Doctors can collaborate better over the Internet. Today, it is possible to obtain experts' opinions within seconds by means of the Internet. Medical professionals sitting on opposite sides of the globe can communicate within minutes by means of the Internet. It is due to computer networking technology that network communication has become easy. Medical practitioners can discuss medical issues in medical forums. They can exchange images and messages in seconds and derive conclusions speedily. They can seek advice and share knowledge in a convenient manner over the Internet.

Computer software is used for diagnosis of diseases. It can be used for the examination of internal organs of the body. Advanced computer-based systems are used to examine delicate organs of the body. Some of the complex surgeries can be performed with the aid of computers. The different types of monitoring equipment in hospitals are often based on computer programming.

How are computers used in health care:

Databases: One of the most obvious ways that computers are used in health care is to keep records. Whether those records are patient files (complete with digital scans and X-rays), or records of payment and debt, computer databases provide an easy, low-space storage option for keeping a huge amount of information accessible to the staff members who need it.

Monitors: Passive monitors, such as those used on EKG machines and other technologically advanced scanners, function off of a computer. The internal computers in the monitors will interpret all of the data being collected (the small surges of electric pulses that are the language of a computer) and then display it in a meaningful way.

Minimally Invasive Tools: Computers are used with a great deal of minimally invasive surgeries. These surgeries cut a small incision, and then place a small surgical tool with an attached camera inside the patient's body. This makes it less likely that a patient will suffer complications from a larger surgical wound, and it helps minimize damage done to the body. Most of these minimally invasive tools use computers to drive the tools, and to relay images from inside the patient's body out to the doctors.

Laboratories: Running tests on tissues and fluids is a basic part of any medical laboratory. However there are automated machines that are attached to computers that will run simple tests that don't require anything more than the completion of simple tasks. Centrifuges and other machines may therefore be run by computers that are programmed for their tasks by lab technicians.

Sanitation: Computer use is so common in the health care field (with some hospitals having a computer in literally every room) that sometimes special cleaning care has to be taken. Computer keyboards especially may transmit bacteria and disease, which can be deadly if the computer is in an operating room. Therefore it becomes very important that computer keyboards are frequently sanitized and kept clean so that there is as little risk as possible.

Remote sensing

Remote sensing is the art and science of making measurements of the earth using sensors on airplanes or satellites. These sensors collect data in the form of images and provide specialized capabilities for manipulating, analyzing, and visualizing those images. Remote sensed imagery is integrated within a GIS. Remote Sensing is a technology for sampling **electromagnetic radiation** comprising a signal emanating from its source target that is used to acquire and interpret non-contiguous *geospatial data* from which to extract information about features, objects, and classes on the Earth's land surface, oceans, and atmosphere (and, where applicable, on the exteriors of other bodies in the solar system, or, in the broadest framework, celestial bodies such as stars and galaxies). remote sensing is a tool for gathering information, usually about what is at the surface of Earth or planets and their moons, but also about the atmosphere, and about celestial bodies. Remote sensing data are commonly combined with other kinds of data (typically, from field or "on-the-spot" studies [commonly called ground truth]) to act together as a system. This next diagram indicates the basic elements involved in an earth survey system:

A variant of this diagram emphasizes the idea that the ultimate goal in applied remote sensing is determined and driven by user requirements. It also shows that in most cases remote sensing data are integrated with other types of data, such as phenomenological and archival.

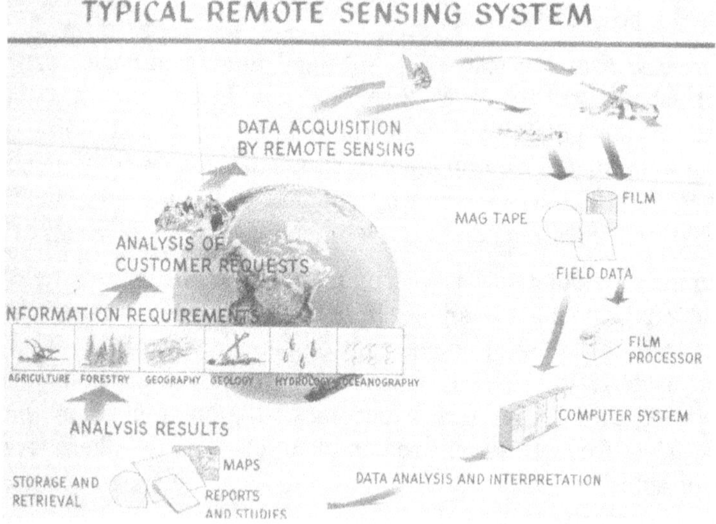

Remote sensing is conducted by means of sensors - in effect, instruments that can pick up (sense) objects and features not in contact with the sensors, by detecting, coordinating, and recording electromagnetic radiation or acoustical (sound) waves. The best known (to the average individual) sensor is the human eye and the human ear. An artificial or manmade instrument familiar to all is the photographic camera (and in the last 80 years, the television camera). Since the beginning of the era of satellite remote sensing, more sophisticated instruments include multispectral scanners, radar, lidar, thermal imagers, and other systems.

Platforms used by Remote Sensors: Aircraft; Balloons; Satellites; Spacecraft; Probes; Rovers;; Launch Vehicles.

Remote Sensing involves four basic inputs: 1. The Target; 2. The Platform; 3. The Sensor(s); and 4. The Signal (usually electromagnetic radiation or acoustical waves). The target is comprised of the features or materials being sensed. Sensors and signals (including the concept of signatures) are treated later in this Section. On this page we will concentrate on the topic of Platforms, the structures that house or support the sensors. In most instances, the platforms will be in motion; by moving they automatically proceed to new positions from whence they sense new targets. A satellite orbiting the Earth is a typical platform. Most of the platforms involved are pictured in this diagram:

Those platforms above Earth's atmosphere and beyond include satellites, spacecraft, space stations, all in orbit around Earth, and planetary satellite orbiters, flyby satellites, probes, and landers/rovers that are used to explore planets, moons, and asteroids/comets.

Remote Sensing Software

Remote Sensing data is processed and analyzed with computer software, known as a remote sensing application. A large number of proprietary and open source applications exist to process remote sensing data. According to an NOAA Sponsored Research by Global Marketing Insights, Inc. the most used applications among Asian academic groups involved in remote sensing are as follows: ERDAS 36% (ERDAS IMAGINE 25% & ERMapper 11%); ESRI 30%; ITT Visual Information Solutions ENVI 17%; MapInfo 17%. Among Western Academic respondents as follows: ESRI 39%, ERDAS IMAGINE 27%, MapInfo 9%, AutoDesk 7%, ITT Visual Information Solutions ENVI 17%. Other important Remote Sensing Software packages include: TNTmips from MicroImages, PCI Geomatica made by PCI Geomatics, the leading remote sensing software package in Canada, IDRISI from Clark Labs, Image Analyst from Intergraph, and the original object based image analysis software eCognition from Definiens. Dragon/ips is one of the oldest remote sensing packages still available, and is in some cases free. Open source remote sensing software includes GRASS GIS, QGIS, OSSIM, Opticks (software) and Orfeo toolbox.

How is Remote Sensing Useful?

Data collection using Remote Sensing offers a variety of advantages compared to other forms of data acquisition. Remote Sensing makes it possible to measure energy (such as ultra-violet, infrared, microwave, etc) at wavelengths that cannot be reached by human vision. Scientific advancements have resulted in use of Remote Sensing in a variety of discipline such as agriculture, forestry, hydrology, geology, cartography, meteorology, etc.

One important application of Remote Sensing is in the field of oceanography. Here Remote Sensing may be used to acquire following information:

- Details about ocean pigmentation
- Particulars pertaining to location, direction and speed of currents
- Determine sea surface temperature
- Locate direction and speed of wind
- Determine location, direction and speed of waves, etc

Although remote sensing is useful in an array of areas, its usage is most significant in the context of terrestrial observations. Global monitoring is possible from any site of earth using Remote Sensing.

Fundamentals of Satellite Remote Sensing

Satellite Remote Sensing involves gathering information about the earth's surface using satellites orbiting around the earth. Satellite remote sensing may be done two ways:

- Using passive sensor systems - Contains an array of small detectors or sensors that can detect electro-magnetic radiations emitted from the earth's surface

- Using active sensor systems - The system sends out electro magnetic radiation towards target object (s) and measures the intensity of the return signal.

Data collected by the satellites are then transmitted to ground stations wherein images of earth's surface are reconstituted to obtain the required information.

Satellite Remote Sensing

In the 1960s, a revolution in remote sensing technology began with the deployment of space satellites. From their high vantage-point, satellites have a greatly extended view of the Earth's surface. The first meteorological satellite, TIROS-1 , was launched by the United States using an Atlas rocket on April 1, 1960. This early weather satellite used vidicon cameras to scan wide areas of the Earth's surface. Early satellite remote sensors did not use conventional film to produce their images. Instead, the sensors digitally capture the images using a device similar to a television camera. Once captured, this data is then transmitted electronically to receiving stations found on the Earth's surface. The image below is from TIROS-7 of a mid-latitude cyclone off the coast of New Zealand.

Today, the GOES (Geostationary Operational Environmental Satellite) system of satellites provides most of the remotely sensed weather information for North America. To cover the complete continent and adjacent oceans two satellites are employed in a geostationary orbit. The western half of North America and the eastern Pacific Ocean is monitored by GOES-10, which is directly above the equator and 135° West longitude. The eastern half of North America and the western Atlantic are cover by GOES-8. The GOES-8 satellite is located overhead of the equator and 75° West longitude. Advanced sensors aboard the GOES satellite produce a continuous data stream so images can be viewed at any instance. The imaging sensor produces visible and infrared images of the Earth's terrestrial surface and oceans. Infrared images can depict weather conditions even during the night. Another sensor aboard the satellite can determine vertical temperature profiles, vertical moisture profiles, total precipitable water, and atmospheric stability.

In the 1970s, the second revolution in remote sensing technology began with the deployment of the Landsat satellites. Since this 1972, several generations of Landsat satellites with their Multispectral Scanners (MSS) have been providing continuous coverage of the Earth for almost 30 years. Current, Landsat satellites orbit the Earth's surface at an altitude of approximately 700 kilometers. Spatial resolution of objects on the ground surface is 79 x 56 meters. Complete coverage of the globe requires 233 orbits and occurs every 16 days. The Multispectral Scanner records a zone of the Earth's surface that is 185 kilometers wide in four wavelength bands: band 4 at 0.5 to 0.6 micrometers, band 5 at 0.6 to 0.7 micrometers, band 6 at 0.7 to 0.8 micrometers, and band 7 at 0.8 to 1.1 micrometers. Bands 4 and 5 receive the green and red wavelengths in the visible light range of the electromagnetic spectrum. The last two bands image near-infrared wavelengths. A second sensing system was added to Landsat satellites launched after 1982. This imaging system, known as the Thematic Mapper, records seven wavelength bands from the visible to far-infrared portions of the electromagnetic spectrum. In addition, the ground resolution of this sensor was enhanced to 30 x 20 meters. This modification allows for greatly improved clarity of imaged objects.

The Landsat 7 enhanced Thematic Mapper instrument.
(*Source: Landsat 7 Home Page*).

The usefulness of satellites for remote sensing has resulted in several other organizations launching their own devices. In France, the SPOT (Satellite Pour l'Observation de la Terre) satellite program has launched five satellites since 1986. Since 1986, SPOT satellites have produced more than 10 million images. SPOT satellites use two different sensing systems to image the planet. One sensing system produces black and white panchromatic images from the visible band (0.51 to 0.73 micrometers) with a ground resolution of 10 x 10 meters. The other sensing device is multispectral capturing green, red, and reflected infrared bands at 20 x 20 meters. SPOT-5, which was launched in 2002, is much improved from the first four versions of SPOT satellites. SPOT-5 has a maximum ground resolution of 2.5 x 2.5 meters in both panchromatic mode and multispectral operation.

Radarsat-1 was launched by the Canadian Space Agency in November, 1995. As a remote sensing device, Radarsat is quite different from the Landsat and SPOT satellites. Radarsat is an active remote sensing system that transmits and receives microwave radiation. Landsat and SPOT sensors passively measure reflected radiation at wavelengths roughly equivalent to those detected by our eyes. Radarsat's microwave energy penetrates clouds, rain, dust, or haze and produces images regardless of the Sun's illumination allowing it to image in darkness. Radarsat images have a resolution between 8 to 100 meters. This sensor has found important applications in crop monitoring, defence surveillance, disaster monitoring, geologic resource mapping, sea-ice mapping and monitoring, oil slick detection, and digital elevation modeling .

Principles of Object Identification

Most people have no problem identifying objects from photographs taken from an oblique angle. Such views are natural to the human eye and are part of our everyday experience. However, most remotely sensed images are taken from an overhead or vertical perspective and from distances quite removed from ground level. Both of these circumstances make the interpretation of natural and human-made objects somewhat difficult. In addition, images obtained from devices that receive and capture electromagnetic wavelengths outside human vision can present views that are quite unfamiliar.

To overcome the potential difficulties involved in image recognition, professional image interpreters use a number of characteristics to help them identify remotely sensed objects. Some of these characteristics include:

Shape: This characteristic alone may serve to identify many objects. Examples include the long linear lines of highways, the intersecting runways of an airfield, the perfectly rectangular shape of buildings, or the recognizable shape of an outdoor baseball diamond.

Size: Noting the relative and absolute sizes of objects is important in their identification. The scale of the image determines the absolute size of an object. As a result, it is very important to recognize the scale of the image to be analyzed.

Image Tone or Color: All objects reflect or emit specific signatures of electromagnetic radiation. In most cases, related types of objects emit or reflect similar wavelengths of radiation. Also, the types of recording device and recording media produce images that are reflective of their sensitivity to particular range of radiation. As a result, the interpreter must be aware of how the object being viewed will appear on the image examined. For example, on color infrared images vegetation has a color that ranges from pink to red rather than the usual tones of green.

Pattern: Many objects arrange themselves in typical patterns. This is especially true of human-made phenomena. For example, orchards have a systematic arrangement imposed by a farmer, while natural vegetation usually has a random or chaotic pattern.

Shadow: Shadows can sometimes be used to get a different view of an object. For example, an overhead photograph of a towering smokestack or a radio transmission tower normally presents an identification problem. This difficulty can be over come by photographing these objects at Sun angles that cast shadows. These shadows then display the shape of the object on the ground. Shadows can also be a problem to interpreters because they often conceal things found on the Earth's surface.

Texture: Imaged objects display some degree of coarseness or smoothness. This characteristic can sometimes be useful in object interpretation. For example, we would normally expect to see textural differences when comparing an area of grass with a field corn. Texture, just like object size, is directly related to the scale of the image.

Advantages of Satellite Remote Sensing

Take a look at few benefits of Satellite remote sensing:

- Enables continuous acquisition of data
- Helps to receive up-to-date information (satellite remote sensing can be programmed to enable regular revisit to object or area under study)
- Offers wide regional coverage and good spectral resolution
- Offers accurate data for information and analysis
- Serves as a large archive of historical data

Data collected using satellite remote sensing can be used for any of the following purposes

- Assessing and observing vegetation types
- Conducting soil surveys
- Carrying out mineral exploration
- Map making to facilitate easy study of information
- Construct thematic maps based on requirement
- Planning and monitoring water resources
- Carry out urban planning
- Assessing crop yields and other agriculture management

Assessing and managing natural disaster, Etc

Geographic Information System(GIS)

GIS is a computer system for capturing, storing, checking, integrating, manipulating, analysing and displaying data related to positions on the Earth's surface. Typically, a Geographical Information System is used for handling maps of one kind or another. These might be represented as several different layers where each layer holds data about a particular kind of feature. Each feature is linked to a position on the graphical image on a map and a record in an attribute table. GIS can relate otherwise disparate on the basis of common geography, revealing hidden patterns, relationships, and trends that are not readily apparent in spreadsheets or statistical packages, often creating new information from existing data resources.

Hidden in most data is a geographical component: an address, postal code, census block, city, county, or latitude/longitude coordinate. With GIS, you can explore the spatial element of your data to display soil types, track crime patterns, analyze animal migration patterns, find the best location for an expanding business, model the path of atmospheric pollution, and make decisions for many types of complicated problems.

A GIS is an information system designed to work with data referenced by spatial / geographical coordinates. In other words, GIS is both a database system with specific capabilities for spatially referenced data as well as a set of operations for working with the data. It may also be considered as a higher order map.

GIS technology integrates common database operations such as query and statistical analysis with the unique visualization and geographic analysis benefits offered by maps. These abilities distinguish GIS from other information systems and make it valuable to a wide range of public and private enterprises for explaining events, predicting outcomes, and planning strategies. (ESRI)

A Geographic Information System is a computer based system which is used to digitally reproduce and analyse the feature present on earth surface and the events that take place on it. In the light of the fact that almost 70% of the data has geographical reference as it's denominator, it becomes imperative to underline the importance of a system which can represent the given data geographically.

A typical GIS can be understood by the help of various definitions given below:-

- A geographic information system (GIS) is a computer-based tool for mapping and analyzing things that exist and events that happen on Earth

- Burrough in 1986 defined GIS as, "Set of tools for collecting, storing, retrieving at will, transforming and displaying spatial data from the real world for a particular set of purposes"

- Arnoff in 1989 defines GIS as, "a computer based system that provides four sets of capabilities to handle geo-referenced data :

- data input

- data management (data storage and retrieval)

- manipulation and analysis

- data output. "

Hence GIS is looked upon as a tool to assist in decision-making and management of attributes that needs to be analysed spatially.

Need of GIS?

Many professionals, such as foresters, urban planners, and geologists, have recognized the importance of spatial dimensions in organising & analysing information. Whether a discipline is concerned with the very practical aspects of business, or is concerned with purely academic research, geographic information system can introduce a perspective, which can provide valuable insights as

1. 70% of the information has geographic location as it's denominator making spatial analysis an essential tool.

2. Ability to assimilate divergent sources of data both spatial and non-spatial (attribute data).

3. Visualization Impact

4. Analytical Capability

5. Sharing of Information

Factors Aiding the rise of GIS.

- Revolution in Information Technology.

- Computer Technology.

- Remote Sensing.

- Global Positioning System.

- Communication Technology.

- Rapidly declining cost of Computer Hardware, and at the same time, exponential growth of operational speed of computers.

- Enhanced functionality of software and their user-friendliness.

- Visualizing impact of GIS corroborating the Chinese proverb "a picture is worth a thousand words."

- Geographical feature and data describing it are part of our everyday lives & most of our everyday decisions are influenced by some facet of Geography.

Components of GIS: GIS constitutes of five key components:

- Hardware

- Software

- Data

- People

- Method

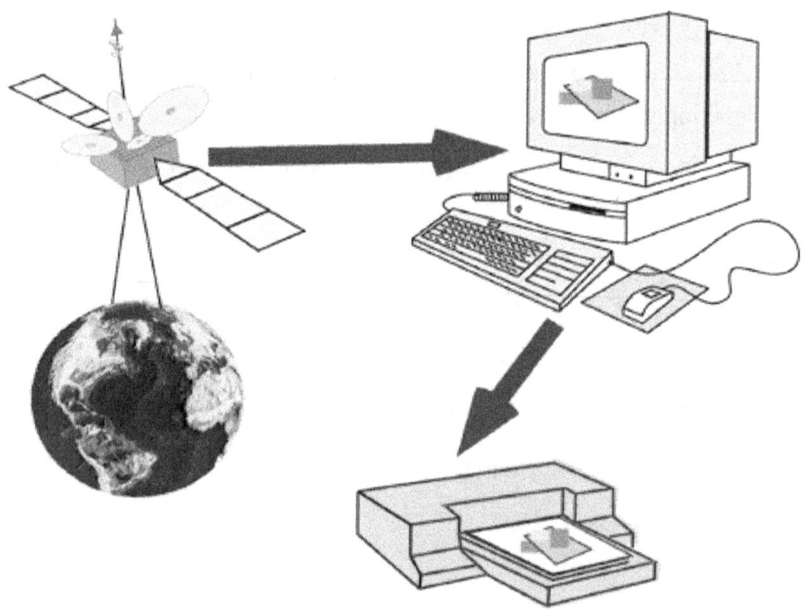

Three major components of a Geographic Information System. These components consist of input, computer hardware and software, and output subsystems.

Hardware

It consists of the computer system on which the GIS software will run. The choice of hardware system range from 300MHz Personal Computers to Super Computers having capability in Tera FLOPS. The computer forms the backbone of the GIS hardware, which gets it's input through the Scanner or a digitizer board. Scanner converts a picture into a digital image for further processing. The output of scanner can be stored in many formats e.g. TIFF, BMP, JPG etc. A digitizer board is flat board used for vectorisation of a given map objects. Printers and plotters are the most common output devices for a GIS hardware setup.

Software

GIS software provides the functions and tools needed to store, analyze, and display geographic information. GIS softwares in use are MapInfo, ARC/Info, AutoCAD Map, etc. The software available can be said to be application specific. When the low cost GIS work is to be carried out desktop MapInfo is the suitable option. It is easy to use and supports many GIS feature. If the user intends to carry out extensive analysis on GIS, ARC/Info is the preferred option. For the people using AutoCAD and willing to step into GIS, AutoCAD Map is a good option.

Data

Geographic data and related tabular data can be collected in-house or purchased from a commercial data provider. The digital map forms the basic data input for GIS. Tabular data related to the map objects can also be attached to the digital data. A GIS will integrate spatial data with other data resources and can even use a DBMS, used by most organization to maintain their data, to manage spatial data.

People

GIS users range from technical specialists who design and maintain the system to those who use it to help them perform their everyday work. The people who useGIS can be broadly classified into two classes. The CAD/GIS operator, whose work is to vectorise the map objects. The use of this vectorised data to perform query, analysis or any other work is the responsibility of a GIS engineer/user.

Method

And above all a successful GIS operates according to a well-designed plan and business rules, which are the models and operating practices unique to each organization. There are various techniques used for map creation and further usage for any project. The map creation can either be automated raster to vector creator or it can be manually vectorised using the scanned images. The source of these digital maps can be either map prepared by any survey agency or satellite imagery.

Advantages of GIS

The Geographic Information System has been an effective tool for implementation and monitoring of municipal infrastructure. The use of GIS has been in vogue primarily due to the advantage mentioned below:

- Planning of project
- Make better decisions
- Visual Analysis

Improve Organizational Integration

GIS Applications

Computerized mapping and spatial analysis have been developed simultaneously in several related fields. The present status would not have been achieved without close interaction between various fields such as utility networks, cadastral mapping, topographic mapping, thematic cartography, surveying and photogrammetery remote sensing, image processing, computer science, rural and urban planning, earth science, and geography.

The GIS technology is rapidly becoming a standard tool for management of natural resources. The effective use of large spatial data volumes is dependent upon the existence of an efficient geographic handling and processing system to transform this data into usable information.

The GIS technology is used to assist decision-makers by indicating various alternatives in development and conservation planning and by modelling the potential outcomes of a series of scenarios. It should be noted that any task begins and ends with the real world. Data are collected about the real world. Of necessity, the product is an abstraction; it is not possible (and not desired) to handle every last detail. After the data are analysed, information is compiled for decision-makers. Based on this information, actions are taken and plans implemented in the real world.

Major areas of application

- *Different streams of planning:* Urban planning, housing, transportation planning architectural conservation, urban design, landscape.

- *Street Network Based Application:* It is an addressed matched application, vehicle routing and scheduling: location and site selection and disaster planning.

- *Natural Resource Based Application:* Management and environmental impact analysis of wild and scenic recreational resources, flood plain, wetlands, acquifers, forests, and wildlife.

- *View Shed Analysis:* Hazardous or toxic factories siting and ground water modelling. Wild life habitat study and migrational route planning.

- *Land Parcel Based:* Zoning, sub-division plans review, land acquisition, environment impact analysis, nature quality management and maintenance etc.

- *Facilities Management:* Can locate underground pipes and cables for maintenance, planning, tracking energy use.

Meteorology

The blanket of air around the earth is called the *atmosphere*. All our weather happens in the bottom layer of the atmosphere called the *troposphere*, which is six to ten miles thick. *Meteorology* is the study of the changes in temperature, air pressure, moisture, and wind direction in the troposphere.

Applications

Boundary layer meteorology: Boundary layer meteorology is the study of processes in the air layer directly above Earth's surface, known as the atmospheric boundary layer (ABL). The effects of the surface – heating, cooling, and friction – cause turbulent mixing within the air layer. Significant fluxes of heat, matter, or momentum on time scales of less than a day are advected by turbulent motions. Boundary layer meteorology includes the study of all types of surface-atmosphere boundary, including ocean, lake, urban land and non-urban land.

Dynamic meteorology: Dynamic meteorology generally focuses on the fluid dynamics of the atmosphere. The idea of air parcel is used to define the smallest element of the atmosphere, while ignoring the discrete molecular and chemical nature of the atmosphere. An air parcel is defined as a point in the fluid continuum of the atmosphere. The fundamental laws of fluid dynamics, thermodynamics, and motion are used to study the atmosphere. The physical quantities that characterize the state of the atmosphere are temperature, density, pressure, etc. These variables have unique values in the continuum.

Agricultural meteorology: Meteorologists, soil scientists, agricultural hydrologists, and agronomists are persons concerned with studying the effects of weather and climate on plant distribution, crop yield, water-use efficiency, phenology of plant and animal development, and the energy balance of managed and natural ecosystems. Conversely, they are interested in the role of vegetation on climate and weather.

Hydrometeorology: Hydrometeorology is the branch of meteorology that deals with the hydrologic cycle, the water budget, and the rainfall statistics of storms. A hydrometeorologist prepares and issues forecasts of accumulating (quantitative) precipitation, heavy rain, heavy snow, and highlights areas with the potential for flash flooding. Typically the range of knowledge that is required overlaps with climatology, mesoscale and synoptic meteorology, and other geosciences.

Nuclear meteorology: Nuclear meteorology investigates the distribution of radioactive aerosols and gases in the atmosphere.

Maritime meteorology: Maritime meteorology deals with air and wave forecasts for ships operating at sea. Organizations such as the Ocean Prediction Center, Honolulu National Weather Service forecast office, United Kingdom Met Office, and JMA prepare high seas forecasts for the world's oceans.

Aviation meteorology: Aviation meteorology deals with the impact of weather on air traffic management. It is important for air crews to understand the implications of weather on their flight plan as well as their aircraft, as noted by the Aeronautical Information Manual.

The effects of ice on aircraft are cumulative-thrust is reduced, drag increases, lift lessens, and weight increases. The results are an increase in stall speed and a deterioration of aircraft performance. In extreme cases, 2 to 3 inches of ice can form on the leading edge of the airfoil in less than 5 minutes. It takes but 1/2 inch of ice to reduce the lifting power of some aircraft by 50 percent and increases the frictional drag by an equal percentage.

Climatology

Climates encompasses the statistics of temperature, humidity, atmospheric pressure, wind, rainfall, atmospheric particle count and other meteorological elements in a given region over long periods of time. Climate can be contrasted to weather, which is the present condition of these same elements and their variations over periods up to two weeks.

The climate of a location is affected by its latitude, terrain, and altitude, as well as nearby water bodies and their currents. Climates can be classified according to the average and the typical ranges of different variables, most commonly temperature and precipitation. The study of this climates is called as climatology.

Climatology is the scientific study of climate and is a major branch of meteorology. Climatology is the tool that is used to develop long-range forecasts. There are three principal approaches to the study of climatology: physical, descriptive, and dynamic.

Types of climatology

Physical Climatology: The physical climatology approach seeks to explain the differences in climate in light of the physical processes influencing climate and the processes producing the various kinds of physical climates, such as marine, desert, and mountain. Physical climatology deals with explanations of climate rather than with presentations.

Descriptive Climatology: Descriptive climatology typically orients itself in terms of geographic regions; it is often referred to as regional climatology. A description of the various types of climates is made on the basis of analyzed statistics from a particular area. A further attempt is made to describe the interaction of weather and climatic elements upon the people and the areas under consideration. Descriptive climatology is presented by verbal and graphic description without going into causes and theory.

Dynamic Climatology: Dynamic climatology attempts to relate characteristics of the general circulation of the entire atmosphere to the climate. Dynamic climatology is used by the theoretical meteorologist and addresses dynamic and thermodynamic effects.

Microclimatology: Microclimatological studies often measure small-scale contrasts, such as between hilltop and valley or between city and surrounding country. They may be of an extremely small scale, such as one side of a hedge contrasted with the other, a plowed furrow versus level soil, or opposite leaf surfaces. Climate in the microscale may be effectively modified by relatively simple human efforts.

Mesoclimatology: Mesoclimatology embraces a rather indistinct middle ground between macroclimatology and microclimatology. The areas are smaller than those of macroclimatology are and larger than those of microclimatology, and they may or may not be climatically representative of a general region.

Macroclimatology: Macroclimatology is the study of the large-scale climate of a large area or country. Climate of this type is not easily modified by human efforts. However, continued pollution of the Earth, its streams, rivers, and atmosphere, can eventually make these modifications. Climate has become increasingly important in other scientific fields. Geographers, hydrologists, and oceanographers use quantitative measures of climate to describe or analyze the influence of our atmospheric environment. Climate classification has developed primarily in the field of geography. The basic role of the atmosphere in the hydrologic cycle is an essential part of the study of hydrology. Both air and water measurements are required to understand the energy exchange between air and ocean (heat budget) as examined in the study of oceanography.

Ecology: Ecology is the study of the mutual relationship between organisms and their environment. Ecology is briefly mentioned here because the environment living organisms is directly affected by weather and climate, including those changes in climate that are gradually being made by man. During our growing years as a nation, our interference with nature by diverting and damming rivers, clearing its lands, stripping its soils, and scarring its landscape has produced changes in climate changes have been on the micro and meso scale and possibly even on the macro scale.

Climatological help in disasters: Climate-related natural disasters cause massive losses of Indian life and property. Droughts, flash floods, cyclones, avalanches, landslides brought on by torrential rains, and snowstorms pose the greatest threats. Other dangers include frequent summer dust storms, which usually track from north to south; they cause extensive property damage in North India[51] and deposit large amounts of dust from arid regions. Hail is also common in parts of India, causing severe damage to standing crops such as rice and wheat.

According to a Policy Brief by ESCAP (United Nations Economic and Social Commission for Asia and the Pacific), telecentres have the potential to play a key role in disaster risk management at the community level. Described as community centres that provide public access to Information and Communication Technologies (ICTs) such as telephones, computers and the Internet, their rapid adoption across the globe has been accompanied by a surge of additional services (e.g. e-learning and training, e-government and financial services) that respond to the needs of the local demand.

The document identifies four main areas of telecentre potential in the field:

- **Capture and disseminate indigenous knowledge** for community-based disaster risk management (DRM), including local knowledge of hazards, vulnerabilities and available resources, using the centre as a knowledge hub in support of preparedness strategies;

- **Support of information bases for disaster risk management**, as telecentres could help organize community inputs into the planning and execution of disaster risk reductions actions (e.g. digitized resource maps, chronological logs of disasters);

- **Provision of awareness raising and training**, based on locally-based needs and priorities and disseminated broadly through telecentre networks and the support of open-source collaboration software, and

- **Communication of risk and last-mile early warning** in local communities, potentially acting as a command centre for disaster response and coordination of efforts.

Computer Gaming

A video game is an electronic game that involves interaction with a user interface to generate visual feedback on a video device. The word video in video game traditionally referred to a raster display device. However, with the popular use of the term "video game," it now implies any type of display device. The electronic systems used to play video games are known as platforms; examples of these are personal computers and video game consoles. These platforms range from large mainframe computers to small handheld devices. Specialized video games such as arcade games, while previously common, have gradually declined in use.

The input device used to manipulate video games is called a game controller, and varies across platforms. For example, a dedicated console controller might consist of only a button and a joystick. Another may feature a dozen buttons and one or more joysticks. Early personal computer games often needed a keyboard for gameplay, or more commonly, required the user to buy a separate joystick with at least one button. Many modern computer games allow, or even require, the player to use a keyboard and mouse simultaneously.

Video games typically also use other ways of providing interaction and information to the player. Audio is almost universal, using sound reproduction devices, such as speakers and headphones. Other feedback may come via haptic peripherals, such as vibration or force feedback, with vibration sometimes used to simulate force feedback.

Early games used interactive electronic devices with various display formats. The earliest example is from 1947—a "Cathode ray tube Amusement Device" was filed for a patent on January 25, 1947 by Thomas T. Goldsmith Jr. and Estle Ray Mann, and issued on December 14, 1948 as U.S. Patent 2455992.

Inspired by radar display tech, it consisted of an analog device that allowed a user to control a vector-drawn dot on the screen to simulate a missile being fired at targets, which were drawings fixed to the screen.

In 1971, Computer Space, created by Nolan Bushnell and Ted Dabney, was the first commercially sold, coin-operated video game. It used a black-and-white television for its display, and the computer system was made of 74 series TTL chips. The game was featured in the 1973 science fiction film Soylent Green. Computer Space was followed in 1972 by the Magnavox Odyssey, the first home console. Modeled after a late 1960s prototype console developed by Ralph H. Baer called the "Brown Box", it also used a standard television. These were followed by two versions of Atari's Pong; an arcade version in 1972 and a home version in 1975. The commercial success of Pong led numerous other companies to develop Pong clones and their own systems, spawning the video game industry.

Multimedia and Animation

Multimedia: The use of computers to present text, graphics, video, animation, and sound in an integrated way. Long touted as the future revolution in computing, multimedia applications were, until the mid-90s, uncommon due to the expensive hardware required. With increases in performance and decreases in price, however, multimedia is now commonplace. Nearly all PCs are capable of displaying video, though the resolution available depends on the power of the computer's video adapter and CPU.

Multimedia is more than one concurrent presentation medium (for example, on CD-ROM or a Web site). Although still images are a different medium than text, multimedia is typically used to mean the combination of text, sound, and/or motion video. Some people might say that the addition of animated images (for example, animated GIF on the Web) produces multimedia, but it has typically meant one of the following:

- Text and sound
- Text, sound, and still or animated graphic images
- Text, sound, and video images
- Video and sound
- Multiple display areas, images, or presentations presented concurrently
- In live situations, the use of a speaker or actors and "props" together with sound, images, and motion video

Multimedia can arguably be distinguished from traditional motion pictures or movies both by the scale of the production (multimedia is usually smaller and less expensive) and by the possibility of audience interactivity or involvement (in which case, it is usually called *interactive multimedia*). Interactive elements can include: voice command, mouse manipulation, text entry, touch screen, video capture of the user, or live participation (in live presentations).

Multimedia tends to imply sophistication (and relatively more expense) in both production and presentation than simple text-and-images. Multimedia presentations are possible in many contexts, including the Web, CD-ROMs, and live theater. A rule-of-thumb for the minimum development cost of a packaged multimedia production with video for commercial presentation (as at trade shows) is: $1,000 a minute of presentation time. Since any Web site can be viewed as a multimedia presentation, however, any tool that helps develop a site in multimedia form can be classed as multimedia software and the cost can be less than for standard video productions.

Application of Multimedia

Multimedia finds its application in various areas including, but not limited to, advertisements, art, education, entertainment, engineering, medicine, mathematics, business, scientific research and spatial temporal applications. this technology is good to use because:

- showing what things look like, how they move and how they change
- keeping an audience's interest,

- establishing personal contact
- establishing the identity and academic credibility of a speaker
- communicating the speaker's enthusiasm for the subject

Below are the several examples where this technology is used :

Entertainment and Fine Arts

Multimedia is heavily used in the entertainment industry, especially to develop special effects in movies and animations. Multimedia games are a popular pastime and are software programs available either as CD-ROMs or online. Some video games also use multimedia features. Multimedia applications that allow users to actively participate instead of just sitting by as passive recipients of information are called Interactive Multimedia.

In the Arts there are multimedia artists, whose minds are able to blend techniques using different media that in some way incorporates interaction with the viewer. One of the most relevant could be Peter Greenaway who is melding Cinema with Opera and all sorts of digital media. Another approach entails the creation of multimedia that can be displayed in a traditional fine arts arena, such as an art gallery. For the most part these artists are using materials that will not hold up over time.

Education

In Education, multimedia is used to produce computer-based training courses (popularly called CBTs) and reference books like encyclopaedia and almanacs. A CBT lets the user go through a series of presentations, text about a particular topic, and associated illustrations in various information formats. Edutainment is an informal term used to describe combining education with entertainment, especially multimedia entertainment. In education they are useful for:

- recorded or broadcast lectures
- bringing in an expert speaker from a distant location
- demonstrating processes that learners may not otherwise have the opportunity to see (such as a rare surgical technique)
- demonstrating techniques that learners will have to try themselves later (such as setting up laboratory equipment)

- recording students' performances to enable feedback and promote reflection
- bringing the real world into the classroom

Engineering

Software engineers may use multimedia in Computer Simulations for anything from entertainment to training such as military or industrial training. Multimedia for software interfaces are often done as collaboration between creative professionals and software engineers.

Industry

In the Industrial sector, multimedia is used as a way to help present information to shareholders, superiors and coworkers. Multimedia is also helpful for providing employee training, advertising and selling products all over the world via virtually unlimited web-based technologies.

Mathematical and Scientific Research

In Mathematical and Scientific Research, multimedia is mainly used for modelling and simulation. For example, a scientist can look at a molecular model of a particular substance and manipulate it to arrive at a new substance. Representative research can be found in journals such as the Journal of Multimedia.

In research they are useful for:
- dissemination of results through:
- recorded or broadcast conference presentations and discussions
- demonstrating new techniques to colleagues,
- publicising and promoting research outcomes to related professionals and to the general public
- and for capturing data - such as focus groups, interviews, behavioural observations.

Medicine

In Medicine, doctors can get trained by looking at a virtual surgery or they can simulate how the human body is affected by diseases spread by viruses and bacteria and then develop techniques to prevent it.

"Graphic Design" encompasses a whole range of media services. Website Outsourcing is your one stop shop for all kinds of graphic designing services. With many years of experience designing high quality professional graphics and advertising material, we are well suited to be your long-term graphics partner. As your company grows and therefore you graphics needs, you will find it makes more sense to associate your firm with a vendor who is experienced in all aspects of graphics designing.

Animations

A simulation of movement created by displaying a series of pictures, or frames. Cartoons on television is one example of animation. Animation on computers is one of the chief ingredients of multimedia presentations. There are many software applications that enable you to create animations that you can display on a computer monitor.

Note the difference between animation and video. Whereas video takes continuous motion and breaks it up into discrete frames, animation starts with independent pictures and puts them together to form the illusion of continuous motion.

Graphics file formats like GIF, MNG and Flash allow animation to be viewed on a computer or over the Internet. Because animation is very time-consuming and often very expensive to produce, the majority of animation for TV and movies comes from professional animation studios. However, the field of independent animation has existed at least since the 1950s, with animation being produced by independent studios (and sometimes by a single person). Several independent animation producers have gone on to enter the professional animation industry.

Limited animation is a way of increasing production and decreasing costs of animation by using "short cuts" in the animation process. This method was pioneered by UPA and popularized (some say exploited) by Hanna-Barbera, and adapted by other studios as cartoons moved from movie theaters to television. It is also the basis of anime.

History of Animation

Picture animation was invented in 1831 by Joseph Antoine Plateau. He used a machine called *phenakistoscope* to create the illusion of movement. The device consisted of a spinning disc that held a series of drawings and windows that framed the user's perception of the drawings.

Many other animating machines were invented since then, but it was not until 1906 when the first complete animated film was produced by J.Steward Blackton. It was called "Humorous Phases of a Funny Face". In 1915, Earl Hurd introduced the technique of *cell animation* which took its name from the transparent sheets of celluloid that was used. The father of animation, Walt Disney produced a huge cartoon world in less than ten years at 1928. The first commercial animated cartoon, "Snow White and the Seven Dwarfs", was then produced. Many people followed, which contributed to this evolution. The results were good, but to a certain point. When very complex animation was required, everything turned out to be extremely difficult. Something was definitely missing and *technology* would give the answer in the following years.

Traditional Animation Techniques

Hand-drawn animation, with each frame individually crafted by an artist, requires a lot of skill, a lot of patience and very little equipment. The drawing is usually done on a *cell* which allows multiple frames to be drawn by the same cells. Each frame can be recorded on film or video, and the amount of work going into an animation is staggering. A feature film containing the production of 250,000 drawings would take fifty years of labour if all were to be drawn by a single artist. So usually it is coordinated by one person but the work is divided among a number of artists. Senior artists will draw the key frames and junior artists will draw in-between ones.

As we said before all the detail can be painted on to every frame; it is more likely that the frame will be compiled from several cells at the point of filming. The *background* may be on one cell, *static characters* on the other and the *moving character* on the top. In this way the bottom two cells can be used in a number of frames. It might also be that the cells are moved relative to one another, in successive frames, without being redrawn. Conventional animation is oriented mainly towards the production of two-dimensional cartoons. Every frame is a flat picture. In order to achieve the multiple frame design by using the same cells the *multiplane* technique is used. Several glass layers are placed beneath the camera at varying distances. On the layers the cells are placed and the frame is filmed. A lot of camera effects can be added into the animation but they are usually difficult to produce and sometimes are very expensive. A few of them are: zooming, fade-in, fade-out, etc.

Computer Assisted Animation

It is very clear that *automation* of the whole animation or even part of it would be very productive. Computers were used for animation for the first time in early sixties but it was mainly for scientific reasons. Ten years later animators started to consider computers to be a very powerful and useful part of their animation systems.

Today, computers can be used in animation in two main ways: as tools to improve the application of traditional methods; and as a means of generating animation which is not possible using traditional methods. Computers can considerably improve the speed, accuracy and at the same time reduce the cost of traditional animation methods. Projects which were impossible to realise in the past could actually be attempted.

Computer animation systems are classified into several different levels. These levels define the depth of the assistance that is provided by the computer. At the lowest level the animator can use software only to design the drawings. On the other hand at the highest level the whole work drawing, modeling and motion control is produced by the system.

The second more important advantage of modern animation systems apart of the fact that make everything easier is the *interactivity*. Animation can not only be a visual effect that one simply sees and waits until it is finished. The user becomes a participant of the whole story and can decide upon the development of the sequence. This has a large amount of applications which give to animation systems a very important existence in life.

There are several animation software packages currently available in the market. They all have a different approach to animation but tend to work on the same principle. There is an interactive graphics interface where the drawing, paint and modeling takes place. An *animation* language takes care of the *motion control* and of any advanced animation that is required. Every language currently available requires different programming skills. However the more advanced a language is, the more enhanced the produced motion will be. The problem that arises here is that computer animators usually don't have strong programming experience since they mostly come from areas of traditional animation.

There is not a single answer to this problem but the most satisfying one is that software should approach differently each user depending on the result that is required to produce.

3 Basic Types of Animation

The basic types of animation are the primary keynote for animation effect. The 3 basic types of animation are cel, stop and computer animation.

Cel Animation

Cel animation refers to the traditional way of animation in a set of hand drawings. In this process of animation, various pictures are created which are slightly different but progressive in nature, to depict certain actions. Trace these drawings on a transparent sheet. This transparent sheet is known as cel and is a medium for drawing frames. Now draw outlines for the images and color them on the back of the cel. The cel is an effective technique that helps to save time by combining characters and backgrounds. You can also put the previous drawings over other backgrounds or cels whenever required. Here, you need not draw the same picture again as it has the facility of saving previous animations that can be used when required. Coloring a background may be a more difficult task than a single drawing, as it covers the whole picture. Background requires shading and lighting and will be viewed for a longer duration. Then use your camera to photograph these drawings. Today, cel animations are made more attractive by using the drawings together with music, matching sound effects and association of timing for each effect. E.g. To display a cartoon show, 10-12 frames are played in rapid succession per second to give a representation of movement in a cel animation.

Stop Animation

Stop animation or stop motion animation is a technique to make objects move on their own. Here, a few images are drawn with some different positions and photographed separately. Puppetry is the one of the most used frame-to-frame animation types. Some famous movies that are animated via stop animation effects are King Kong, The Dinosaur and the Missing Link, The Curse of the Were-Rabbit and and The Lost World.

Computer Animation

Computer Animation is the latest technique of animation that includes 2D and 3D animation. These animations not only enhance the hand-drawn characters but also make them appear real as compared to the above mentioned animations.

2D Animation: It is used through Powerpoint and Flash animations. Though its features are similar to cel animation, 2D animation has become popular due to simple application of scanned drawings into the computer like in a cartoon film.

3D Animation: It is used in film making where we require unusual objects or characters that are not easy to display. Use of 3D animation can create a crowd of people in a disaster like earthquake, flood or war. There are different shapes, support of mathematical codes, display of actions and colors which are mind-blowing as if copied from an actual picture.

The uses of animation

Cartoons: The most common use of animation, and perhaps the origin of it, is cartoons. Cartoons appear all the time on television and the cinema and can be used for entertainment, advertising, presentations and many more applications that are only limited by the imagination of the designer. The most important factor about making cartoons on a computer is *reusability* and *flexibility*. The system that will actually do the animation needs to be such that all the actions that are going to be performed can be repeated easily, without much fuss from the side of the animator. Speed here is not of real importance, as once the sequence is complete, it can be recorded on film or video, frame by frame and played back at an acceptable speed.

Simulations: Many times it is much cheaper to train people to use certain machines on a *virtual environment* (i.e. on a computer simulation), than to actually train them on the machines themselves. Simulations of all types that use animation are supposed to respond to real-time stimuli, and hence the events that will take place are non-deterministic. The response to real-time stimuli requires a fast response and the non-determinism, requires a fast system to deal with it. This means that speed is the most important factor in simulation systems.

Scientific Visualisation: Graphical visualisation is very common in all areas of science. The usual form that is takes is x-y plots and when things get more complicated three dimensional graphs are used. However there are many cases that something is more complex to be visualised in a three dimensional plot, even if that has been enhanced with some other effect (e.g. colour). Here is where animation comes in. Data is represented in multiple images (frames) which differ a little from each other, and displayed one after the other to give the illusion of motion. This adds a fourth dimension and increases the information conveyed. Speed here is again the most important factor, as huge sets of data might have to be displayed in real-time. Someone might argue, that results maybe filmed and played back, but that depends on how often the sequence has to be recalculated. For example it might take a few days or weeks to generate an animation of a *fractal*, which zooms in slowly, and it might be distressing to realise that it has zoomed in at the wrong place.

The uses of *scientific visualisation* can be classified into two main categories: analysis and teaching. Both of these are described below

Analysis and Understanding

Very frequently, scientists have large sets of data (often in the form of lists of numbers) that need to be understood and often a theory needs to be formulated that explains their relationship. It would be very difficult to go through these lists manually or otherwise and make any sense out of them, unless some graphical technique is used for the initial approach. If the data set is massive, a short (or long) animation of the data can give the scientists a first idea of how to approach the situation.

Examples of the different uses of animation:

- Astronomers use computers to do animations if high speed jets penetrating different gases, to determine why a few galaxies flare dramatically. (This research has given out valuable information about why some galaxies flare into broad plumes and why others remain extremely straight and narrow).

- British Telecom uses sophisticated programs that plot on a map of the UK, the density of telephone fault reports using different colours. When a storm was plotted on top of this map and the whole system was animated it could be seen that the density of faults increased significantly at areas from which the storm had just passed.

- Animation can be used in software engineering, where an algorithm can be animated, in order to understand how it works or to debug it. Spotting errors using animation, becomes much easier.

Teaching and Communicating

One of the most difficult aspects of teaching is communicating ideas effectively. When this becomes too difficult using the classical teaching tools (speech, blackboard etc.) animation can be used to convey information. From its nature, an animation sequence contains much more information than a single image or page of text. This, and the fact that an animation can be very *"pleasing to the eye"*, makes animation the perfect tool for learning.

Two examples of the use of animation for learning are:

- Programs that show the planetary system in action in three dimensions make it very easy for kids to understand rather than using tables of sizes, periods and diameters.

- Astrophysicists at the National Center for Supercomputing Applications, work with artists, in order to explain some phenomena which cannot be seen such as the visualisation of the gravitational field of a Schwarzchild black hole. The latter is not visible as it absorbs all light that falls onto it. The only way of experimenting with it is to animate it on a computer.

Exercises

Fill in the Blanks

1. First generation computer based on ______________.

2. A set of Instruction called __________.

3. Random access memory having two types __________ , __________.

4. Memory unit is one part of ______________.

5. EPROM can be used for ______________.

Answers

1.Vacuum tube 2. Program 3. Static and Dynamic 4.Central Processing Unit 5.Erasing and reconstructing the contents of ROM

Questions

1. Explain the classification of computer.

2. What do you mean by storage devices .

3. What is system software.

4. Describe Computer Ethics.

5. Explain Animation.

6. Discuss Climatology.
7. What are the types of Multimedia.
8. What do you understand by remote sensing.
9. Explain Types of Printer.
10. Draw Bus Architecture and Explain.

CHAPTER - 2

Fundamental of Operating System and Programming Generation and Approach

Objectives

At the end of this session, the learner will be able to:

Define operating system.

Outline the function and types of OS.

Distinguish file, process and memory management.

Explain generation of programming languages.

Tell the characteristics and categorization of Programming language.

Compare Procedure and Object oriented Programming

Write features and merits of OOPS.

***Definition*:** An operating system is a system software which may be viewed as an organized collection of software consisting of procedures for operating a computer and providing an environment for execution of programs. It acts as an interface between users and hardware of a computer system.

There are many important reasons for studying operating system. *Some of them are*:

1. User interacts with the computer through the operating system in order to accomplish his task since it is his primary interface with a computer.

2. It helps the user to understand the inner functions of a computer very closely.

3. Many concepts and techniques found in the operating system have general applicability in other applications.

What is an Operating System?

An operating system is an essential component of a computer system. the primary objective of an operating system are to make the computer system convenient to use and to utilise computer hardware in an efficient manner.

An operating system is a large collection of software, which manages the resources of the computer system, such as memory, processor, file system and input/output devices. It keeps track of the status of each resources and decides who will have control over computer resources, for how long and when. The positioning of the overall computer system is shown in figure.

From the figure, it is clear that the operating system directly controls the computer hardware resources. Other programs rely on facilities provided by the operating system gain access to computer system resources. There are two ways to interact with the computer system:

1. By means of operating **System Call** in a program.

2. Directly by means of Operating System Commands.

***System Call*:** System call provides the interface to a running program and the operating system. The user program receives operating system service through the set of system calls. Earlier these calls were available in assembly language instructions, but now a days these features are supported through high level language like C, Pascal, etc., which replace assembly language for system programming. The use of system calls in C or Pascal programs very much resemble pre-defined functions or subroutine calls.

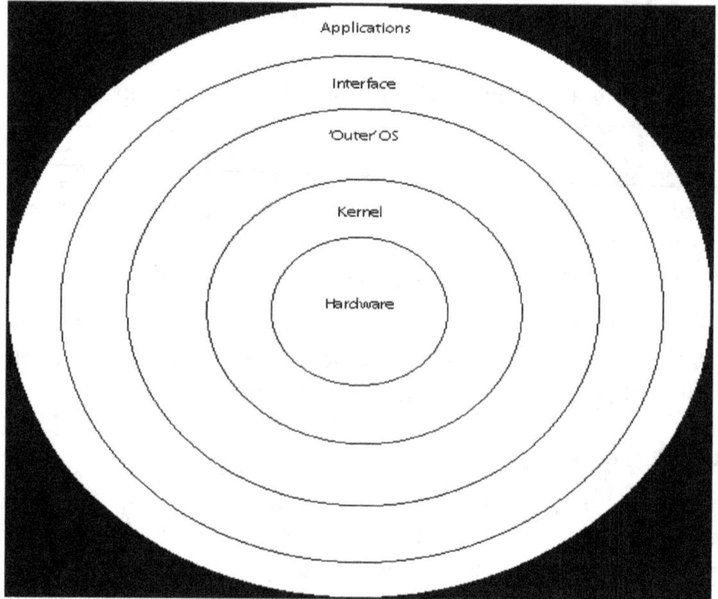

As an example of how system calls are used, let us consider a simple program to copy data from one file to another. In an interactive system, the following system calls will be generated by the operating system.

- Prompt message for inputting two files names and reading it from the terminal.

- Open source and destination files.

- Prompt error message in case of source file cannot be open because it is protected against access or because the destination file cannot be created since there is already a file of this name.

- Read the source file.

- Write into the destination file.

- Display status information regarding various read/write error conditions. For ex., the program may find that the end of the file has been reached or that there was a hardware failure. The write operation may encounter various errors, depending upon the output device.

- Close both files after the entire file is copied.

As we can observe, a user program makes heavy use of the operating system. All interaction between the program and its environment must occur as a result of request from the program to the operating system.

Operating System Commands: Apart from system calls users may interact with the operating system directly by means of operating system commands.

For ex., if you want to list files or sub-directories in MS-DOS, you invoke Dir command. In either case the operating system acts as an interface between users and the hardware of the computer system. The fundamental goal of the computer system is to solve user problems. Towards this goal computer hardware is designed. Since the bare hardware alone is not very easy to use, programs (software) were developed. These programs require certain common operations, such as controlling peripheral devices. The command function of controlling and allocating resources are then brought together into one piece of software, the operating system.

Types of Operating System: Operating system can be classified into various categories with respect to the type of processing it supports. Following are the main type of OS:

1. ***Batch OS:*** This the most primitive type of operating system. In batch processing a program, its related data and control commands should be submitted together in a form of job(coded on a punch card). Batch OS allows no interaction between the user and the executing programs. Thus, the programs that needed large execution time(like payroll, forecasting, scientific researches and structural analysis etc.) and less interaction with user were well served by batch processing. But, due to long time needed for execution and probability of less online debugging, the batch processing is not at all suitable for software development. The typical features of Batch OS were:

   - *Scheduling*: the scheduling of jobs was according to their arrival i.e. First Come First Served(FCFS) basis. This criteria provides a fair deal to the jobs but, because of the long turn around time and the average waiting time, the short jobs have to wait for very large time to get executed if some long jobs preceded them in the queue. To overcome this controversy another criteria known as "shortest job next", was evolved which provided preference to shorter jobs over longer jobs. This offered much better turn around time and average waiting time to the pending jobs.

- *Memory Management*: In Batch OS memory was divided into two permanent partitions, one permanently occupied by the resident portion of the OS and the other was used to load the transient program for execution. When this program gets executed it vacant the memory space occupied by it, so that another program waiting for execution may reside into it.

- *I/O Management*: Since, only one program is under execution at a time so, there was no contention for the allocation of the I/O devices. Hence, the program which is under execution only used the I/O devices.

- *File Management*: the program which is executing can only access the files at a time without providing any concurrency between other jobs.

Thus, Batch OS proved to be limited to some simpler and loader device drivers.

Multi-Programming OS: A multi-programming system permits multiple programs to be loaded into the memory and execute the programs concurrently. The program in execution is called a "Process" or "Task". Thus the concurrency helps in improving the potentiality of the OS by allowing the utilisation of system resources, and enhancing the system throughput as compared to the serial and batch OS.

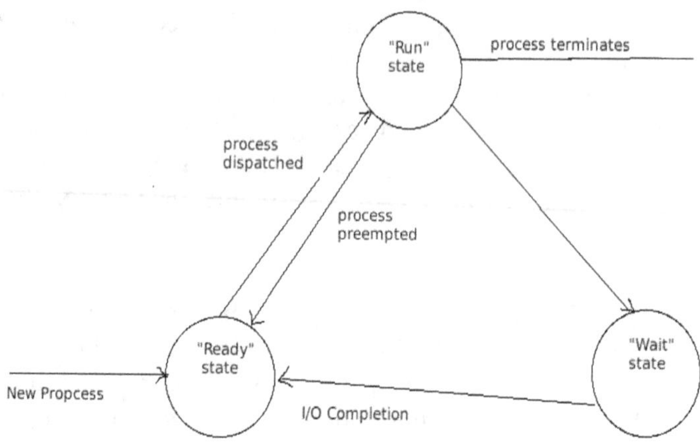

When a running process request for some I/O, it goes to the "Wait" state. Then another ready process is scheduled to "Run". So, when a process goes for I/O, the CPU is not idle. When a process in I/O has completed, the process which was in waiting state is allotted I/O i.e. it is transferred from "Waiting" state to the "Ready" state. This can be well understood from the above figure.

Multitasking: The concept of managing a multitude of simultaneously active programs, competing with each other for accessing the system resources, is called multitasking. A multitasking OS is characterized by its capability to support concurrent execution of more than one task. This is achieved by simultaneous maintenance of code and data of several processes in the memory at the same time, and by multiplexing the CPU and I/O resources among the active tasks. The multitasking OS monitors the state of all the task that are active.

The multitasking supports following features:

- User authentication by user-id and password.
- Resource usage accounting for the interactive users.
- Protection of users environments.

Multitasking without multi-user support, is usually found in real-time systems.

Time-Sharing: The time-sharing OS belongs to the period of Mainframe systems, where large number of users were allowed to access concurrently in an interactive mode. In this every user had its own terminal to access with. In this system the user enters his program with the source code and compiles it to run the program to get the output. In this OS the user can interact with the software while the program is in executable mode, and also can debug the program online. Thus, this reduced the time that was needed to first develop the program, then run and after its executing debug the program. But, now the user can simultaneously do this job. In time-Sharing OS the OS, served the users in a Round-Robin fashion. This process is so slow in I/O device that every user thinks that he is given full attention.

So, time-sharing systems were large multi-programmed, multi-user systems, designed for program development. One of the major requirement in this system is good terminal response. Most time-sharing systems use time-sliced, non-preemptive scheduling. It has FCFS queue. The main features of the time-sharing interactive OS are:

- *Memory Management:* The memory management in time sharing systems provides isolation and protection of co-resident programs. Since the programs are executed by different users, which do not involve inter process communication.

- *I/O Device Management:* The I/O management in this system must be good enough to maintain the requirements of the multiple users. In most of the system the allocation and de-allocation of devices provides system integrity.

- *File Management:* Since multiple users must be accessing multiple files, the file management must provide protection and access control.

Real-time OS: In this system the processing of the inputed data is carried out in a specific time interval. The data to be fed is received from the real world while, the data outputed controls some real world processes i.e. an air defense system receiving information from radars about the enemies aircraft and movements thus, controls weapons to target that aircraft. In this type of example it is very critical situation so, the inputed data should be correct, secure and within time limits so, that it can be well appreciated.

So, the real time systems are well managed in this system. This system mostly processes the application which are from the real world like control in industry viz.. thermal plants, petro-chemical plants and nuclear plants etc., military systems for processing of sensor information, weapon control, telephone switching equipment, flight control, etc.

- *Scheduling:* The primary objective of this system is quick response to external events, to meet the deadlines provided by the system. So, this type of systems are multi-tasking. The scheduling is priority based pre-emptive in which the inputs provided from real world is given higher priority so that it becomes ready to run, while the running program is given the lower priority. Such systems are expected to handle thousands of interrupts per second.

- *Memory Management:* In this the memory is so designed so as to get quick response as most of the programs may be residing in the memory always. This requires features which will enable programs to share memory as well as secure them from each other. The programs are mostly ROM resident.

- *I/O devices:* Time critical I/O device management is used in this system as, the external events and data is to be accepted and processed in time bound manner. The system calls allows the users to connect the devices and access Interrupt Service Routines(ISRs) directly.

- *File Management:* The file management is not so critical as , most of the programs are memory resident. The dynamic databases are maintained in ROM. The primary objective in this systemis the fast access.

The real time systems can be categorized into:

1. *Hard Real time OS*: In this the task given has to be completed within the specified time limits. Not meeting the deadlines can be catastrophic. The delays must be bounded. The interrupts must be optimized to respond real world inputs.

2. *Soft Real Time OS*: This is less restrictive type of real time OS. In this the results may not be catastrophic if the data are not processed within specified time interval but, the output may lose its utility. Ex. If the air craft system is monitoring the path of a flight and delays the information about landing then the information afterwards is of no use. This type of systems are not suitable for scientific and defense purpose

Combination OS: Different types of OS are combined to form combination OS. In this the computer system serves to be a software development platform as well as a target machine in a real time environment. So, Unix, VMS etc. are designed to provide a large set of services in various environments.

Distributed OS: A distributed system caters for a distributed environment, wherein a collection of autonomous computer systems, capable of communicating with each other through network that are connected via LAN/WAN. A distributed system provide means for sharing resources like computational capacity, I/O devices, and files etc. thus it should also provide following services.

- Global naming of resources.
- Distribution of computations.
- Enabling processes to access remote sources.
- Enabling processes to communicate with remote processes.

Functions of an Operating System: The Operating system is a manager of system resources, performing the following functions.

1. Process Management
2. Main memory Management
3. I/O device Management
4. File Management

1. **Process Management:** A process is an instance of a program in execution. A process is an active entity performing the functions of its related programs. To do its task it requires certain resources like CPU, memory, files and I/O devices. These resources are allocated to the process either at the time of its creation or at the time of processing. In multi-programming concept there are many system processes as well as user   processes running simultaneously.

   OS Functions Related to Process Management:
   - Process creation which involves loading the program from secondary storage to memory and executing it.
   - Transferring the program from ready state to run state when, CPU is controlled.
   - Suspending a process, which involves transferring a process from run state to wait state.
   - Providing mechanism for sharing resources.
   - Providing mechanism for inter-process communication.
   - Providing mechanism for deadlock handling.
   - Process deletion or process termination can be done when either the process has finish executing or there are some errors in the process.

2. **Main Memory Management:** For a program to be executed it is compulsory that it should be given absolute address and loaded into memory. As the program executes it calls the data from the memory by generating absolute address. When the program has finished execution it releases this memory space for others to occupy it. In multi-programing environment multiple programs are maintained in the memory.

   OS functions related to memory management:
   - Relocation
   - Protection
   - Sharing
   - Logical organization
   - Physical organization

3. **I/O Devices Management:** Every peripheral device has a unique identity. A stub on the local machine understands the NOS I/O port protocol and translates the protocol to the series of local operating

system calls to manage the local peripheral. The results are then returned back through the port.

Sample peripheral devices might include printers, CDROMs, disks, tapes, CD Recorders, and floppy disks.

Peripheral actions might include load or unload device driver and allocated or unallocated device. Some device specific actions might include read, write, and seek.

4. **File Management:** Computers can store information on different media like Hard Disk, Floppy Disk, CD,Magnetic Tape etc. All of them have different organization, capacity, access methods, Data transfer rates etc. But, for convenience OS provides a logical view and storage unit called File. A file is a collection of related information. The files can be organized into directories and sub-directories.

   OS function related to File Management:
   - Creating and deleting files.
   - Creating and deleting directories and sub-directories.
   - Support manipulation of files and directories.
   - Mapping files onto secondary storage.
   - Backing up files onto media like tapes.

Programming Languages: Language in which a computer programmer writes instructions for a computer to execute. The different notations used to communicate algorithms to a computer. A computer executes a sequence of instructions (a program) in order to perform some task. The set of instructions and the order in which they have to be performed is known as an algorithm. The result of expressing the algorithm in a programming language is called a program. The process of writing the algorithm using a programming language is called programming, and the person doing this is the programmer.

Many programming languages have some form of written specification of their syntax (form) and semantics (meaning). Some languages are defined by a specification document. For example, the C programming language is specified by an ISO Standard. Other languages, such as Perl, have a dominant implementation that is used as a reference. Most programming languages describe computation in an imperative style, i.e., as a sequence of commands, although some languages, such as those that support functional programming or logic programming, use alternative forms of description.

Generations

1GL or first-generation language: The main benefit of programming in a first-generation programming language is that the code a user writes can run very fast and efficiently, since it is directly executed by the CPU. However, machine language is a lot more difficult to learn than higher generational programming languages, and it is far more difficult to edit if errors occur.

2GL or second-generation language is called "assembly" language. A typical 2GL instruction looks like this:

ADD   12,8

which is in assembly language and, is converted by assembler to machine language.

Assembler: An assembler is a program that takes basic computer instructions and converts them into a pattern of bits that the computer's processor can use to perform its basic operations. An assembler converts the assembler language statements into machine language.

Second-generation languages are sometimes used in kernels and device drivers, but more often find use in extremely intensive processing such as games, video editing, graphic manipulation / rendering. The second generation of programming languages brought logical structure to software.

3GL or third-generation language is a "high-level" programming language, such as PL/I, C, or Java. Java language statements look like this:

```
public boolean handleEvent (Event evt) {
    switch (evt.id)  {
        case Event.ACTION_EVENT:  {
            if ("Try me" .equald(evt.arg)) {
```

which is then compiled and errors if present are shown to programmer.

A **compiler** converts the statements of a specific high-level programming language into machine language. In Java, the output is called bytecode, which is converted into appropriate machine language by a Java virtual machine that runs as part of an operating system platform.

A 3GL language requires a considerable amount of programming knowledge.   The third generation brought refinements to make the languages more programmer-friendly. This includes features like good support for data types, and expressing concepts in a way that favors the programmer, not the computer. Also English language was used to write syntax which became easier for the programmer.

FORTRAN, ALGOL, and COBOL are early examples of this sort of language. Most popular general-purpose languages today are C, C++, C#, Java, Delphi, and Python. Most 3GLs support structured programming.

4GL or fourth-generation language: Languages for accessing databases are often described as 4GLs. A 4GL language statement might look like this:

EXTRACT ALL CUSTOMERS WHERE "PREVIOUS PURCHASES"
TOTAL MORE THAN $1000

All 4GLs are designed to reduce programming effort, it takes less time to develop software, and the cost of software development is also very low as compared to 3GL and 4GL.

A number of different types of 4GLs *exist*:

- Table-driven (codeless) programming
- Report-generator programming languages
- forms generators
- Data management

5GL or fifth-generation language is programming that uses a visual or graphical development interface to create source language that is usually compiled with a 3GL or 4GL language compiler.In the 1990s, fifth-generation languages were considered to be the wave of the future, and some predicted that they would replace all other languages for system development, with the exception of low-level languages. Most notably, from 1982 to 1993 put much research and money into their fifth generation computer systems project, hoping to design a massive computer network of machines using these tools.

However, as larger programs were built, the flaws of the approach became more apparent. It turns out that, starting from a set of constraints defining a particular problem, deriving an efficient algorithm to solve it is a very difficult problem in itself. This crucial step cannot yet be automated and still requires the insight of a human programmer.

Example of 5GL can be given as Microsoft, Borland, IBM, and other companies make 5GL visual programming products for developing applications in Java, for example. Visual programming allows you to easily envision object-oriented programming class hierarchies and drag icons to assemble program components.

Some examples of widely used languages

Here is a non-exhaustive list of current programming languages:

Language	Main application area	Compiled/interpreted
ADA	Real-time	Compiled language
BASIC	Programming for educational purposes	Interpreted language
C	System programming	Compiled language
C++	System object programming	Compiled language
Cobol	Management	Compiled language
Fortran	Calculation	Compiled language
Java	Internet oriented programming	Intermediary language
MATLAB	Mathematical calculations	Interpreted language
Mathematica	Mathematical calculations	Interpreted language
LISP	Artificial intelligence	Intermediary language
Pascal	Education	Compiled language
PHP	Dynamic website development	Interpreted language
Prolog	Artificial intelligence	Interpreted language
Perl	Processing character strings	Interpreted language

General Characteristics of Programming Languages: Programming languages fall into two fundamental categories-low and high-level languages. Low-level languages are machine-dependent; that is, they are designed to be run on a particular computer. In contrast, high-level languages (for example, COBOL and BASIC) are machine-independent and can run on a variety of computers. The first two generations were low-level and the next two high-level generations of programming languages.

The higher-level languages do not provide us a greater programming capabilities, but they do provide a more sophisticated programmer/computer interaction. In short, the higher the level of the language, the easier it is to understand and use. For example, in a fourth-generation language you need only instruct the computer system what to do, not necessarily how to do it.

While programming in one of the first three generations of languages, you have to tell the computer what to do and how to do it. What comprises a new generation is less clear; therefore, languages after the fourth generation are referred to as a very high level languages.

Introduction to Programming: The set of techniques, methods, theories and standards that together represent the way of thinking for a problem solving is called programming. Since the invention of the computer, many approaches of program development have evolved. These include modular programming, top-down programming, bottom-up programming and structured programming. The main theme of all these programming was to handle the complexity of programs to be reliable and maintainable.

The earliest computers were programmed in machine language using 0 and 1. but, it was tedious to prepare a program in this language and also prone to error which, could not be easily debugged. To overcome these difficulties high level language came into existence. These languages are simple and easy to use. However these programs suffered the limitation of re-usability, flow control, difficulty due to global variables, understanding and maintainability. To sustain this feature a approach known as object oriented programming was insisted. This can be well understood from the figure below,

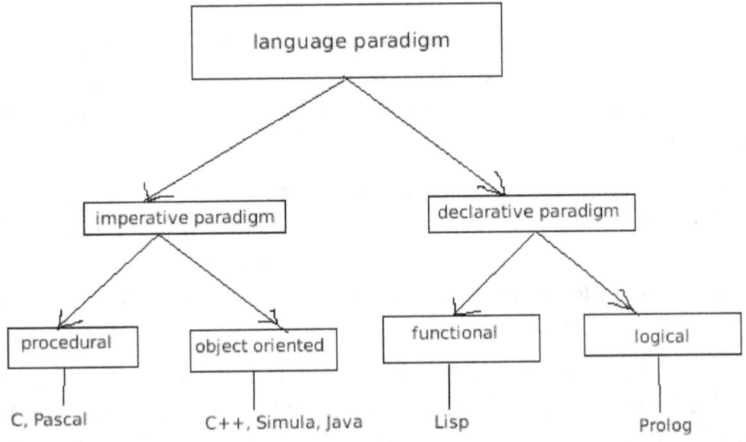

Procedure Oriented Programming: A program in a procedural language is a list of instructions. Each statement in the language tells the computer to do something. Get some input, do some computational task and finally display the output. This computational task is a function or

Procedure. The program structure can be viewed as shown in figure.

All conventional programming languages like **Pascal, C, FORTRAN, COBOL** used to model program based on the procedures re-oriented approach. In the procedure oriented approach, the problem is divided into **sub-programs** or **modules**. Then functions are defined for each subprogram. Each function can have its own data and logic. Information is passed between functions using **parameters** and **global variables**. Functions can have local variables that cannot be accessed outside the function.

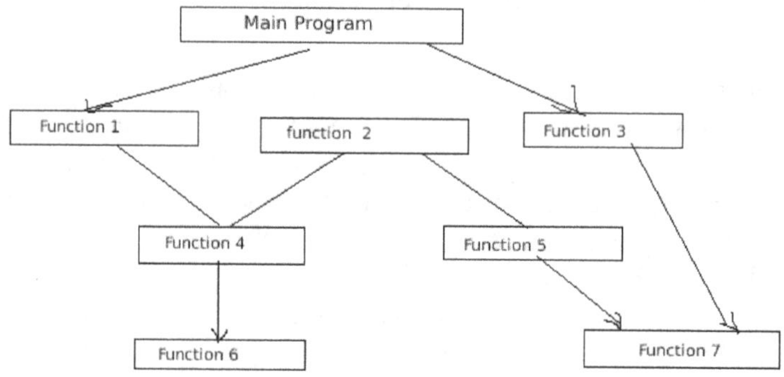

Procedure Oriented Approach

The programmer starts thinking *"what should be done to solve this problem?"*. Typically it starts with a pseudo code, a flow chart or a data flow diagram and changes the design into code. The concentration is more on development of functions.

Procedural languages have certain properties, which gives rise to some difficulties. The first and the foremost problem is the manner in which functions access global variables. Many important data items are placed as global so that they may be accessed by all the functions. Each function may have its own local data.

The next issue is in which way procedural language specifies user-defined data types, operations that are to be performed on this type of user-defined data types are left unspecified. As a result it may not be clear how to operate this type of variable.

The next issue is re-usability. Since procedural languages are strongly typed, their functions are highly dependent on the type of variables that are being used. This property hampers re-usability.

Finally the serious drawback of the procedural approach is that it does not model the real world problems very well. The emphasis is more on the functions that represents the action or activity and does not really correspond to the elements of the problem.

The major characteristics of the Procedure Oriented Programming are:

- More emphasis is on doing things.
- It is based on the problem at hand. Sequence or procedure or functionality is paramount.
- Most of the functions share global data which may lead to the following problems:
  - It will not produce software that is easy to maintain.
  - The risk of unwanted access and modification increases.
- It will not result in reusable software.
- It employs top down approach in program design.
- Works well in small systems.

Object Oriented Programming: The major factor, which leads to the development of Object Oriented programming is to resolve many problems encountered in the procedural programming. It is a programming language model organized around "objects" rather than "actions" and data rather than logic.

In this programming, we decompose a problem into a number of entities called objects and then build data and function around these entities. *"A collection of data and its operation is referred to as an object"*. Data is the vital element in the program development. Data is local to an object. These objects know ow to interact with another object through the interface. The organization of data and functions in Object Oriented Programs is shown in figure.

The salient features of Object Oriented programming are:

- More emphasis is on data rather than procedure.
- Programs are modularized into entities called objects.
- Data structures method characterize the objects of the problem.
- Since the data is not global, there is no question of any operations other than those defined within the objects, accessing the data. Therefore there is no scope of any accidental modification of data.

- It is easier to maintain programs. The manner in which the objects implement its operation is internal to it. Therefore any change within the objects could not affect the external objects.

- Objects re-usability, which can save many human hours of effort, is possible. An application developer can use objects like 'array', 'list', 'windows', 'menus', 'event' and many other components, which were developed by other programmers, in their program and thus can reduce program development time.

- It employs bottom-up approach in program design.

- Since a class defines only the data it needs to be concerned with, when an instance of that class (an object) is run, the code will not be able to accidentally access other program data. This characteristic of data hiding provides greater system security and avoids unintended data corruption.

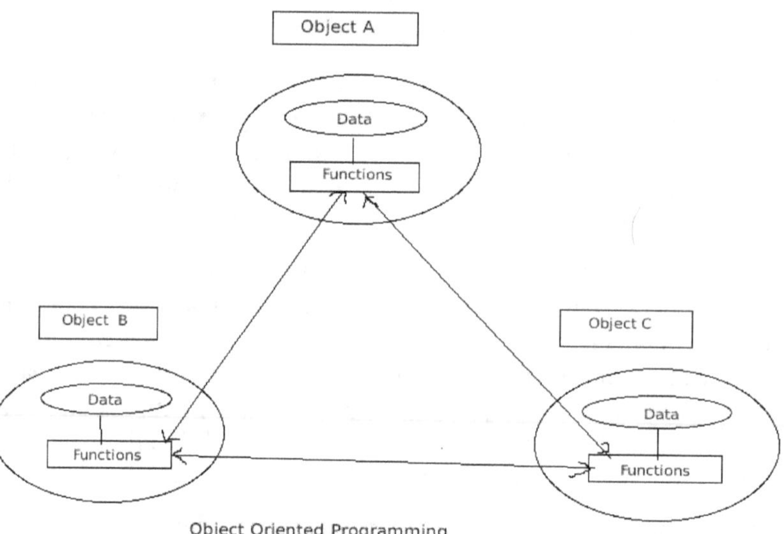

Object Oriented Programming

Simula was the first object-oriented programming language. Java, Python, C++, Visual Basic .NET and Ruby are the most popular OOP languages today. The Java programming language is designed especially for use in distributed applications on corporate networks and the Internet. Ruby is used in many Web applications. Curl, Smalltalk, Delphi and Eiffel are also examples of object-oriented programming languages.

OOPS features: The main component of Object-oriented programming (OOP) is a programming paradigm that uses "objects" and their interactions to design applications and computer programs. Programming techniques may include features such as abstraction, encapsulation, inheritance, and polymorphism. It is very important for you to understand this concept.

Object: Basically an object is anything that is identifiable as an single material item. You can see around and find many objects like Camera, Monitor, Laptop etc. In OOP perspective, an object is nothing but an instance of a class that contains real values instead of variables. Each object contains data and functions that operate on the data. Objects can interact without knowing details of each other. Thus an oops can be considered as network of operating objects which interact with each other by sending messages as shown in fig.

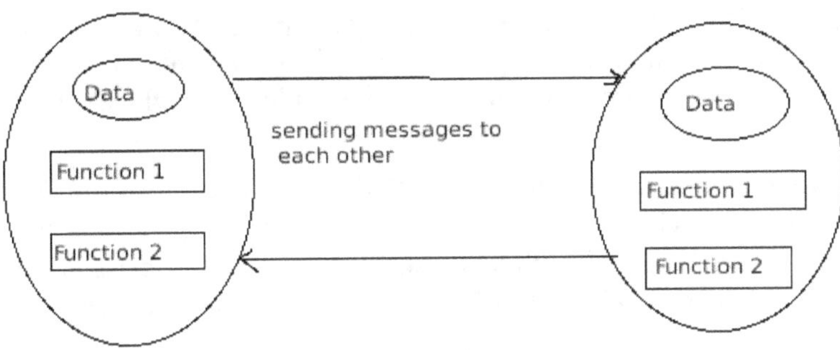

Message passing

Class: Objects of similar type can be group together to form a class. A class serves as a plan or template.A class is a template definition of the methods and variables for a particular kind of object. In other words, class is the blue print from which an individual objects are created. The programmer has to define the entire set of data and function for various operations on data for an object as an user-defined type in the form of a class. The compiler of that language does not know about this user defined data type. Ex. In a collection of potatoes each individual potato is an object and belongs to the class potato.

Data Abstraction: It refers to the act of representing essential features without including the background details to distinguish objects/functions from other objects/functions. With data abstraction, data structures can be used without having to be concerned about the exact details of implementation. In object-oriented software, complexity is managed by using abstraction. Abstraction is a process that involves identifying the critical behavior of an object and eliminating irrelevant and complex details. A well thought-out abstraction is usually simple, and easy to use in the perspective of the user, the person who is using your object. For ex. In case of built in data types like integer, floating point, etc. the programmer only knows about the operations but, how they are carried out by the hardware or software is hidden from the programmer. In oops the classes act as abstract data types.

Encapsulation: The wrapping up of data and functions into a single unit is known as encapsulation. This is one of the strong features of OOPS. The data is not directly accessible to the outside world but, only the functions which are wrapped in the class can access it. Functions are accessible to the outside world. These functions provide the interface to access the data. If one wants to modify the data of an object, s/he should know exactly what functions are available to interact with it. This insulation of the data from direct access by the program is known as **data hiding.** For example, the Laptop is an object that encapsulates many technologies, hardware that might not be understood clearly by most people who use it.

Inheritance: Inheritance is the ability to define a new class or object that inherits the behavior and the properties of an existing class. The new class or object is called a child or subclass or derived class while the original class is called parent or base class. For ex. The scooter is a type

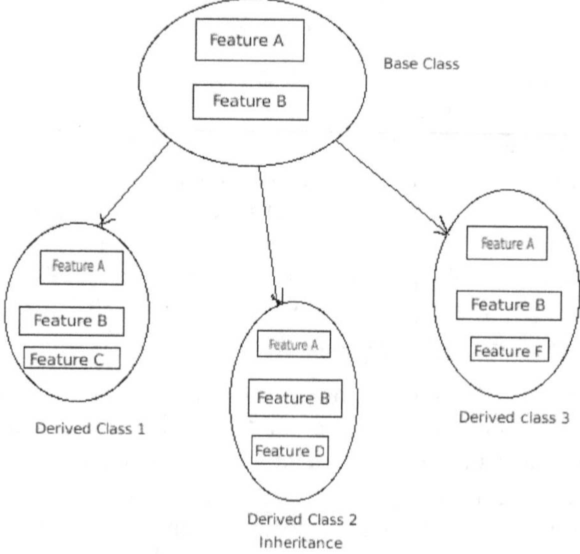

Inheritance

of the class two-Wheeler, which is again a type of the class motor vehicles.

New class can be built from the existing classes. It means that we can add additional features to an existing class without modifying it. Therefore the concept of inheritance provides the idea of re-usability. This inheritance mechanism allows the programmer to reuse a class that is made almost, but not exactly, similar to the required one by adding a few more features to it. As shown in the figure below.

Polymorphism: Polymorphism means **the ability to take more than one form of the same property.** In OOP, it is a language's ability to handle objects differently based on their run time type and use. Polymorphism is briefly described as "one interface, many implementations".Polymorphism is a characteristic of being able to assign a different meaning or usage to something in different contexts - specifically, to allow an entity such as a variable, a function, or an object to have more than one form.

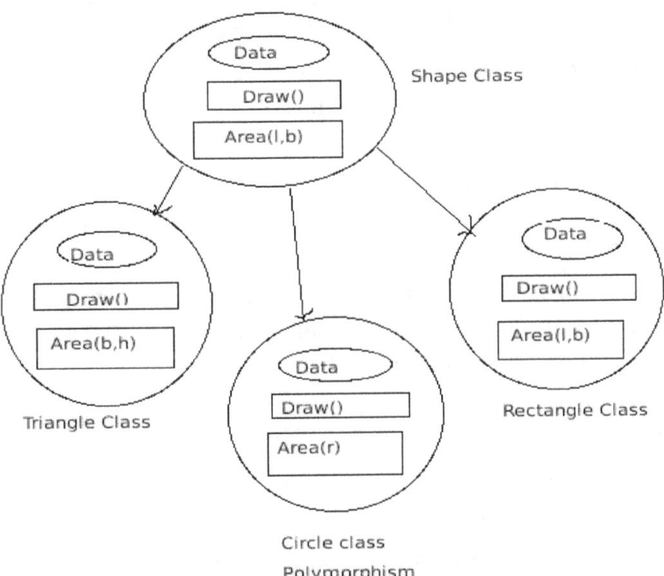

Polymorphism

There are two types of polymorphism.

1. Compile time polymorphism - It is achieved by overloading functions and operators.

2. Run time polymorphism - It is achieved by overriding virtual functions.

For ex. We used a function area which was inherited by all the three derived classes, i.e. triangle, circle and rectangle. Here the name is the same but, the functionality differs. This is known as function overriding, which is a type of polymorphism. As shown in the fig.

Benefits of OOPS: OOP offers several benefits to both the program developer and the user. The new technology provides greater programmer productivity, better quality of software and lesser maintenance cost. The major benefits are:

- **Ease in division of job**: Since it is possible to map objects of the problem domain to those objects in the program, the work can be easily partitioned based on objects.

- **Reduce complexity**: Software complexity can be easily managed.

- **Provide extensibility:** Object Oriented systems can be easily upgraded from small to large systems.

- **Eliminate redundancy:** through inheritance we can eliminate redundant code and extend the use of existing classes.

- **Saves development time and increase productivity:** Instead of writing code from scratch, solutions can be built from standard working modules.

- **Allows building secure programs:** Data hiding principle helps programmer to build secure programs that cannot be accessed by code in other parts of the program.

- **Allows designing simpler interfaces:** Message passing techniques between objects allows making simpler interface description with external systems.

OOPS Merits

1. Testability/Increased Quality (automated testing can increase speed of testing and increase quality)
2. Code re-use (Polymorphism, Generics, Interfaces)
3. Code extensibility
4. Catch errors at compile time rather than at runtime.
5. Maintainability: If designed correctly, any tier of the application can be replaced by another that implements the correct interface(s), and the application will still work (can use multiple user interfaces, can swap out data providers, etc.).

6. Reduces large problems to smaller, more manageable ones.

7. Fits the way the real world works. It is easy to map a real world problem to a solution in OO code.

Applications of OOPS

1. Real time systems
2. Simulations and modeling
3. Object oriented database
4. Hypertext, hypermedia and hypertext
5. AI and expert systems
6. Neural networks and parallel programming
7. Decision support and office automation systems
8. CIM / CAM /CAD systems

Exercises

Fill in the Blanks

- __________ language has the synonym mnemonic language.

- An operating system is a____________ software.

- System call provides the __________ to a running program and the operating system.

- A________converts the statements of a specific high-level programming language into machine language.

- An______ is anything that is identifiable as an single material item.

- The Hardware mechanism that enables a device to notify the CPU is called __________.

Answers

1.	Assembly	2.	System	3.	Interface
4.	Compiler	5.	Object	6.	Interrupt

Questions

1. List and describe briefly four of the characteristics of modern operating systems

2. Compare batch multiprogramming systems and time-sharing systems. Discuss their similarities and differences.
3. Write Application of OOPS.
4. What are the basic functions of an operating system? –
5. Explain procedure Oriented Programming.
6. What is virtual memory?
7. Give features of OOPS.
8. Write different generations of Programming language.
9. Give the differences between procedure Oriented and Object Oriented Programming.
10. Give demerits of Procedure Oriented Programming.

CHAPTER - 3

Basics of C++ and Object Oriented Approach

Objectives

At the end of this session, the learner will be able to:

List features, character, tokens.

Write precedence.

Illustrate program structure.

Define Data types, Operator, Expression.

Explain Statements and Control Statements.

Implement I/O operations, Array, Structures and Unions.

Demonstrate Object and Classes.

Apply Constructors and Destructors.

Illustrate overloading and Inheritance.

Features: The C++ is an extensive version of C-language. The C++ is built on C because of C's suitability to complex programming situation. C++ (pronounced see plus plus) is a statically typed, free-form, multi-paradigm, compiled, general-purpose programming language. It comprises a combination of both high-level and low-level language features. C++ has more versatile and useful features like:

- It provides functions for both input and output statements.
- It allows single line comments.
- The variable should be declared at the point of use.
- It allows for declaration of constants.
- It has no. of function programs.
- It provides technique of object based programming.
- It allows use of objects and classes to store large data.
- It provides new simplified methods for file operations.
- He database operation can be performed using array of objects.

History of C++: C was developed by Dennis Ritchie at Bell Laboratories and was first put to use in 1972. it proved to be very popular and was used by numerous users on variety of computers. This led to some variations in the language and affected its portability. A standard version of c was in great demand. In 1983 a technical committee was setup under the "American National Standard Committee on Computers and Information Processing" (ANSI) to standardize C. the standard was known as ANSI C.

C++ is the extension of C. it was developed by Bjarne Stroustrup in 1980's at Bell Laboratories in Murray Hill, New Jersey. It was initially stated as C with classes. In 1983 the name was changed to C++. Since its advent in 1980, C++ has undergone three major revisions, the first in 1985,the second in 1989 and the third in 1994 and the latest in 1997. still some work is going on the C++.

Stroustrup, the author of C++, added some features to original C to support Object Oriented programming. This feature helps you to approach a programming task in a new way. The problem is broken down into subgroups of related parts and encapsulate the data and code related to each group. Then these groups are organized into hierarchical structure and then translated into self-contained units called objects. Thus object oriented programming allows programs to be structured for clarity, extensibility, and ease of maintenance without loss of efficiency.

New features were added including virtual functions, function name and operator overloading, references, constants, user-controlled free-store memory control, improved type checking, and BCPL style single-line comments with two forward slashes (//). In 1985, the first edition of The C++ Programming Language was released, providing an important reference to the language, since there was not yet an official standard. Late addition of features included templates, exceptions, namespaces, new casts, and a Boolean type.

As the C++ language evolved, the standard library evolved with it. The first addition to the C++ standard library was the stream I/O library which provided facilities to replace the traditional C functions such as printf and scanf. Later, among the most significant additions to the standard library, was the Standard Template Library.

C++ Tokens: A token is the smallest element of a C++ program that is meaningful to the compiler. The C++ parser recognizes these kinds of tokens: identifiers, keywords, literals, operators, punctuators, and other separators. A stream of these tokens makes up a translation unit. Tokens are usually separated by "white space." White space can be one or more.

Operator Precedence and Associativity

Precedence Rules: The *precedence rules* of a language specify which operator is evaluated first when two operators with different precedence are adjacent in an expression. Adjacent operators are separated by a single operand.

Associativity Rules: The *associativity rules* of a language specify which operator is evaluated first when two operators with the same precedence are adjacent in an expression.

This table shows the priority and associativity of each operator in Pike, with the highest priority at the top:

Operators	**Associativity**
::a a::b	left to right
a() a[b] a->b a[b..c] ({}) ([]) (<>)	left to right
a++ a--	left to right
!a ~a (*type*)a ++a --a	right to left!

a*b a/b a%b	left to right
a+b a-b	left to right
a>>b a<<b	left to right
a>b a>=b a<b a<=b	left to right
a==b a!=b	left to right
a&b	left to right
a^b	left to right
a|b	left to right
&&	left to right
||	left to right
a?b:c	right to left!
=	right to left!
+=	
-=	
*=	
/=	
%=	
<<=	
>>=	
&=	
|=	
^=	
@a	right to left!
,	left to right

Structure of a program:

```
#include <iostream.h>
```

```
int main ()


{


  cout << "Hello World!";


  return 0;


}
```

In C++ language, to use C++ commands a header file "iostream.h" must be included in every program. The C++ functions are available in header file "iostream.h" which are accessible in the program.

#include<iostream.h>

Every file of C++ must be written with ".cpp" extension name.

Lines beginning with a hash sign (#) are directives for the preprocessor. They are not regular code lines. With expressions but indications for the compiler's preprocessor. In this case the directive #include<iostream> tells the preprocessor to include the iostream standard file. This specific file (iostream) includes the declarations of the basic standard input-output library in C++, and it is included because its functionality is going to be used later in the program.

int main ()

This line corresponds to the beginning of the definition of the main function. The main function is the point by where all C++ programs start their execution, independently of its location within the source code. It does not matter whether there are other functions with other names defined before or after it - the instructions contained within this function's definition will always be the first ones to be executed in any C++ program. For that same reason, it is essential that all C++ programs have a main function. The word main is followed in the code by a pair of parentheses (()). That is because it is a function declaration: In C++, what differentiates a function declaration from other types of expressions are these parentheses that follow its name. Optionally, these parentheses may enclose a list of parameters within them.

Right after these parentheses we can find the body of the main function enclosed in braces ({}). What is contained within these braces is what the function does when it is executed.

```
cout << "Hello World!";
```

This line is a C++ statement. A statement is a simple or compound expression that can actually produce some effect. In fact, this statement performs the only action that generates a visible effect in our first program. cout represents the standard output stream in C++, and the meaning of the entire statement is to insert a sequence of characters (in this case the Hello World sequence of characters) into the standard output stream (which usually is the screen. cout is declared in the iostream standard file within the std namespace, so that's why we needed to include that specific file and to declare that we were going to use this specific namespace earlier in our code.

Notice that the statement ends with a semicolon character (;). This character is used to mark the end of the statement and in fact it must be included at the end of all expression statements in all C++ program (one of the most common syntax errors is indeed to forget to include some semicolon after a statement).

```
return 0;
```

The return statement causes the main function to finish. return may be followed by a return code (in our example is followed by the return code 0). A return code of 0 for the main function is generally interpreted as the program worked as expected without any errors during its execution. This is the most usual way to end a C++ console program.

You may have noticed that not all the lines of this program perform actions when the code is executed. There were lines containing only comments (those beginning by //). There were lines with directives for the compiler's preprocessor (those beginning by #). Then there were lines that began the declaration of a function (in this case, the main function) and, finally lines with statements (like the insertion into cout), which were all included within the block delimited by the braces ({}) of the main function.

The program has been structured in different lines in order to be more readable, but in C++, we do not have strict rules on how to separate instructions in different lines. For example, instead of

```cpp
int main ()

{

    cout << " Hello World!";

    return 0;

}
```

We could have written:

```cpp
int main () { cout << "Hello World!"; return 0; }
```

Comments

Comments are parts of the source code disregarded by the compiler. They simply do nothing. Their purpose is only to allow the programmer to insert notes or descriptions embedded within the source code.

C++ supports two ways to insert comments:

```cpp
// line comment
```

```cpp
/* block comment */
```

The first comment starts with the double slash symbol(//) and terminates at the end of the line. ex.

// This is C++ programming

while, the second comment is written within the block i.e. started with a slash and star, and ended again with a slash and star. ex.

/*This is C++ programming*/

Fundamental Data Types

During programming, we store the variables in our computer's memory, but how the computer will know that how much space should be allotted to particular variable because the variables might be small, a letter, or a big name. So computer should know how much space will be needed unless all the memory will get full. So, to overcome this problem the concept of data types was introduced.

The memory in our computers is organized in bytes. A byte is the minimum amount of memory that we can manage in C++. A byte can store a relatively small amount of data: one single character or a small integer (generally an integer between 0 and 255). In addition, the computer can manipulate more complex data types that come from grouping several bytes, such as long numbers or non-integer numbers.

Here we have the summary of all fundamental data types in C++ and their range of storing the values in the memory:

Name	Description	Size*	Range*
char	Character or small integer.	1byte	signed: -128 to 127 unsigned: 0 to 255
short int (short)	Short Integer.	2bytes	signed: -32768 to 32767 unsigned: 0 to 65535
int	Integer.	4bytes	signed: -2147483648 to 2147483647 unsigned: 0 to 4294967295
long int (long)	Long integer.	4bytes	signed: -2147483648 to 2147483647 unsigned: 0 to 4294967295
bool	Boolean value. It can take one of two values: true or false.	1byte	true or false
float	Floating point number.	4bytes	+/- 3.4e +/- 38 (~7 digits)

double	Double precision floating point number.	8bytes	+/- 1.7e +/- 308 (~15 digits)
long double	Long double precision floating point number.	8bytes	+/- 1.7e +/- 308 (~15 digits)
wchar_t	Wide character.	2 *or* 4 bytes	1 wide character

* The values of the columns *Size* and *Range* depend on the system the program is compiled for. The values shown above are those found on most 32-bit systems. But for other systems, the general specification is that **int** has the natural size suggested by the system architecture (one *"word"*) and the four integer types **char**, **short**, **int** and **long** must each one be at least as large as the one preceding it, with **char** being always one byte in size. The same applies to the floating point types **float**, **double** and **long double**, where each one must provide at least as much precision as the preceding one.

Variables: If it is said to store some numbers in your memory you can do it but, when after some time you are been told to recall what values you had stored you, would be unable to recall it one by one. Also in computer the same concept is there how you will recall only a particular value. It is very difficult unless a name is provided to that value. This provision of providing names to the value which we want to store in computers memory is called initializing variables.

This is also helpful with respect to programming. As here we will need lots and lots of things to be stored in memory. This process can be expressed in C++ with the following instruction set:

```
1    a = 6;
2    b = 2;
3
     a = a -2;
4
     result = a / b;
```

Obviously, this is a very simple example since we have only used two small integer values, but consider that your computer can store millions of numbers like these at the same time and conduct sophisticated mathematical operations with them. Therefore, we can define a variable as a portion of memory to store a determined value.

Each variable needs an identifier that distinguishes it from the others. For example, in the previous code the *variable identifiers* were a, b and result, but we could have called the variables any names we wanted to invent, as long as they were valid identifiers.

Identifiers: In C++ we provide names for the entities we create, the variables, functions and types in our programs. These names, or identifiers, are required to conform to some simple rules. An identifier must start with a letter and is comprised of a sequence of letters and digits. Somewhat surprisingly, in this context the underscore _ is considered to be a letter (although there are conditions associated with its use).

There's no restriction on the length of an identifier. Identifiers beginning with an underscore followed by an upper case letter are reserved for use by the implementation, as are identifiers beginning with a two consecutive underscores, so to avoid problems you should refrain from using them for your own identifiers. C++ is case sensitive, so upper case and lower case characters are distinct. This means that the names userInput and userinput are recognised as two different identifiers.

Another rule that you have to consider when inventing your own identifiers is that they cannot match any keyword of the C++ language nor your compiler's specific ones, which are *reserved keywords*. The standard reserved keywords are:

asm, auto, bool, break, case, catch, char, class, const, const_cast, continue, default, delete, do, double, dynamic_cast, else, enum, explicit, export, extern, false, float, for, friend, goto, if, inline, int, long, mutable, namespace, new, operator, private, protected, public, register, reinterpret_cast, return, short, signed, sizeof, static, static_cast, struct, switch, template, this, throw, true, try, typedef, typeid, typename, union, unsigned, using, virtual, void, volatile, wchar_t, while.

Additionally, alternative representations for some operators cannot be used as identifiers since they are reserved words under some circumstances:

and, and_eq, bitand, bitor, compl, not, not_eq, or, or_eq, xor, xor_eq

Examples of acceptable identifiers are:

calculate_height, readWindSpeed, channel42, foo, BAR

Examples of unacceptable identifiers:

calculate height, delete, 2letters, _HELLO_

Declaration of variables: Every variable in a C++ program must be declared before it is used. The syntax is

specifier type name initializer:

where *specifier* is an optional keyword such as *const, type* is one of the C++ data types such as *int, name* is the name of the variable, and *initializer* is an optional.

The purpose of the declaration is to introduce a name to the program ; i.e.; to explain to the compiler what the name means. The *type* tells the compiler what range of values the variable may have and what operations can be performed on the variable.

The location of the declaration within the program determines the *scope* of the variables, the part of the program where variable must be used. In general, the scope of a variable extends from its point of declaration to the end of the immediate block in which it is declared or which it controls.

For ex.

int a;

int b;

int c;

The integer data types char, short, long and int can be either signed or unsigned depending on the range of numbers needed to be represented. Signed types can represent both positive and negative values, whereas unsigned types can only represent positive values (and zero). This can be specified by using either the specifier signed or the specifier unsigned before the type name. For example:

unsigned short int NumberOfSisters;

signed int MyAccountBalance;

Scope of variables: All the variables that we intend to use in a program must have been declared with its type specifier in an earlier point in the code, like we did in the previous code at the beginning of the body of the function main when we declared that a, b, and result were of type int.

A variable can be either of global or local scope. A global variable is a variable declared in the main body of the source code, outside all functions, while a local variable is one declared within the body of a function or a block.

Global variables can be referred from anywhere in the code, even inside functions, whenever it is after its declaration.

The scope of local variables is limited to the block enclosed in braces ({}) where they are declared. For example, if they are declared at the beginning of the body of a function (like in function main) their scope is between its declaration point and the end of that function. In the example above, this means that if another function existed in addition to main, the local variables declared in main could not be accessed from the other function and vice-verse.

Initialization of variables: Initializing variable means storing some value in the variable, which can be done through two methods. One is like how it is done in C, using assignment operator the syntax for which is:

type identifier = initial_value ;

For example, if we want to declare an int variable called a initialized with a value of 5 at the moment in which it is declared, we could write:

int a=5;

The second method is called constructor initialization in which the value to be stored is placed in the parenthesis (()):

type identifier (initial_value) ;

For example if we want to declare an int variable and initialize value to it we have to write:

int a(5);

Constants: C++ constants are values used in a program and will not change during the operation of the program and are important for any programmer in the operation of their programs.

C++ constants are not very different from any C++ variable. They are defined in a similar way and have the same data types and the same memory limitations. However, there is one major difference - once a constant has been created and value assigned to it then that value may not be changed.

Defining Constants with C++: There are actually three ways of defining a constant in a C++ program:

- by using the preprocessor
- by using the *const* key word
- by using enumerators - these will have a range of integer values

It's also worth noting that there are two types of constant: literal and symbolic.

Literal constants can be divided in *Integer Numerals, Floating-Point Numerals, Characters, Strings* and *Boolean Values. Integer Numerals*

1564

704

-286

These are numerical constants which are identified as a integer decimal value. For, this we do not have to write any quotes("") or any special character.

In addition to decimal numbers C++ allows the use as literal constants of octal numbers (*base 8*) and hexadecimal numbers (*base 16*). If we want to express an octal number we have to precede it with a 0 (a *zero* character). And in order to express a hexadecimal number we have to precede it with the characters 0x (*zero, x*). For example, the following literal constants are all equivalent to each other:

75   *// decimal*

0113   *// octal*

0x4b   *// hexadecimal*

By default, integer literals are of type int. However, we can force them to either be unsigned by appending the u character to it, or long by appending l:

75   *// int*

75u   *// unsigned int*

75l   *// long*

75ul   *// unsigned long*

the suffix can be specified using either upper or lowercase letters.

Floating Point Numbers: These describe the numbers with decimals or exponents where the numbers are expressed with the help of decimal numbers or e character. The e character is expressed by xth height where x is the integer value that follows the e character. Examples are,

3.14159   // 3.14159

6.02e23   // 6.02 x 10^23

1.6e-19   // 1.6 x 10^-19

3.0   // 3.0

These are four valid numbers with decimals expressed in C++. The first number is PI, the second one is the number of Avogadro, the third is the electric charge of an electron (an extremely small number) -all of them approximated- and the last one is the number three expressed as a floating-point numeric literal.

The default type for floating point literals is *double*. If you explicitly want to express a *float* or a *long double* numerical literal, you can use the f or l suffixes respectively:

3.14159L // *long double*

6.02e23f // *float*

Any of the letters that can be part of a floating-point numerical cons*tant (e, f, l)* can be written using either lower or uppercase letters without any difference in their meanings.

Character and string literals: There also exist non-numerical constants, like:

'z'

'p'

"Hello world"

"How do you do?"

The first two expressions represent single character constants, and the following two represent string literals composed of several characters. Notice that to represent a single character we enclose it between single quotes (') and to express a string (which generally consists of more than one character) we enclose it between double quotes (").

When writing both single character and string literals, it is necessary to put the quotation marks surrounding them to distinguish them from possible variable identifiers or reserved keywords. Notice the difference between these two expressions:

x

'x'

x alone would refer to a variable whose identifier is x, whereas 'x' (enclosed within single quotation marks) would refer to the character constant 'x'.

Character and string literals have certain peculiarities, like the escape codes. These are special characters that are difficult or impossible to express otherwise in the source code of a program, like newline (\n) or tab (\t). All of them are preceded by a backslash (\). Here you have a list of some of such escape codes:

ln	newline
lr	carriage return
lt	tab
lv	vertical tab
lb	backspace
lf	form feed (page feed)
la	alert (beep)
l'	single quote (')
l"	double quote (")
l?	question mark (?)
ll	backslash (l)

For example:

'ln'

'lt'

"Left lt Right"

"one ln two ln three"

Additionally, you can express any character by its numerical ASCII code by writing a backslash character (l) followed by the ASCII code expressed as an octal (*base-8*) or hexadecimal (*base-16*) number. In the first case (octal) the digits must immediately follow the backslash (for example 123 or 140), in the second case (hexadecimal), an x character must be written before the digits themselves (for example lx20 or lx4A).

String literals can extend to more than a single line of code by putting a backslash sign (l) at the end of each unfinished line.

"string expressed in\

  two lines"

You can also concatenate several string constants separating them by one or several blank spaces, tabulators, newline or any other valid blank character:

  "this forms" "a single" "string" "of characters"

Finally, if we want the string literal to be explicitly made of wide characters (*wchar_t* type), instead of narrow characters (*char* type), we can precede the constant with the L prefix:

L"This is a wide character string"

Wide characters are used mainly to represent non-English or exotic character sets.

Boolean literals

There are only two valid Boolean values: *true* and *false*. These can be expressed in C++ as values of type *bool* by using the Boolean literals true and false.

Defined constants (#define): You can define your own names for constants that you use very often without having to resort to memory-consuming variables, simply by using the #define preprocessor directive. Its format is:

#define identifier value

For example: #define PI 3.14159

#define NEWLINE '\n'

This defines two new constants: *PI* and *NEWLINE*. Once they are defined, you can use them in the rest of the code as if they were any other regular constant, for example:

```
// defined constants: calculate circumference

#include <iostream>
using namespace std;

#define PI 3.14159
#define NEWLINE '\n'

int main ()
{
  double r=5.0;                        // radius
  double circle;

  circle = 2 * PI * r;
  cout << circle;
  cout << NEWLINE;

  return 0;
}
```

In fact the only thing that the compiler preprocessor does when it encounters #define directives is to literally replace any occurrence of their identifier (in the previous example, these were PI and NEWLINE) by the code to which they have been defined (3.14159 and '\n' respectively).

The #define directive is not a C++ statement but a directive for the preprocessor; therefore it assumes the entire line as the directive and does not require a semicolon (;) at its end. If you append a semicolon character (;) at the end, it will also be appended in all occurrences of the identifier within the body of the program that the preprocessor replaces.

Declared constants (const): With the const prefix you can declare constants with a specific type in the same way as you would do with a variable: *const int* pathwidth = 100;

const char tabulator = '¥t';

Operators: C++ integrates operators. Unlike other languages whose operators are mainly keywords, operators in C++ are mostly made of signs that are not part of the alphabet but are available in all keyboards. This makes C++ code shorter and more international, since it relies less on English words, but requires a little of learning effort in the beginning.

Assignment (=)

The assignment operator assigns a value to a variable.

a = 5;

This statement assigns the integer value 5 to the variable a. The part at the left of the assignment operator (=) is known as the lvalue (left value) and the right one as the rvalue (right value). The lvalue has to be a variable whereas the rvalue can be either a constant, a variable, the result of an operation or any combination of these.

The most important rule when assigning is the right-to-left rule: The assignment operation always takes place from right to left, and never the other way:

a = b;

Arithmetic operators (+, -, *, /, %)

The five arithmetical operations supported by the C++ language are:

+   addition

-   subtraction

*   multiplication

/   division

%   modulo

Operations of addition, subtraction, multiplication and division literally correspond with their respective mathematical operators. The only one that you might not be so used to see is *modulo*; whose operator is the percentage sign (%). Modulo is the operation that gives the remainder of a division of two values. For example, if we write:

a = 11 % 3;

the variable a will contain the value 2, since 2 is the remainder from dividing 11 between 3.

Compound assignment (+=, -=, *=, /=, %=, >>=, <<=, &=, ^=, |=)

When we want to modify the value of a variable by performing an operation on the value currently stored in that variable we can use compound assignment operators:

expression	**is equivalent to**
value += increase;	value = value + increase;
a -= 5;	a = a - 5;
a /= b;	a = a / b;
price *= units + 1;	price = price * (units + 1);

and the same for all other operators. For example:

```
// compound assignment operators

#include <iostream>
using namespace std;

int main ()
{
  int a, b=3;
  a = b;
  a+=2;        // equivalent to a=a+2
  cout << a;
  return 0;
}
```

Increase and decrease (++, --)

Shortening even more some expressions, the increase operator (++) and the decrease operator (--) increase or reduce by one the value stored in a variable. They are equivalent to +=1 and to -=1, respectively. Thus:

```
c++;

c+=1;

c=c+1;
```

are all equivalent in its functionality: the three of them increase by one the value of c.

In the early C compilers, the three previous expressions probably produced different executable code depending on which one was used. Nowadays, this type of code optimization is generally done automatically by the compiler, thus the three expressions should produce exactly the same executable code.

A characteristic of this operator is that it can be used both as a prefix and as a suffix. That means that it can be written either before the variable identifier (++a) or after it (a++). Although in simple expressions like a++ or ++a both have exactly the same meaning, in other expressions in which the result of the increase or decrease operation is evaluated as a value in an outer expression they may have an important difference in their meaning: In the case that the increase operator is used as a prefix (++a) the value is increased **before** the result of the expression is evaluated and therefore the increased value is considered in the outer expression; in case that it is used as a suffix (a++) the value stored in a is increased after being evaluated and therefore the value stored before the increase operation is evaluated in the outer expression. Notice the difference:

Example 1	**Example 2**
B=3; A=++B; // A contains 4, B contains 4	B=3; A=B++; // A contains 3, B contains 4

In Example 1, B is increased before its value is copied to A. While in Example 2, the value of B is copied to A and then B is increased.

Relational and equality operators (==, !=, >, <, >=, <=):

In order to evaluate a comparison between two expressions we can use the relational and equality operators. The result of a relational operation is a Boolean value that can only be true or false, according to its Boolean result.

We may want to compare two expressions, for example, to know if they are equal or if one is greater than the other is. Here is a list of the relational and equality operators that can be used in C++:

    $==$ Equal to

    $!=$ Not equal to

    $>$ Greater than

    $<$ Less than

    $>=$ Greater than or equal to

    $<=$ Less than or equal to

Some examples are:

    $(7 == 5)$ *// evaluates to false.*
    $(5 > 4)$ *// evaluates to true.*
    $(3 != 2)$ *// evaluates to true.*
    $(6 >= 6)$ *// evaluates to true.*
    $(5 < 5)$ *// evaluates to false.*

Of course, instead of using only numeric constants, we can use any valid expression, including variables. Suppose that a=2, b=3 and c=6,(a == 5)   *// evaluates to false since a is not equal to 5.*

(a*b >= c) *// evaluates to true since (2*3 >= 6) is true.*

(b+4 > a*c) *// evaluates to false since (3+4 > 2*6) is false.*

((b=2) == a) *// evaluates to true.*

The operator = (one equal sign) is not the same as the operator == (two equal signs), the first one is an assignment operator (assigns the value at its right to the variable at its left) and the other one (==) is the equality operator that compares whether both expressions in the two sides of it are equal to each other. Thus, in the last expression ((b=2) == a), we first assigned the value 2 to b and then we compared it to a, that also stores the value 2, so the result of the operation is true.

Logical operators (!, &&, ||): The Operator ! is the C++ operator to perform the Boolean operation NOT, it has only one operand, located at its right, and the only thing that it does is to inverse the value of it, producing false if its operand is true and true if its operand is false. Basically, it returns the opposite Boolean value of evaluating its operand. For example:

!(5 == 5)   *// evaluates to false because the expression at its right (5 == 5) is true.*

!(6 <= 4)   *// evaluates to true because (6 <= 4) would be false.*

!true   *// evaluates to false*

!false   *// evaluates to true.*

The logical operators && and || are used when evaluating two expressions to obtain a single relational result. The operator && corresponds with Boolean logical operation AND. This operation results true if both its two operands are true, and false otherwise. The following panel shows the result of operator && evaluating the expression a && b:

&& OPERATOR

a	b	a && b
true	true	true
true	false	false
false	true	false
false	false	false

The operator || corresponds with Boolean logical operation OR. This operation results true if either one of its two operands is true, thus being false only when both operands are false themselves. Here are the possible results of a || b:

|| OPERATOR

a	b	a || b
true	true	true
true	false	true

              false   true   true

              false   false   false

For example:

((5 == 5) && (3 > 6)) *// evaluates to false (true && false).*

((5 == 5) || (3 > 6)) *// evaluates to true (true || false).*

***Conditional operator* (? :):** The conditional operator evaluates an expression returning a value if that expression is true and a different one if the expression is evaluated as false. Its format is:

              condition ? result1 : result2

If condition is true the expression will return result1, if it is not it will return result2.

    7==5 ? 4 : 3   // returns 3, since 7 is not equal to 5.

    7==5+2 ? 4 : 3   // returns 4, since 7 is equal to 5+2.

    5>3 ? a : b   // returns the value of a, since 5 is greater than 3.

    a>b ? a : b   // returns whichever is greater, a or b.

we can consider a small program to better understand it.


```cpp
// conditional operator


#include <iostream>
using namespace std;


int main ()
{
   int a,b,c;


   a=2;
   b=7;
   c = (a>b) ? a : b;
```

```
cout << c;


return 0;

}
```

the program returns the value 7.In this example a was 2 and b was 7, so the expression being evaluated (a>b) was not true, thus the first value specified after the question mark was discarded in favor of the second value (the one after the colon) which was b, with a value of 7.

Comma operator (,): The comma operator (,) is used to separate two or more expressions that are included where only one expression is expected. When the set of expressions has to be evaluated for a value, only the rightmost expression is considered. For example, the following code:

```
a = (b=3, b+2);
```

Would first assign the value 3 to b, and then assign b+2 to variable a. So, at the end, variable a would contain the value 5 while variable b would contain value 3.

Bitwise Operators (&, |, ^, ~, <<, >>): Bitwise operators modify variables considering the bit patterns that represent the values they store.

operator	asm equivalent	description
&	AND	Bitwise AND
|	OR	Bitwise Inclusive OR
^	XOR	Bitwise Exclusive OR
~	NOT	Unary complement (bit inversion)
<<	SHL	Shift Left
>>	SHR	Shift Right

Explicit type casting operator: Type casting operators allow you to convert a datum of a given type to another. There are several ways to do this in C++. The simplest one, which has been inherited from the C language, is to precede the expression to be converted by the new type enclosed between parentheses (()):

int i;

float f = 3.14;

i = (*int*) f;

The previous code converts the float number 3.14 to an integer value (3), the remainder is lost. Here, the typecasting operator was (int). Another way to do the same thing in C++ is using the functional notation: preceding the expression to be converted by the type and enclosing the expression between parentheses:

i = *int* (f);

Both ways of type casting are valid in C++.

sizeof(): This operator accepts one parameter, which can be either a type or a variable itself and returns the size in bytes of that type or object:

a = *sizeof* (*char*);

This will assign the value 1 to a because char is a one-byte long type. The value returned by sizeof is a constant, so it is always determined before program execution.

Precedence of operators: When writing complex expressions with several operands, we may have some doubts about which operand is evaluated first and which later. For example, in this expression:

a = 5 + 7 % 2

we may doubt if it really means:

a = 5 + (7 % 2)   // with a result of 6, or

a = (5 + 7) % 2   // with a result of 0

The correct answer is the first of the two expressions, with a result of 6. There is an established order with the priority of each operator, and not only the arithmetic ones (those whose preference come from mathematics) but for all the operators which can appear in C++. From greatest to lowest priority, the priority order is as follows:

Level	Operator	Description	Grouping
1	::	scope	Left-to-right
2	() [] . -> ++ -- dynamic_cast static_cast reinterpret_cast const_cast typeid	postfix	Left-to-right
3	++ -- ~ ! sizeof new delete	unary (prefix)	
	* &	indirection and reference (pointers)	Right-to-left
	+ -	unary sign operator	
4	(type)	type casting	Right-to-left
5	.* ->*	pointer-to-member	Left-to-right
6	* / %	multiplicative	Left-to-right
7	+ -	additive	Left-to-right
8	<< >>	shift	Left-to-right
9	< > <= >=	relational	Left-to-right
10	== !=	equality	Left-to-right
11	&	bitwise AND	Left-to-right
12	^	bitwise XOR	Left-to-right
13	|	bitwise OR	Left-to-right
14	&&	logical AND	Left-to-right
15	||	logical OR	Left-to-right
16	?:	conditional	Right-to-left
17	= *= /= %= += -= >>= <<= &= ^= |=	assignment	Right-to-left
18	,	comma	Left-to-right

Grouping defines the precedence order in which operators are evaluated in the case that there are several operators of the same level in an expression. All these precedence levels for operators can be manipulated or become more legible by removing possible ambiguities using parentheses signs (and), as in this example:

    a = 5 + 7 % 2;

might be written either as:

    a = 5 + (7 % 2);a = (5 + 7) % 2;

depending on the operation that we want to perform. If you want to write complicated expressions and you are not completely sure of the precedence levels, always include parentheses. It will also become a code easier to read.

Basic Input/Output: In C++ the basic input-output statements are "cout", "cin". C++ uses a convenient abstraction called *streams* to perform input and output operations in sequential media such as the screen or the keyboard. A stream is an object where a program can either insert or extract characters to/from it. The standard C++ library includes the header file iostream, where the standard input and output stream objects are declared.

Standard Output (cout): By default, the standard output of a program is the screen, and the C++ stream object defined to access it is cout. cout is used in conjunction with the insertion operator, which is written as << (two "less than" signs).

    cout << "Output sentence"; // prints Output sentence on screen

    cout << 120;   // prints number 120 on screen

    cout << x;   // prints the content of x on screen

The << operator inserts the data that follows it into the stream preceding it. In the examples above it inserted the constant string Output sentence, the numerical constant 120 and variable x into the standard output stream cout. Notice that the sentence in the first instruction is enclosed between double quotes (") because it is a constant string of characters. Whenever we want to use constant strings of characters we must enclose them between double quotes (") so that they can be clearly distinguished from variable names. For example, these two sentences have very different results:

    cout << "Hello"; // prints Hello

cout << Hello;   // prints the content of Hello variable

The insertion operator (<<) may be used more than once in a single statement:

cout << "Hello, " << "I am " << "a C++ statement";

This last statement would print the message Hello, I am a C++ statement on the screen. The utility of repeating the insertion operator (<<) is demonstrated when we want to print out a combination of variables and constants or more than one variable:

cout << "Hello, I am " << age << " years old and my zipcode is " << zipcode;

if we assume the age variable to contain the value 24 and the zipcode variable to contain 90064 the output of the previous statement would be:

Hello, I am 24 years old and my zipcode is 90064

It is important to notice that cout does not add a line break after its output unless we explicitly indicate it, therefore, the following statements:

cout << "This is a sentence.";

cout << "This is another sentence.";

will be shown on the screen one following the other without any line break between them:

This is a sentence. This is another sentence.

even though we had written them in two different insertions into cout. In order to perform a line break on the output we must explicitly insert a new-line character into cout. In C++ a new-line character can be specified as \n (backslash, n):

cout << "First sentence.\n";

cout << "Second sentence.\nThird sentence.";

This produces the following output:

First sentence.

Second sentence.

Third sentence.

Additionally, to add a new-line, you may also use the endl manipulator. For example:

cout << "First sentence." << endl;

cout << "Second sentence." << endl; would print out:

First sentence.
Second sentence.

The endl manipulator produces a newline character, exactly as the insertion of '\n' does, but it also has an additional behavior when it is used with buffered streams: the buffer is flushed. Anyway, cout will be an unbuffered stream in most cases, so you can generally use both the \n escape character and the endl manipulator in order to specify a new line without any difference in its behavior.

Standard Input (cin): The standard input device is usually the keyboard. Handling the standard input in C++ is done by applying the overloaded operator of extraction (>>) on the cin stream. The operator must be followed by the variable that will store the data that is going to be extracted from the stream. For example:

int age;

cin >> age;

The first statement declares a variable of type int called age, and the second one waits for an input from cin (the keyboard) in order to store it in this integer variable.

cin can only process the input from the keyboard once the RETURN key has been pressed. Therefore, even if you request a single character, the extraction from cin will not process the input until the user presses RETURN after the character has been introduced.

You must always consider the type of the variable that you are using as a container with cin extractions. If you request an integer you will get an integer, if you request a character you will get a character and if you request a string of characters you will get a string of characters.

// i/o example

```cpp
#include <iostream>
using namespace std;
```

```
int main ()
{
  int i;
  cout << "Please enter an integer value: ";
  cin >> i;
  cout << "The value you entered is " << i;
  cout << " and its double is " << i*2 << ".\n";
  return 0;
}
```

The user of a program may be one of the factors that generate errors even in the simplest programs that use cin (like the one we have just seen). Since if you request an integer value and the user introduces a name (which generally is a string of characters), the result may cause your program to misoperate since it is not what we were expecting from the user. So when you use the data input provided by cin extractions you will have to trust that the user of your program will be cooperative and that he/she will not introduce his/her name or something similar when an integer value is requested. A little ahead, when we see the stringstream class we will see a possible solution for the errors that can be caused by this type of user input.

You can also use cin to request more than one datum input from the user:

cin >> a >> b;is equivalent to:cin >> a;

cin >> b;

In both cases the user must give two data, one for variable a and another one for variable b that may be separated by any valid blank separator: a space, a tab character or a newline.

cin and strings: We can use cin to get strings with the extraction operator (>>) as we do with fundamental data type variables:

cin >> mystring;

However, as it has been said, cin extraction stops reading as soon as if finds any blank space character, so in this case we will be able to get just one word for each extraction. This behavior may or may not be what we want; for example if we want to get a sentence from the user, this extraction operation would not be useful.

Control Structures: A program is usually not limited to a linear sequence of instructions. During its process it may bifurcate, repeat code or take decisions. For that purpose, C++ provides control structures that serve to specify what has to be done by our program, when and under which circumstances.

With the introduction of control structures we are going to have to introduce a new concept: the *compound-statement* or *block*. A block is a group of statements which are separated by semicolons (;) like all C++ statements, but grouped together in a block enclosed in braces: { }:

{statement1; statement2; statement3; }

Most of the control structures that we will see in this section require a generic statement as part of its syntax. A statement can be either a simple statement (a simple instruction ending with a semicolon) or a compound statement (several instructions grouped in a block), like the one just described. In the case that we want the statement to be a simple statement, we do not need to enclose it in braces ({}). But in the case that we want the statement to be a compound statement it must be enclosed between braces ({}), forming a block.

Conditional structure: The if statement:

The if statement allows conditional execution that means the if keyword is used to execute a statement or block only if a condition is fulfilled. Its syntax is:

if (condition)

    statement;

where condition is integral expression and statement is any executable statement. The statement will be executed only if the value of the integral expression is nonzero. Notice the required parenthesis around the condition.

For example, the following code fragment prints x is 100 only if the value stored in the x variable is indeed 100:

if (x == 100)

cout << "x is 100";

If we want more than a single statement to be executed in case that the condition is true we can specify a block using braces { }:

The syntax for that is,

```
if (condition)
{
    statement1;
    statement2;
    -------------
    statement n;
}
```

for example

```
if (x == 100)
{
  cout << "x is ";
  cout << x;
}
```

The if and else statement: We can additionally specify what we want to happen if the condition is not fulfilled by using the keyword else. Its form used in conjunction with if is:

```
if (condition)
    statement1
else
    statement2
```

For example:

```
if (x == 100)
  cout << "x is 100";
else
  cout << "x is not 100";
```

prints on the screen x is 100 if indeed x has a value of 100, but if it has not -and only if not- it prints out x is not 100.

The nested if and else statement: The if + else structures can be concatenated with the intention of verifying a range of values. The following example shows its use telling if the value currently stored in x is positive, negative or none of them (i.e. zero):the syntax is,

```
if(condition)
{
    else if(condition)
        else if(condition)
            else

                statements;
}
```

if (x > 0)

  cout << "x is positive";

else if (x < 0)

  cout << "x is negative";

else

  cout << "x is 0";

Remember that in case that we want more than a single statement to be executed, we must group them in a block by enclosing them in braces { }. for example,

```
#include<iostream>
#include<cstdlib>

using namespace std;

int main()
{
int magic;
int guess;
magic =r and ();        //enter a random no.
```

```cpp
cout << "Enter your guess: ";
cin >> guess;

if(guess==magic)
{
cout<<"**Right**\n";
cout<<magic<<"is the magic number.\n";
}
else {
cout<"...Sorry,you're wrong.";
if(guess>magic)
cout<<"Your guess is too high.\n";
}

else
cout<<Your guess is too low.\n";}
return 0;
}
```

Iteration structures (loops): Loops have as purpose to repeat a statement a certain number of times or while a condition is fulfilled.

The while loop: Its format is:

    while (expression)

        statement;

and its functionality is simply to repeat statement while the condition set in expression is true.

For example, we are going to make a program to countdown using a while-loop:

```cpp
// custom countdown using while

#include <iostream>

using namespace std;

int main ()
{
```

```cpp
int n;

 cout << "Enter the starting number > ";
//Enter the starting number > 8

                               8, 7, 6, 5, 4, 3,
2, 1, FIRE!
 cin >> n;
while (n>0) {

   cout << n << ", ";

   --n;

 }


 cout << "FIRE!\n";

 return 0;

}
```

When the program starts the user is prompted to insert a starting number for the countdown. Then the while loop begins, if the value entered by the user fulfills the condition n>0 (that n is greater than zero) the block that follows the condition will be executed and repeated while the condition (n>0) remains being true.

The whole process of the previous program can be interpreted according to the following script (beginning in main):

1. User assigns a value to n

2. The while condition is checked (n>0). At this point there are two posibilities:
    * condition is true: statement is executed (to step 3)
    * condition is false: ignore statement and continue after it (to step 5)

3. Execute statement:
   cout << n << ", ";

   --n;(prints the value of n on the screen and decreases n by 1)

4. End of block. Return automatically to step 2

5. Continue the program right after the block: print FIRE! and end program.

When creating a while-loop, we must always consider that it has to end at some point, therefore we must provide within the block some method to force the condition to become false at some point, otherwise the loop will continue looping forever. In this case we have included --n; that decreases the value of the variable that is being evaluated in the condition (n) by one - this will eventually make the condition (n>0) to become false after a certain number of loop iterations: to be more specific, when n becomes 0, that is where our while-loop and our countdown end.

Of course this is such a simple action for our computer that the whole countdown is performed instantly without any practical delay between numbers.

The do-while loop: Its format is:

do statement

   while (condition);

Its functionality is exactly the same as the while loop, except that condition in the do-while loop is evaluated after the execution of statement instead of before, granting at least one execution of statement even if condition is never fulfilled. For example, the following example program echoes any number you enter until you enter 0.

```cpp
// number echoer

#include <iostream>
using namespace std;

int main ()
{
  unsigned long n;
  do {
    cout << "Enter number (0 to end): ";
    cin >> n;
  cout << "You entered: " << n << "\n";
  } while (n != 0);
  return 0;
```

```
}
Enter number (0 to end): 12345
You entered: 12345
Enter number (0 to end): 160277
You entered: 160277
Enter number (0 to end): 0
You entered: 0
```

The do-while loop is usually used when the condition that has to determine the end of the loop is determined **within** the loop statement itself, like in the previous case, where the user input within the block is what is used to determine if the loop has to end. In fact if you never enter the value 0 in the previous example you can be prompted for more numbers forever.

The for loop:

Its format is:

for (initialization; condition; increase/decrease) statement;

and its main function is to repeat statement while condition remains true, like the while loop. But in addition, the for loop provides specific locations to contain an initialization statement and an increase statement. So this loop is specially designed to perform a repetitive action with a counter which is initialized and increased on each iteration. It works in the following way:

1. initialization is executed. Generally it is an initial value setting for a counter variable. This is executed only once.

2. condition is checked. If it is true the loop continues, otherwise the loop ends and statement is skipped (not executed).

3. statement is executed. As usual, it can be either a single statement or a block enclosed in braces { }.

4. finally, whatever is specified in the increase field is executed and the loop gets back to step 2.

Here is an example of countdown using a for loop:

```
// countdown using a for loop
#include <iostream>
```

```cpp
using namespace std;
int main ()
{
  for (int n=10; n>0; n--) {
    cout << n << ", ";
  }
  cout << "FIRE!\n";
  return 0;
}
```

The initialization and increase fields are optional. They can remain empty, but in all cases the semicolon signs between them must be written. For example we could write: for (;n<10;) if we wanted to specify no initialization and no increase; or for (;n<10;n++) if we wanted to include an increase field but no initialization (maybe because the variable was already initialized before).

Optionally, using the comma operator (,) we can specify more than one expression in any of the fields included in a for loop, like in initialization, for example. The comma operator (,) is an expression separator, it serves to separate more than one expression where only one is generally expected. For example, suppose that we wanted to initialize more than one variable in our loop:

```cpp
for ( n=0, i=100 ; n!=i ; n++, i-- )
{
  // whatever here...
}
```

This loop will execute for 50 times if neither n or i are modified within the loop: n starts with a value of 0, and i with 100, the condition is n!=i (that n is not equal to i). Because n is increased by one and i decreased by one, the loop's condition will become false after the 50th loop, when both n and i will be equal to 50.

Jump statements:

The break statement: Using break we can leave a loop even if the condition for its end is not fulfilled. It can be used to end an infinite loop, or to force it to end before its natural end. For example, we are going to stop the count down before its natural end (maybe because of an engine check failure?):

```cpp
// break loop example
#include <iostream>
using namespace std;

int main ()
{
   int n;
   for (n=10; n>0; n--)
   {
     cout << n << ", ";
     if (n==3)
     {
       cout << "countdown aborted!";
       break;
     }
   }
   return 0;
}
```

The continue statement. The continue statement causes the program to skip the rest of the loop in the current iteration as if the end of the statement block had been reached, causing it to jump to the start of the following iteration. For example, we are going to skip the number 5 in our countdown:

```cpp
// continue loop example

#include <iostream>
using namespace std;

int main ()
{
```

```
for (int n=10; n>0; n--) {
  if (n==5) continue;
  cout << n << ", ";
}
cout << "FIRE!\n";
return 0;
```

The goto statement: goto allows to make an absolute jump to another point in the program. You should use this feature with caution since its execution causes an unconditional jump ignoring any type of nesting limitations.

The destination point is identified by a label, which is then used as an argument for the goto statement. A label is made of a valid identifier followed by a colon (:).

Generally speaking, this instruction has no concrete use in structured or object oriented programming aside from those that low-level programming fans may find for it. For example, here is our countdown loop using goto:

```
// goto loop example

#include <iostream>
using namespace std;

int main ()
{
  int n=10;
  loop:
  cout << n << ", ";
  n--;
  if (n>0) goto loop;
  cout << "FIRE!\n";
```

```
return 0;
```

The exit function: exit is a function defined in the cstdlib library. The purpose of exit is to terminate the current program with a specific exit code. Its prototype is:

    void exit (int exitcode);

The exitcode is used by some operating systems and may be used by calling programs. By convention, an exit code of 0 means that the program finished normally and any other value means that some error or unexpected results happened.

The selective structure: switch.

The syntax of the switch statement is a bit peculiar. Its objective is to check several possible constant values for an expression. Something similar to what we did at the beginning of this section with the concatenation of several if and else if instructions. Its form is the following:

```
switch (expression)
{
  case constant1:
     group of statements 1;
     break;
  case constant2:
     group of statements 2;
     break;
     .
     .
     .
  default:
     default group of statements
}
```

It works in the following way: switch evaluates expression and checks if it is equivalent to constant1, if it is, it executes group of statements 1 until it finds the break statement. When it finds this break statement the program jumps to the end of the switch selective structure.

If expression was not equal to constant1 it will be checked against constant2. If it is equal to this, it will execute group of statements 2 until a break keyword is found, and then will jump to the end of the switch selective structure.

Finally, if the value of expression did not match any of the previously specified constants (you can include as many case labels as values you want to check), the program will execute the statements included after the default: label, if it exists (since it is optional).

Both of the following code fragments have the same behavior:

```
switch (x) {
  case 1:
    cout << "x is 1";
    break;
  case 2:
    cout << "x is 2";
    break;
  default:
    cout << "value of x unknown
}
```

The switch statement is a bit peculiar within the C++ language because it uses labels instead of blocks. This forces us to put break statements after the group of statements that we want to be executed for a specific condition. Otherwise the remainder statements -including those corresponding to other labels- will also be executed until the end of the switch selective block or a break statement is reached.

For example, if we did not include a break statement after the first group for case one, the program will not automatically jump to the end of the switch selective block and it would continue executing the rest of statements until it reaches either a break instruction or the end of the switch selective block. This makes unnecessary to include braces { } surrounding the statements for each of the cases, and it can also be useful to execute the same block of instructions for different possible values for the expression being evaluated. For example:

```cpp
//program to find the square, cube, square root
and cube root of a number
#include<iostream>
#include<cmath>
#define PI 3.1416
using namespace std;
void main()
{
    int option;
    float x;
    cout<< "enter any number";
    cin>> x;
    cout<< "1: square"<<endl ;
    cout<< "2: cube"<< endl ;
    cout<<"3: square root"<< endl ;
    cout<<"4: cube root"<< endl ;
    cout<< "your option";
    cin>> option;
    switch(option)
        {
      case 1:
        cout<< "square of" <<x<< "is"<<x*x<< endl ;
        break;
      case 2:
        cout<< "cube of" <<x<< "is"<<x*x*x<< endl ;
        break;
      case 3:
        cout<< "square  root  of"<<x<<"is"<<  sqrt
```

```
(x)<< endl;
    break;

   case 4:
       cout<<"cube        root        of"<<x<<"is"<<pow
(x,1/3.00)<<endl;
     break;

  }

}
```

Notice that switch can only be used to compare an expression against constants. Therefore we cannot put variables as labels (for example case n: where n is a variable) or ranges (case (1..3):) because they are not valid C++ constants.

If you need to check ranges or values that are not constants, use a concatenation of if and else if statements.

Arrays: An array is a sequence of objects all of which have the same type. The objects are called elements of the array and are numbered consecutively 0,1,2,3,...... . These numbers are called index values or subscripts of the array. The term "subscript" is used because as a mathematical sequence, an array would be written with subscripts: a0,a1,a2,...... The subscripts locate the elements position within the array, thereby giving direct access into the array.

If the name of the array is a, then a[0] is the name of the element that is in position 0, a[1] is the name of the element that is in the position 1, etc. in general the ith element is in position i-1. So, if the array has n elements then their position will be a[0], a[1], a[2], ...a[n-1].

Declaration of Array: As other variables the array must be declared before they are used in C++. the syntax for this is:

data_type array_name[size]

Example:

int marks [25];

in this the data items are integer type i.e. in marks array we can only store integer type data. Array can be given any names but we should remember that the name must specify what we have stored in the array and also it should be according to the identifier rule. While the size defines how big the array size is. In the above example the size of array is 25 so, we can store 25 integer values in this array.

This can be explained well by using following example

string stu_name [5];

for this the memory location reserved is 5, but from 0 to 4.

Initialization of Array: The array can be initialized in the following ways:

data-type array-name [size]={value1,value2,........,value n};

Example:

int marks[5]={25,34,30,45,22};

char value[2]={"t", "f"};

similarly we can use this into loops as,

for(i=0; i>=29; i++)

cin>> marks[i];

through this statement we can assign the values into array through keyboard.

Accessing elements of an array: The syntax for accessing array is,

array-name [index or subscript];

Example:

int marks [3];

in this example 3 is assigned to the first element of the array as

marks[0]=3;

if we want to see what is written in the particular array we can write as,

cout << marks[4];

this statement will give the result as

marks[4]=22;

similarly we can use this into loops as,

for(i=0; i>=29; i++)

cout<< marks[i];

through this statement we can access the values of an array.

Two dimensional arrays: Data that is in rows and columns is usually stored in *2-dimensional* arrays.

Declaring of 2-dimensional arrays: Two-dimensional arrays are declared by specifying the number of rows then the number of columns.

int a[30][10];   // declares an int array of 30 rows and 10 columns.

char ticTacToeBoard[3][3];   // three rows and three columns of chars.

Initializing 2-dimensional arrays: Unless specified, all initial values of arrays are *garbage*. You can specify initial values by enclosing each row in curly braces like this:

```
char ticTacToeBoard[3][3] = {{'x', 'x', 'o'},
                {'o', 'o', 'x'},
                {'x', 'o', ' '}
                };
```

If some elements are omitted in the initialization list, they are set to zero.

Subscripting 2-dimensional arrays: Write subscripts as $x[row][col]$. Passing over all elements of a two-dimensional array is usually done with two *nested* for loops.

```
// clear the board
for (int row=0; row<3; row++) {
   for (int col=0; col<3; col++) {
      ticTacToeBoard[row][col] = ' ';
   }
}
```

Functions: A function is a group of statements that is executed when it is called from some point of the program. Functions are building blocks of the programs. They make the programs more modular and easy to read and manage. All C++ programs must contain the function main( ). The execution of the program starts from the function main( ). A C++ program can contain any number of functions according to the needs. The general form of the function is: -

```
      return_type function_name(parameter list)
{

    body of the function

}
```

The function of consists of two parts function header and function body. The function header is:-

return_type function_name(parameter list)

The return_type specifies the type of the data the function returns. The return_type can be void which means function does not return any data type. The function_name is the name of the function. The name of the function should begin with the alphabet or underscore. The parameter list consists of variables separated with comma along with their data types. The parameter list could be empty which means the function do not contain any parameters. The parameter list should contain both data type and name of the variable. For example,

int factorial(int n, float j)

is the function header of the function factorial. The return type is of integer which means function should return data of type integer. The parameter list contains two variables n and j of type integer and float respectively. The body of the function performs the computations.

Function Declaration: A function declaration is made by declaring the return type of the function, name of the function and the data types of the parameters of the function. A function declaration is same as the declaration of the variable. The function declaration is always terminated by the semicolon. A call to the function cannot be made unless it is declared. The general form of the declaration is:-

return_type function_name(parameter list);

For example function declaration can be

int factorial(int n1,float j1);

The variables name need not be same as the variables of parameter list of the function. Another method can be

int factorial(int , float);

The variables in the function declaration can be optional but data types are necessary.

Function Arguments: The information is transferred to the function by the means of arguments when a call to a function is made. Arguments contain the actual value which is to be passed to the function when it is called. The sequence of the arguments in the call of the function should be same as the sequence of the parameters in the parameter list of the declaration of the function. The data types of the arguments should correspond with the data types of the parameters. When a function call is made arguments replace the parameters of the function.

The Return Statement and Return values: A return statement is used to exit from the function where it is. It returns the execution of the program to the point where the function call was made. It returns a value to the calling code. The general form of the return statement is:-

    return expression;

The expression evaluates to a value which has type same as the return type specified in the function declaration. For example the statement,

    return(n);

the return statement of the factorial function. The type of variable n should be integer as specified in the declaration of the factorial function. If a function has return type as void then return statement does not contain any expression. It is written as:-

    return;

The function with return type as void can ignore the return statement. The closing braces at the end indicate the exit of the function. Here is a program which illustrates the working of functions.

```cpp
#include<iostream>
using namespace std;
int factorial(int n);
int main ()
{
   int n1,fact;
    cout <<"Enter the number whose factorial has
to be calculated" << endl;
    cin >> n1;
```

```cpp
    fact=factorial(n1);
    cout << "The factorial of " << n1 << " is : "
<< fact << endl;
    return(0);


}
int factorial(int n)
{
    int i=0,fact=1;
    if(n<=1)
    {
    return(1);
    }
    else
    {
      for(i=1;i<=n;i++)
        {
          fact=fact*i;
        }
        return(fact);
    }
}
```

The function factorial calculates the factorial of the number entered by the user. If the number is less than or equal to 1 then function returns 1 else it returns the factorial of the number. The statement

    int factorial(int n);

is a declaration of the function. The return type is of integer. The parameter list consists of one data type which is integer. The statement

    cout <<"Enter the number whose factorial has to be calculated" <<
endl;

    cin >> n1;

makes the user enter the number whose factorial is to be calculated. The variable n1 stores the number entered by the user. The user has entered number 5. The statement

    fact=factorial(n1);

makes a call to the function. The variable n1 is now argument to the function factorial. The argument is mapped to the parameters in the parameter list of the function. The function header is

    int factorial(int n)

The body of the function contains two return statements. If the value entered by the user is less than and equal to 1 then value 1 is returned else computed factorial is returned. The type of the expression returned is integer.

Parameter passing: There are two parameter passing mechanisms for passing arguments to functions such as pass by value and pass by reference.

Pass by value: In pass be value mechanism copies of the arguments are created and which are stored in the temporary locations of the memory. The parameters are mapped to the copies of the arguments created. The changes made to the parameter do not affect the arguments. Pass by value mechanism provides security to the calling program. Here is a program which illustrates the working of pass by value mechanism.

```cpp
#include<iostream>
using namespace std;
int add(int n);
int main()
{
    int number,result;
    number=5;
    cout << " The initial value of number : " <<
number << endl;
    result=add(number);
    cout << " The final value of number : " <<
```

```cpp
number << endl;
    cout << " The result is : " << result << endl;
    return(0);
}
int add(int number)
{
   number=number+100;
    return(number);
}
```

Pass by reference: Pass by reference is the second way of passing parameters to the function. The address of the argument is copied into the parameter. The changes made to the parameter affect the arguments. The address of the argument is passed to the function and function modifies the values of the arguments in the calling function. Here is a program which illustrates the working of pass by reference mechanism.

```cpp
#include<iostream>
using namespace std;
int add(int &number);
int main ()
{
    int number;
    int result;
    number=5;
    cout << "The value of the variable number before calling the function : " << number << endl;
    result=add(&number);
    cout << "The value of the variable number after the function is returned : " << number << endl;
    cout << "The value of result : " << result <<
```

```cpp
endl;
    return(0);
}
int add(int &p)
{
    *p=*p+100;
    return(*p);
}
```

Default values in parameters: When declaring a function we can specify a default value for each of the last parameters. This value will be used if the corresponding argument is left blank when calling to the function. To do that, we simply have to use the assignment operator and a value for the arguments in the function declaration. If a value for that parameter is not passed when the function is called, the default value is used, but if a value is specified this default value is ignored and the passed value is used instead. For example:

```cpp
// default values in functions
#include <iostream>
using namespace std;

int divide (int a, int b=2)
{
   int r;
   r=a/b;
   return (r);
}

int main ()
{
   cout << divide (12);
```

```
cout << endl;
cout << divide (20,4);
return 0;
}
```

As we can see in the body of the program there are two calls to function divide. In the first one:

divide (12)

we have only specified one argument, but the function divide allows up to two. So the function divide has assumed that the second parameter is 2 since that is what we have specified to happen if this parameter was not passed (notice the function declaration, which finishes with int b=2, not just int b). Therefore the result of this function call is 6 (12/2). In the second call:

divide (20,4)

there are two parameters, so the default value for b (int b=2) is ignored and b takes the value passed as argument, that is 4, making the result returned equal to 5 (20/4).

Overloaded functions: In C++ two different functions can have the same name if their parameter types or number are different. That means that you can give the same name to more than one function if they have either a different number of parameters or different types in their parameters.

For example:

```
// overloaded function
#include <iostream>
using namespace std;

int operate (int a, int b)
{
   return (a*b);
}
```

```cpp
float operate (float a, float b)
{
  return (a/b);
}


int main ()
{
  int x=5,y=2;
  float n=5.0,m=2.0;
  cout << operate (x,y);
  cout << "\n";
  cout << operate (n,m);
  cout << "\n";
  return 0;
}
```

In this case we have defined two functions with the same name, operate, but one of them accepts two parameters of type int and the other one accepts them of type float. The compiler knows which one to call in each case by examining the types passed as arguments when the function is called. If it is called with two ints as its arguments it calls to the function that has two int parameters in its prototype and if it is called with two floats it will call to the one which has two float parameters in its prototype.

In the first call to operate the two arguments passed are of type int, therefore, the function with the first prototype is called; This function returns the result of multiplying both parameters. While the second call passes two arguments of type float, so the function with the second prototype is called. This one has a different behavior: it divides one parameter by the other. So the behavior of a call to operate depends on the type of the arguments passed because the function has been *overloaded*.

Notice that a function cannot be overloaded only by its return type. At least one of its parameters must have a different type.

Inline functions: The inline specifier indicates the compiler that inline substitution is preferred to the usual function call mechanism for a specific function. This does not change the behavior of a function itself, but is used to suggest to the compiler that the code generated by the function body is inserted at each point the function is called, instead of being inserted only once and perform a regular call to it, which generally involves some additional overhead in running time.

The   format   for   its   declaration   is:
inline type name (arguments ...) { instructions ... }

and the call is just like the call to any other function. You do not have to include the inline keyword when calling the function, only in its declaration.

Most compilers already optimize code to generate inline functions when it is more convenient. This specifier only indicates the compiler that inline is preferred for this function.

Recursivity: Recursivity is the property that functions have to be called by themselves. It is useful for many tasks, like sorting or calculate the factorial of numbers. For example, to obtain the factorial of a number (n!) the mathematical formula would be:

$$n! = n * (n-1) * (n-2) * (n-3) ... * 1$$

more concretely, 5! (factorial of 5) would be:

$$5! = 5 * 4 * 3 * 2 * 1 = 120$$

and a recursive function to calculate this in C++ could be:

```cpp
// factorial calculator
#include <iostream>
using namespace std;

long factorial (long a)
{
  if (a > 1)
   return (a * factorial (a-1));
  else
   return (1);
}
```

```
int main ()
{
  long number; cout << "Please type a number: ";
  cin >> number;
  cout << number << "! = " << factorial (number);
  return 0;
}
```

Notice how in function factorial we included a call to itself, but only if the argument passed was greater than 1, since otherwise the function would perform an infinite recursive loop in which once it arrived to 0 it would continue multiplying by all the negative numbers (probably provoking a stack overflow error on runtime).

This function has a limitation because of the data type we used in its design (long) for more simplicity. The results given will not be valid for values much greater than 10! or 15!, depending on the system you compile it.

Declaring functions: Until now, we have defined all of the functions before the first appearance of calls to them in the source code. These calls were generally in function main which we have always left at the end of the source code. If you try to repeat some of the examples of functions described so far, but placing the function main before any of the other functions that were called from within it, you will most likely obtain compiling errors. The reason is that to be able to call a function it must have been declared in some earlier point of the code, like we have done in all our examples.

But there is an alternative way to avoid writing the whole code of a function before it can be used in main or in some other function. This can be achieved by declaring just a prototype of the function before it is used, instead of the entire definition. This declaration is shorter than the entire definition, but significant enough for the compiler to determine its return type and the types of its parameters. Its form is:

type name (argument_type1, argument_type2, ...);

It is identical to a function definition, except that it does not include the body of the function itself (i.e., the function statements that in normal definitions are enclosed in braces { }) and instead of that we end the prototype declaration with a mandatory semicolon (;).

The parameter enumeration does not need to include the identifiers, but only the type specifiers. The inclusion of a name for each parameter as in the function definition is optional in the prototype declaration. For example, we can declare a function called protofunction with two int parameters with any of the following declarations:

int protofunction (*int* first, *int* second);

int protofunction (*int, int*);

Anyway, including a name for each variable makes the prototype more legible.

```cpp
// declaring functions prototypes
#include <iostream>
using namespace std;


void odd (int a);
void even (int a);


int main ()
{
  int i;
  do {
    cout << "Type a number (0 to exit): ";
    cin >> i;
    odd (i);
  } while (i!=0);
  return 0;
}


void odd (int a)
{
  if ((a%2)!=0) cout << "Number is odd.\n";
```

```
    else even (a);
}


void even (int a)
{
    if ((a%2)==0) cout << "Number is even.\n";
    else odd (a);
}
```

This example is indeed not an example of efficiency. I am sure that at this point you can already make a program with the same result, but using only half of the code lines that have been used in this example. Anyway this example illustrates how prototyping works. Moreover, in this concrete example the prototyping of at least one of the two functions is necessary in order to compile the code without errors. The first things that we see are the declaration of functions odd and even:

void odd (*int* a);

void even (*int* a);

This allows these functions to be used before they are defined, for example, in main, which now is located where some people find it to be a more logical place for the start of a program: the beginning of the source code.

Anyway, the reason why this program needs at least one of the functions to be declared before it is defined is because in odd there is a call to even and in even there is a call to odd. If none of the two functions had been previously declared, a compilation error would happen, since either odd would not be visible from even (because it has still not been declared), or even would not be visible from odd (for the same reason).

Having the prototype of all functions together in the same place within the source code is found practical by some programmers, and this can be easily achieved by declaring all functions prototypes at the beginning of a program.

Structures: Structure is a collection of variables under a single name. Variables can be of any type: int, float, char etc. The main difference between structure and array is that arrays are collections of the same data type and structure is a collection of variables under a single name. A *structure* contains an ordered group of data objects. Unlike the elements of an array, the data objects within a structure can have varied data types. Each data object in a structure is a *member* or *field*.

```
struct tag_name
{
data type member1;
data type member2;
...

...
}

Example:
struct lib_books
{
char title[20];
char author[15];
int pages;
float price;
};
```

Declaring a Structure: The structure is declared by using the keyword struct followed by structure name, also called a tag. Then the structure members (variables) are defined with their type and variable names inside the open and close braces { and }. Finally, the closed braces end with a semicolon denoted as ; following the statement. The above structure declaration is also called a Structure Specifier.

Example: Three variables: *custnum* of type int, *salary* of type int, *commission* of type float are structure members and the structure name is Customer. This structure is declared as follows:

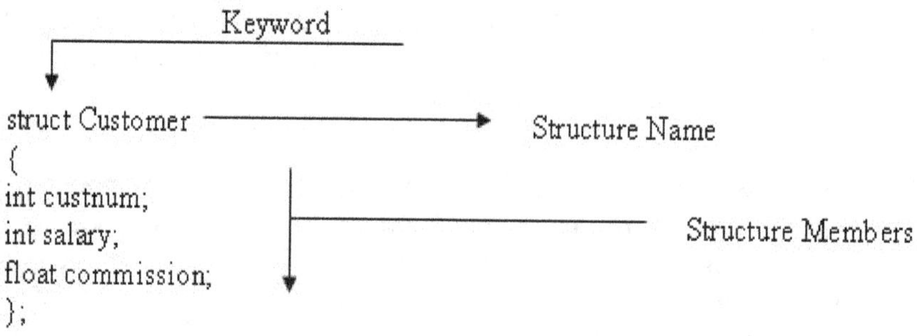

```
                    Keyword

struct Customer  ─────────────►  Structure Name
{
int custnum;
int salary;                      Structure Members
float commission;
};
```

In the above example, it is seen that variables of different types such as int and float are grouped in a single structure name Customer.

Arrays behave in the same way, declaring structures does not mean that memory is allocated. Structure declaration gives a skeleton or template for the structure.

After declaring the structure, the next step is to define a structure variable.

Declaring Structure Variable: This is similar to variable declaration. For variable declaration, data type is defined followed by variable name. For structure variable declaration, the data type is the name of the structure followed by the structure variable name. In the above example, structure variable cust1 is defined as:

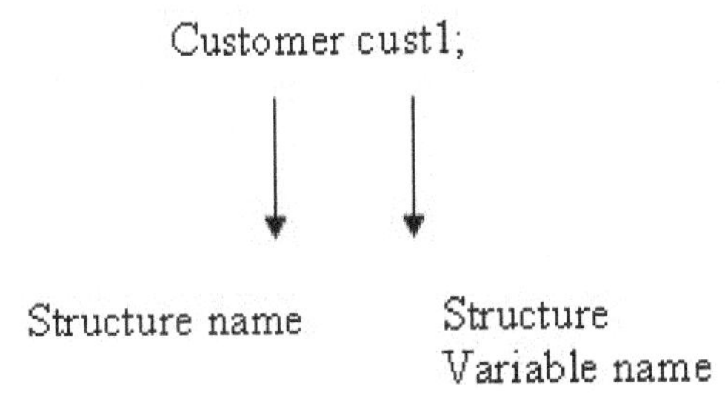

What happens when this is defined? When structure is defined, it allocates or reserves space in memory. The memory space allocated will be cumulative of all defined structure members. In the above example, there are 3 structure members: custnum, salary and commission. Of these, two are of type in and one is of type float. If integer space allocated by a system is 2 bytes and float four bytes the above would allocate 2bytes for custnum, 2 bytes for salary and 4 bytes for commission.

Accessing structure variable: To access structure members, the operator used is the dot operator denoted by (.). The dot operator for accessing structure members is used as,

structure variable name.member name

For example:

A programmer wants to assign 2000 for the structure member *salary* in the above example of structure *Customer* with structure variable *cust1* this is written as

cust1.salary=2000;

where cust1 is the structure variable name, then the dot operator, and then the member name.

Unions: A union is a user-defined data or class type that, at any given time, contains only one object from its list of members (although that object can be an array or a class type).

union [tag] { member-list } [declarators];

[union] tag declarators;

Declaring a Union: Begin the declaration of a union with the union keyword, and enclose the member list in curly braces:

```
// declaring_a_union.cpp
union DATATYPE                    // Declare union type
{
    char  ch;
    int   i;
    long  l;
    float f;
    double d;
} var1;        // Optional declaration of union variable

int main()
{
}
```

Using a Union: A C++ union is a limited form of the class type. It can contain access specifiers (public, protected, private), member data, and member functions, including constructors and destructors. It cannot contain virtual functions or static data members. It cannot be used as a base class, nor can it have base classes. Default access of members in a union is public.

A C union type can contain only data members.

In C, you must use the union keyword to declare a union variable. In C++, the union keyword is unnecessary:

```
union DATATYPE var2;   // C declaration of a union variable

DATATYPE var3;         // C++ declaration of a union variable
```

A variable of a union type can hold one value of any type declared in the union. Use the member-selection operator (.) to access a member of a union:

```
var1.i = 6;         // Use variable as integer

var2.d = 5.327;     // Use variable as double
```

You can declare and initialize a union in the same statement by assigning an expression enclosed in braces. The expression is evaluated and assigned to the first field of the union.

Example

```cpp
// using_a_union.cpp
#include <stdio.h>


union NumericType
{
    int      iValue;
    long     lValue;
    double   dValue;
};


int main()
{
    union NumericType Values = { 10 };   // iValue = 10
    printf_s("%d\n", Values.iValue);
    Values.dValue = 3.1416;
    printf_s("%f\n", Values.dValue);
}
```

Access Control and Constraints of Structures, Classes and Unions

Structures	Classes	Unions
class key is struct	class key is class	class key is union
Default access is public	Default access is private	Default access is public
No usage constraints	No usage constraints	Use only one member at a time

Objects: In a object oriented programming language C++, the data and functions are bundled together as a self-contained unit called objects. An object is any entity that can be manipulated by the commands of a programming language, such as a value, variable, function, or data structure. (With the later introduction of object oriented programming the same word, "object", refers to a particular instance of a class)

Classes: A class is an expanded concept of a data structure: instead of holding only data, it can hold both data and functions. An object is an instantiate of a class. In terms of variables, a class would be the type, and an object would be the variable. Classes are generally declared using the keyword class, with the following format:

```
class class_name {
  access_specifier_1:
    member1;
  access_specifier_2:
    member2;
  ...
} object_names;
```

Where class_name is a valid identifier for the class, object_names is an optional list of names for objects of this class. The body of the declaration can contain members, that can be either data or function declarations, and optionally access specifiers.

All is very similar to the declaration on data structures, except that we can now include also functions and members, but also this new thing called *access specifier*. An access specifier is one of the following three keywords: private, public or protected. These specifiers modify the access rights that the members following them acquire:

- private members of a class are accessible only from within other members of the same class or from their *friends*.
- protected members are accessible from members of their same class and from their friends, but also from members of their derived classes.
- Finally, public members are accessible from anywhere where the object is visible.

By default, all members of a class declared with the class keyword have private access for all its members. Therefore, any member that is declared before one other class specifier automatically has

private access. For example:

```
class CRectangle {
    int x, y;
  public:
    void set_values (int,int);
    int area (void);
  } rect ;
```

Declares a class (i.e., a type) called CRectangle and an object (i.e., a variable) of this class called rect. This class contains four members: two data members of type int (member x and member y) with private access (because private is the default access level) and two member functions with public access: set_values() and area(), of which for now we have only included their declaration, not their definition.

Notice the difference between the class name and the object name: In the previous example, CRectangle was the class name (i.e., the type), whereas rect was an object of type CRectangle. It is the same relationship int and a have in the following declaration:*int* a;where int is the type name (the class) and a is the variable name (the object).

After the previous declarations of CRectangle and rect, we can refer within the body of the program to any of the public members of the object rect as if they were normal functions or normal variables, just by putting the object's name followed by a dot (.) and then the name of the member. All very similar to what we did with plain data structures before. For example:

rect.set_values (3,4);

myarea = rect.area();

The only members of rect that we cannot access from the body of our program outside the class are x and y, since they have private access and they can only be referred from within other members of that same class.

Here is the complete example of class CRectangle:// *classes example*

```cpp
#include <iostream>
using namespace std;

class CRectangle {
    int x, y;
  public:
    void set_values (int,int);
    int area () {return (x*y);}
};

void CRectangle::set_values (int a, int b) {
  x = a;
  y = b;
}
int main () {
  CRectangle rect;
  rect.set_values (3,4);
  cout << "area: " << rect.area();
  return 0;
}
```

The most important new thing in this code is the operator of scope (::, two colons) included in the definition of set_values(). It is used to define a member of a class from outside the class definition itself.

You may notice that the definition of the member function area() has been included directly within the definition of the CRectangle class given its extreme simplicity, whereas set_values() has only its prototype declared within the class, but its definition is outside it. In this outside declaration, we must use the operator of scope (::) to specify that we are defining a function that is a member of the class CRectangle and not a regular global function.

The scope operator (::) specifies the class to which the member being declared belongs, granting exactly the same scope properties as if this function definition was directly included within the class definition. For example, in the function set_values() of the previous code, we have been able to use the variables x and y, which are private members of class CRectangle, which means they are only accessible from other members of their class.

The only difference between defining a class member function completely within its class or to include only the prototype and later its definition, is that in the first case the function will automatically be considered an inline member function by the compiler, while in the second it will be a normal (not-inline) class member function, which in fact supposes no difference in behavior.

Members x and y have private access (remember that if nothing else is said, all members of a class defined with keyword class have private access). By declaring them private we deny access to themfrom anywhere outside the class. This makes sense, since we have already defined a member function to set values for those members within the object: the member function set_values(). Therefore, the rest of the program does not need to have direct access to them. Perhaps in a so simple example as this, it is difficult to see an utility in protecting those two variables, but in greater projects it may be very important that values cannot be modified in an unexpected way (unexpected from the point of view of the object).

One of the greater advantages of a class is that, as any other type, we can declare several objects of it. For example, following with the previous example of class CRectangle, we could have declared the object rectb in addition to the object rect:

```
// example: one class, two objects
```

```cpp
#include <iostream>
using namespace std;


class CRectangle {
    int x, y;
  public:
    void set_values (int,int);
    int area () {return (x*y);}
};


void CRectangle::set_values (int a, int b) {
  x = a;
  y = b;
}


int main () {
  CRectangle rect, rectb;
  rect.set_values (3,4);
  rectb.set_values (5,6);
  cout << "rect area: " << rect.area() << endl;
  cout << "rectb area: " << rectb.area() << endl;
  return 0;
}
```

In this concrete case, the class (type of the objects) to which we are talking about is CRectangle, of which there are two instances or objects: rect and rectb. Each one of them has its own member variables and member functions.

Notice that the call to rect.area() does not give the same result as the call to rectb.area(). This is because each object of class CRectangle has its own variables x and y, as they, in some way, have also their own function members set_value() and area() that each uses its object's own variables to operate.

That is the basic concept of *object-oriented programming*: Data and functions are both members of the object. We no longer use sets of global variables that we pass from one function to another as parameters, but instead we handle objects that have their own data and functions embedded as members. Notice that we have not had to give any parameters in any of the calls to rect.area or rectb.area. Those member functions directly used the data members of their respective objects rect and rectb.

Constructors and Destructors: Objects generally need to initialize variables or assign dynamic memory during their process of creation to become operative and to avoid returning unexpected values during their execution. For example, what would happen if in the previous example we called the member function area() before having called function set_values()? Probably we would have gotten an undetermined result since the members x and y would have never been assigned a value. In order to avoid that, a class can include a special function called constructor, which is automatically called whenever a new object of this class is created. This constructor function must have the same name as the class, and cannot have any return type; not even void. We are going to implement CRectangle including a constructor:

```cpp
// example: class constructor
#include <iostream>
using namespace std;


class CRectangle {
    int width, height;
  public:
    CRectangle (int,int);
    int area () {return (width*height);}
};


CRectangle::CRectangle (int a, int b) {
  width = a;
  height = b;
}
```

```cpp
int main () {
  CRectangle rect (3,4);
  CRectangle rectb (5,6);
  cout << "rect area: " << rect.area() << endl;
  cout << "rectb area: " << rectb.area() << endl;
  return 0;
}
```

As you can see, the result of this example is identical to the previous one. But now we have removed the member function set_values(), and have included instead a constructor that performs a similar action: it initializes the values of width and height with the parameters that are passed to it.

Notice how these arguments are passed to the constructor at the moment at which the objects of this class are created:

CRectangle rect (3,4);

CRectangle rectb (5,6);

Constructors cannot be called explicitly as if they were regular member functions. They are only executed when a new object of that class is created.

You can also see how neither the constructor prototype declaration (within the class) nor the latter constructor definition include a return value; not even void.

The *destructor* fulfills the opposite functionality. It is automatically called when an object is destroyed, either because its scope of existence has finished (for example, if it was defined as a local object within a function and the function ends) or because it is an object dynamically assigned and it is released using the operator delete.

The destructor must have the same name as the class, but preceded with a tilde sign (~) and it must also return no value.

The use of destructors is especially suitable when an object assigns dynamic memory during its lifetime and at the moment of being destroyed we want to release the memory that the object was allocated.

```cpp
// example on constructors and destructors
```

```cpp
#include <iostream>
using namespace std;

class CRectangle {
    int *width, *height;
  public:
    CRectangle (int,int);
    ~CRectangle ();
    int area () {return (*width * *height);}
};

CRectangle::CRectangle (int a, int b) {
  width = new int;
  height = new int;
  *width = a;
  *height = b;
}

CRectangle::~CRectangle () {
  delete width;
  delete height;
}

int main () {
  CRectangle rect (3,4), rectb (5,6);
  cout << "rect area: " << rect.area() << endl;
  cout << "rectb area: " << rectb.area() << endl;
  return 0;
}
```

Overloading Constructors: Like any other function, a constructor can also be overloaded with more than one function that have the same name but different types or number of parameters. Remember that for overloaded functions the compiler will call the one whose parameters match the arguments used in the function call. In the case of constructors, which are automatically called when an object is created, the one executed is the one that matches the arguments passed on the object declaration:

```cpp
// overloading class constructors
#include <iostream>
using namespace std;

class CRectangle {
    int width, height;
  public:
    CRectangle ();
    CRectangle (int,int);
    int area (void) {return (width*height);}
};

CRectangle::CRectangle () {
  width = 5;
  height = 5;
}

CRectangle::CRectangle (int a, int b) {
  width = a;
  height = b;
}

int main () {
  CRectangle rect (3,4);
```

```
CRectangle rectb;
cout << "rect area: " << rect.area() << endl;
cout << "rectb area: " << rectb.area() << endl;
return 0;
}
```

In this case, rectb was declared without any arguments, so it has been initialized with the constructor that has no parameters, which initializes both width and height with a value of 5. Important: Notice how if we declare a new object and we want to use its default constructor (the one without parameters), we do not include parentheses ():

CRectangle rectb;　 *// right*

CRectangle rectb(); *// wrong*

Default constructor: If you do not declare any constructors in a class definition, the compiler assumes the class to have a default constructor with no arguments. Therefore, after declaring a class like this one:

class CExample {

 public:

　int a,b,c;

　void multiply (*int* n, *int* m) { a=n; b=m; c=a*b; };

 };

The compiler assumes that CExample has a default constructor, so you can declare objects of this class by simply declaring them without any arguments:

CExample ex;

But as soon as you declare your own constructor for a class, the compiler no longer provides an implicit default constructor. So you have to declare all objects of that class according to the constructor prototypes you defined for the class:

class CExample {

 public:

　int a,b,c;

CExample (*int* n, *int* m) { a=n; b=m; };

void multiply () { c=a*b; };

};

Here we have declared a constructor that takes two parameters of type int. Therefore the following object declaration would be correct:

CExample ex (2,3);

But,

CExample ex;

Would not be correct, since we have declared the class to have an explicit constructor, thus replacing the default constructor.

But the compiler not only creates a default constructor for you if you do not specify your own. It provides three special member functions in total that are implicitly declared if you do not declare your own. These are the *copy constructor*, the *copy assignment operator*, and the default destructor.

The copy constructor and the copy assignment operator copy all the data contained in another object to the data members of the current object. For CExample, the copy constructor implicitly declared by the compiler would be something similar to:

Cexample::CExample (*const* CExample& rv) {

  a=rv.a; b=rv.b; c=rv.c;

}

Therefore, the two following object declarations would be correct:

CExample ex (2,3);

CExample ex2 (ex);   *// copy constructor (data copied from ex)*

Pointers to classes: It is perfectly valid to create pointers that point to classes. We simply have to consider that once declared, a class becomes a valid type, so we can use the class name as the type for the pointer. For example:

CRectangle * prect;

is a pointer to an object of class CRectangle.

As it happened with data structures, in order to refer directly to a member of an object pointed by a pointer we can use the arrow operator (->) of indirection. Here is an example with some possible combination :

```cpp
// pointer to classes example
#include <iostream>
using namespace std;

class CRectangle {
    int width, height;
  public:
    void set_values (int, int);
    int area (void) {return (width * height);}
};

void CRectangle::set_values (int a, int b) {
  width = a;
  height = b;
}
int main () {
  CRectangle a, *b, *c;
  CRectangle * d = new CRectangle[2];
  b= new CRectangle;
  c= &a;
  a.set_values (1,2);
  b->set_values (3,4);
  d->set_values (5,6);
  d[1].set_values (7,8);
  cout << "a area: " << a.area() << endl;
  cout << "*b area: " << b->area() << endl;
  cout << "*c area: " << c->area() << endl;
  cout << "d[0] area: " << d[0].area() << endl;
  cout << "d[1] area: " << d[1].area() << endl;
  delete[] d;
```

```
delete b;

return 0;
```
}

Next you have a summary on how can you read some pointer and class operators (*, &, ., ->, [ ]) that appear in the previous example:

expression	can be read as
*x	pointed by x
&x	address of x
x.y	member y of object x
x->y	member y of object pointed by x
(*x).y	member y of object pointed by x (equivalent to the previous one)
x[0]	first object pointed by x
x[1]	second object pointed by x
x[n]	(n+1)th object pointed by x

Be sure that you understand the logic under all of these expressions before proceeding with the next sections. If you have doubts, read again this section and/or consult the previous sections about pointers and data structures.

Classes defined with struct and union: Classes can be defined not only with keyword class, but also with keywords struct and union.

The concepts of class and data structure are so similar that both keywords (struct and class) can be used in C++ to declare classes (i.e. structs can also have function members in C++, not only data members). The only difference between both is that members of classes declared with the keyword struct have public access by default, while members of classes declared with the keyword class have private access. For all other purposes both keywords are equivalent.

Overloading functions: A function is overloaded when same name is given to different function. However, the two functions with the same name will differ at least in one of the following.

(a)   The number of parameters

(b)   The data type of parameters

(c)   The order of appearance

These three together are referred to as the function signature. For example if we have two functions:

```
void foo(int i,char a);
void boo(int j,char b);
```

Their signature is the same (int ,char) but a function

```
void moo(int i,int j) ;
```

has a signature (int, int) which is different.

Function overloading is the practice of declaring the same function with different signatures. The same function name will be used with different number of parameters and parameters of different type. But overloading of functions with different return types are not allowed.

```
//C++ Tutorial - Sample code for function overloading
void AddAndDisplay(int x, int y)
{
    cout<<" C++ Tutorial - Integer result: "<<(x+y);
}

void AddAndDisplay(double x, double y)
{
    cout<< " C++ Tutorial - Double result: "<<(x+y);
}

void AddAndDisplay(float x, float y)
{
    cout<< " C++ Tutorial - float result: "<<(x+y);

}
```

Overloading Operators: You can redefine or overload the function of most built-in operators in C++. These operators can be overloaded globally or on a class-by-class basis. Overloaded operators are implemented as functions and can be member functions or global functions. C++ overloading is the mechanism by which the language standard operators are used for customized operations of the classes. For example if we are trying to write a string class, we would very simply ask for "+" operator to handle string concatenation,

```
//C++ overloading sample
class MyString
{
 public:
    char member1[100];
    void operator +(MyString val)
    {
        strcat(member1, val.member1);
    }
}
```

Derived Classes: C++ allows you to use one class declaration, known as a base class, as the basis for the declaration of a second class, known as a derived class

Creating or deriving a new class using another class as a base is called inheritance in C++. The new class created is called a Derived class and the old class used as a base is called a Base class in C++ inheritance terminology.

The derived class will inherit all the features of the base class in C++ inheritance. The derived class can also add its own features, data etc., It can also override some of the features (functions) of the base class, if the function is declared as virtual in base class.

```
class vehicle //Sample base class for c++ inheritance tutorial
    {
    protected:
    char colorname[20];
    int number_of_wheels;
    public:
    vehicle();
    ~vehicle(); void start();
    void stop();
    void run();
    };
    class Car: public vehicle //Sample derived class for C++ inheritance
tutorial
```

```
{
protected:
char type_of_fuel;
public:
Car();
};
```

The derived class Car will have access to the protected members of the base class. It can also use the functions start, stop and run provided the functionalities remain the same. In case the derived class needs some different functionalities for the same functions start, stop and run, then the base class should implement the concept of virtual functions.

Inheritance: *Inheritance* is a mechanism of reusing and extending existing classes without modifying them, thus producing hierarchical relationships between them. *Inheritance* is the process by which new classes called *derived* classes are created from existing classes called *base* classes. The derived classes have all the features of the base class and the programmer can choose to add new features specific to the newly created derived class.

Features or Advantages of Inheritance

Reusability: Inheritance helps the code to be reused in many situations. The base class is defined and once it is compiled, it need not be reworked. Using the concept of inheritance, the programmer can create as many derived classes from the base class as needed while adding specific features to each derived class as needed.

Saves Time and Effort: The above concept of reusability achieved by inheritance saves the programmer time and effort. Since the main code written can be reused in various situations as needed.

General Format for implementing the concept of Inheritance:

class derived_classname: access specifier baseclassname

Inheritance is almost like embedding an object into a class. Suppose that you declare an object x of class A in the class definition of B. As a result, class B will have access to all the public data members and member functions of class A. However, in class B, you have to access the data members and member functions of class A through object x. The following example demonstrates this:

```
#include <iostream>
```

```cpp
using namespace std;

class A {
    int data;
public:
    void f(int arg) { data = arg; }
    int g() { return data; }
};

class B {
public:
    A x;
};

int main() {
    B obj;
    obj.x.f(20);
    cout << obj.x.g() << endl;
//   cout << obj.g() << endl;
}
```

Multiple inheritance: You can derive a class from any number of base classes. Deriving a class from more than one direct base class is called *multiple inheritance*. In the following example, classes A, B, and C are direct base classes for the derived class X:

```cpp
class A { /* ... */ };
class B { /* ... */ };
class C { /* ... */ };
class X : public A, private B, public C { /* ... */ };
```

The following *inheritance graph* describes the inheritance relationships of the above example. An arrow points to the direct base class of the class at the tail of the arrow:

The order of derivation is relevant only to determine the order of default initialization by constructors and cleanup by destructorsA direct base class cannot appear in the base list of a derived class more than once:

class B1 { /* ... */ };   // direct base class

class D : public B1, private B1 { /* ... */ }; // error

However, a derived class can inherit an indirect base class more than once, as shown in the following example:

class L { /* ... */ };   // indirect base class

class B2 : public L { /* ... */ };

class B3 : public L { /* ... */ };

class D : public B2, public B3 { /* ... */ }; // valid

In the above example, class D inherits the indirect base class L once through class B2 and once through class B3. However, this may lead to ambiguities because two subobjects of class L exist, and both are accessible through class D. You can avoid this ambiguity by referring to class L using a qualified class name. For example:

B2::L

Virtual base classes: Suppose you have two derived classes B and C that have a common base class A, and you also have another class D that inherits from B and C. You can declare the base class A as *virtual* to ensure that B and C share the same subobject of A.

In the following example, an object of class D has two distinct subobjects of class L, one through class B1 and another through class B2. You can use the keyword virtual in front of the base class specifiers in the *base lists* of classes B1 and B2 to indicate that only one subobject of type L, shared by class B1 and class B2, exists.

For example:

```
class L { /* ... */ }; // indirect base class

class B1 : virtual public L { /* ... */ };

class B2 : virtual public L { /* ... */ };

class D : public B1, public B2 { /* ... */ }; // valid
```

Using the keyword virtual in this example ensures that an object of class D inherits only one subobject of class L.

A derived class can have both virtual and nonvirtual base classes. For example:

```
class V { /* ... */ };

class B1 : virtual public V { /* ... */ };

class B2 : virtual public V { /* ... */ };

class B3 : public V { /* ... */ };

class X : public B1, public B2, public B3 { /* ... */
};
```

In the above example, class X has two subobjects of class V, one that is shared by classes B1 and B2 and one through class B3.

Multiple access: In an inheritance graph containing virtual base classes, a name that can be reached through more than one path is accessed through the path that gives the most access.

For example:

```
class L {
public:
  void f();
};


class B1 : private virtual L { };


class B2 : public virtual L { };
```

```
class D : public B1, public B2 {
public:
  void f() {
    // L::f() is accessed through B2
    // and is public
    L::f();
  }
};
```

In the above example, the function f() is accessed through class B2. Because class B2 is inherited publicly and class B1 is inherited privately, class B2 offers more access.

Ambiguous base classes: When you derive classes, ambiguities can result if base and derived classes have members with the same names. Access to a base class member is ambiguous if you use a name or qualified name that does not refer to a unique function or object. The declaration of a member with an ambiguous name in a derived class is not an error. The ambiguity is only flagged as an error if you use the ambiguous member name.

For example, suppose that two classes named A and B both have a member named x, and a class named C inherits from both A and B. An attempt to access x from class C would be ambiguous. You can resolve ambiguity by qualifying a member with its class name using the scope resolution (::) operator.

```
class B1 {
public:
  int i;
  int j;
  void g(int) { }
};

class B2 {
```

```cpp
public:
  int j;
  void g() { }
};

class D : public B1, public B2 {
public:
  int i;
};

int main() {
  D dobj;
  D *dptr = &dobj;
  dptr->i = 5;
// dptr->j = 10;
  dptr->B1::j = 10;
// dobj.g();
  dobj.B2::g();
}
```

The statement dptr->j = 10 is ambiguous because the name j appears both in B1 and B2. The statement dobj.g() is ambiguous because the name g appears both in B1 and B2, even though B1::g(int) and B2::g() have different parameters.

The compiler checks for ambiguities at compile time. Because ambiguity checking occurs before access control or type checking, ambiguities may result even if only one of several members with the same name is accessible from the derived class.

Name hiding: Suppose two subobjects named A and B both have a member name x. The member name x of subobject B *hides* the member name x of subobject A if A is a base class of B. The following example demonstrates this:

```cpp
struct A {
```

```
    int x;
};
struct C: A, B {
    void f() { x = 0; }
};


int main() {
    C i;
    i.f();
}
```

The assignment x = 0 in function C::f() is not ambiguous because the declaration B::x has hidden A::x. However, the compiler will warn you that deriving C from A is redundant because you already have access to the subobject A through B. A base class declaration can be hidden along one path in the inheritance graph and not hidden along another path. The following example demonstrates this:

```
struct A { int x; };
struct B { int y; };
struct C: A, virtual B { };
struct D: A, virtual B {
    int x;
    int y;
};
struct E: C, D { };


int main() {
    E e;
//    e.x = 1;
    e.y = 2;
}
```

The assignment e.x = 1 is ambiguous. The declaration D::x hides A::x along the path D::A::x, but it does not hide A::x along the path C::A::x. Therefore the variable x could refer to either D::x or A::x. The assignment e.y = 2 is not ambiguous. The declaration D::y hides B::y along both paths D::B::y and C::B::y because B is a virtual base class.

Ambiguity and using declarations:

Suppose you have a class named C that inherits from a class named A, and x is a member name of A. If you use a using declaration to declare A::x in C, then x is also a member of C; C::x does not hide A::x. Therefore using declarations cannot resolve ambiguities due to inherited members. The following example demonstrates this:

```cpp
struct A {
    int x;
};


struct B: A { };


struct C: A {
    using A::x;
};


struct D: B, C {
    void f() { x = 0; }
};


int main() {
    D i;
    i.f();
}
```

The compiler will not allow the assignment x = 0 in function D::f() because it is ambiguous. The compiler can find x in two ways: as B::x or as C::x.

Unambiguous class members: The compiler can unambiguously find static members, nested types, and enumerators defined in a base class A regardless of the number of subobjects of type A an object has. The following example demonstrates this:

```cpp
struct A {
    int x;
    static int s;
    typedef A* Pointer_A;
    enum { e };
};

int A::s;

struct B: A { };

struct C: A { };

struct D: B, C {
    void f() {
        s = 1;
        Pointer_A pa;
        int i = e;
//      x = 1;
    }
};

int main() {
    D i;
    i.f();
}
```

The compiler allows the assignment s = 1, the declaration Pointer_A pa, and the statement int i = e. There is only one static variable s, only one typedef Pointer_A, and only one enumerator e. The compiler would not allow the assignment x = 1 because x can be reached either from class B or class C.

Pointer conversions: Conversions (either implicit or explicit) from a derived class pointer or reference to a base class pointer or reference must refer unambiguously to the same accessible base class object. (An *accessible base class* is a publicly derived base class that is neither hidden nor ambiguous in the inheritance hierarchy.) For example:

```cpp
class W { /* ... */ };
class X : public W { /* ... */ };
class Y : public W { /* ... */ };
class Z : public X, public Y { /* ... */ };
int main ()
{
    Z z;
    X* xptr = &z;     // valid
    Y* yptr = &z;     // valid
    W* wptr = &z;     // error, ambiguous reference to class W
              // X's W or Y's W ?
}
```

You can use virtual base classes to avoid ambiguous reference. For example:

```cpp
class W { /* ... */ };
class X : public virtual W { /* ... */ };
class Y : public virtual W { /* ... */ };
class Z : public X, public Y { /* ... */ };
int main ()
{
    Z z;
```

```
    X* xptr = &z;     // valid
    Y* yptr = &z;     // valid
    W* wptr = &z;     // valid, W is virtual therefore only one
                      // W subobject exists
}
```

A pointer to a member of a base class can be converted to a pointer to a member of a derived class if the following conditions are true:

The conversion is not ambiguous. The conversion is ambiguous if multiple instances of the base class are in the derived class.

A pointer to the derived class can be converted to a pointer to the base class. If this is the case, the base class is said to be *accessible*.

Member types must match. For example suppose class A is a base class of class B. You cannot convert a pointer to member of A of type int to a pointer to member of type B of type float.

The base class cannot be virtual.

Overload resolution: Overload resolution takes place *after* the compiler unambiguously finds a given function name. The following example demonstrates this:

```
struct A {
    int f() { return 1; }
};


struct B {
    int f(int arg) { return arg; }
};


struct C: A, B {
    int g() { return f(); }
};
```

The compiler will not allow the function call to f() in C::g() because the name f has been declared both in A and B. The compiler detects the ambiguity error before overload resolution can select the base match A::f().

Virtual functions: By default, C++ matches a function call with the correct function definition at compile time. This is called *static binding*. You can specify that the compiler match a function call with the correct function definition at run time; this is called *dynamic binding*. You declare a function with the keyword virtual if you want the compiler to use dynamic binding for that specific function.

The following examples demonstrate the differences between static and dynamic binding. The first example demonstrates static binding:

```cpp
#include <iostream>
using namespace std;
struct A {
   void f() { cout << "Class A" << endl; }
};


struct B: A {
   void f() { cout << "Class B" << endl; }
};


void g(A& arg) {
   arg.f();
}


int main() {
   B x;
   g(x);
}
```

The following is the output of the above example:

Class A

When function g() is called, function A::f() is called, although the argument refers to an object of type B. At compile time, the compiler knows only that the argument of function g() will be a reference to an object derived from A; it cannot determine whether the argument will be a reference to an object of type A or type B. However, this can be determined at run time. The following example is the same as the previous example, except that A::f() is declared with the virtual keyword:

```cpp
#include <iostream>
using namespace std;

struct A {
    virtual void f() { cout << "Class A" << endl;
}
};

struct B: A {
    void f() { cout << "Class B" << endl; }
};

void g(A& arg) {
    arg.f();
}

int main() {
    B x;
    g(x);
}
```

The following is the output of the above example:

Class B

The virtual keyword indicates to the compiler that it should choose the appropriate definition of f() not by the type of reference, but by the type of object that the reference refers to.

Therefore, a *virtual function* is a member function you may redefine for other derived classes, and can ensure that the compiler will call the redefined virtual function for an object of the corresponding derived class, even if you call that function with a pointer or reference to a base class of the object.

A class that declares or inherits a virtual function is called a *polymorphic class*.

You redefine a virtual member function, like any member function, in any derived class. Suppose you declare a virtual function named f in a class A, and you derive directly or indirectly from A a class named B. If you declare a function named f in class B with the same name and same parameter list as A::f, then B::f is also virtual (regardless whether or not you declare B::f with the virtual keyword) and it *overrides* A::f. However, if the parameter lists of A::f and B::f are different, A::f and B::f are considered different, B::f does not override A::f, and B::f is not virtual (unless you have declared it with the virtual keyword). Instead B::f *hides* A::f. The following example demonstrates this:

```cpp
#include <iostream>
using namespace std;

struct A {
    virtual void f() { cout << "Class A" << endl;
}
};

struct B: A {
    void f(int) { cout << "Class B" << endl; }
};

struct C: B {
    void f() { cout << "Class C" << endl; }
```

```
};

int main() {
   B b; C c;
   A* pa1 = &b;
   A* pa2 = &c;
// b.f();
   pa1->f();
   pa2->f();
}
```

The following is the output of the above example:

Class A

Class C

The function B::f is not virtual. It hides A::f. Thus the compiler will not allow the function call b.f(). The function C::f is virtual; it overrides A::f even though A::f is not visible in C.

If you declare a base class destructor as virtual, a derived class destructor will override that base class destructor, even though destructors are not inherited.

The return type of an overriding virtual function may differ from the return type of the overridden virtual function. This overriding function would then be called a *covariant virtual function*. Suppose that B::f overrides the virtual function A::f. The return types of A::f and B::f may differ if all the following conditions are met:

The function B::f returns a reference or pointer to a class of type T, and A::f returns a pointer or a reference to an unambiguous direct or indirect base class of T.

The const or volatile qualification of the pointer or reference returned by B::f has the same or less const or volatile qualification of the pointer or reference returned by A::f.

The return type of B::f must be complete at the point of declaration of B::f, or it can be of type B.

The following example demonstrates this:

```cpp
#include <iostream>
using namespace std;

struct A { };

class B : private A {
    friend class D;
    friend class F;
};

A global_A;
B global_B;

struct C {
    virtual A* f() {
        cout << "A* C::f()" << endl;
        return &global_A;
    }
};

struct D : C {
    B* f() {
        cout << "B* D::f()" << endl;
        return &global_B;
    }
};

struct E;
```

```
struct F : C {

//    Error:
//    E is incomplete
//    E* f();
};

struct G : C {

//    Error:
//    A is an inaccessible base class of B
//    B* f();
};

int main() {
    D d;
    C* cp = &d;
    D* dp = &d;

    A* ap = cp->f();
    B* bp = dp->f();
};
```

The following is the output of the above example:

B* D::f()

B* D::f()

The statement A* ap = cp->f() calls D::f() and converts the pointer returned to type A*. The statement B* bp = dp->f() calls D::f() as well but does not convert the pointer returned; the type returned is B*. The compiler would not allow the declaration of the virtual function F::f() because E is not a complete class. The compiler would not allow the declaration of the virtual function G::f() because class A is not an accessible base class of B (unlike friend classes D and F, the definition of B does not give access to its members for class G).

A virtual function cannot be global or static because, by definition, a virtual function is a member function of a base class and relies on a specific object to determine which implementation of the function is called. You can declare a virtual function to be a friend of another class.

If a function is declared virtual in its base class, you can still access it directly using the scope resolution (::) operator. In this case, the virtual function call mechanism is suppressed and the function implementation defined in the base class is used. In addition, if you do not override a virtual member function in a derived class, a call to that function uses the function implementation defined in the base class.

A virtual function must be one of the following:

- Defined

- Declared pure

- Defined and declared pure

A base class containing one or more pure virtual member functions is called an *abstract class*.

Abstract classes: An *abstract class* is a class that is designed to be specifically used as a base class. An abstract class contains at least one *pure virtual function*. You declare a pure virtual function by using a *pure specifier* (= 0) in the declaration of a virtual member function in the class declaration.

The following is an example of an abstract class:

```
class AB {
public:
  virtual void f() = 0;
};
```

Function AB::f is a pure virtual function. A function declaration cannot have both a pure specifier and a definition. For example, the compiler will not allow the following:

```
struct A {
  virtual void g() { } = 0;
};
```

You cannot use an abstract class as a parameter type, a function return type, or the type of an explicit conversion, nor can you declare an object of an abstract class. You can, however, declare pointers and references to an abstract class. The following example demonstrates this:

```cpp
struct A {
  virtual void f() = 0;
};


struct B : A {
  virtual void f() { }
};


// Error:
// Class A is an abstract class
// A g();


// Error:
// Class A is an abstract class
// void h(A);
A& i(A&);


int main() {

// Error:
// Class A is an abstract class
//    A a;


   A* pa;
   B b;


// Error:
```

```
// Class A is an abstract class
//    static_cast<A>(b);
}
```

Class A is an abstract class. The compiler would not allow the function declarations A g() or void h(A), declaration of object a, nor the static cast of b to type A.

Virtual member functions are inherited. A class derived from an abstract base class will also be abstract unless you override each pure virtual function in the derived class.

For example:

```
class AB {
public:
  virtual void f() = 0;
};


class D2 : public AB {
  void g();
};


int main() {
  D2 d;
}
```

The compiler will not allow the declaration of object d because D2 is an abstract class; it inherited the pure virtual function f()from AB. The compiler will allow the declaration of object d if you define function D2::f(), as this overrides the inherited pure virtual function AB::f(). Function AB::f() needs to be overridden if you want to avoid the abstraction of D2.

Note that you can derive an abstract class from a nonabstract class, and you can override a non-pure virtual function with a pure virtual function.

You can call member functions from a constructor or destructor of an abstract class. However, the results of calling (directly or indirectly) a pure virtual function from its constructor are undefined. The following example demonstrates this:

```
struct A {
  A() {
    direct();
    indirect();
  }
  virtual void direct() = 0;
  virtual void indirect() { direct(); }
};
```

The default constructor of A calls the pure virtual function direct() both directly and indirectly (through indirect()).

The compiler issues a warning for the direct call to the pure virtual function, but not for the indirect call.

Exercises

Fill in the Blanks

1. C++ was originally developed by ____________________

2. The standard c++ comment ______________

3. The operator << is called __________

4. C++ name was suggested by__________.

5. A constructor is called whenever ________________.

6. A destructor takes__________.

7. The fields in a class of a c++ program are by default ______________

Answers

1. Bjarne Stroustrup

2. //

3. A insertion operator or put to operator

4. Rrick Mascitti

5. A object is declared

6. Zero arguments 7.private

Questions

1. What is C++ ?
2. Explain Token.
3. How do I compile .m files with the GNU C compiler ?
4. What is the difference between self and super ?
5. What is function overloading and operator overloading?
6. What is the difference between declaration and definition?
7. Explain Types of Inheritance.
8. Give difference between Structure and Unions.
9. Describe Constructors.
10. Write various data types.

CHAPTER - 4

Introduction to Database Management System

Objectives

At the end of this session, the learner will be able to:

Define DBMS.

Compare File and Database approach.

Discuss Architecture of Database system.

Define Data Model.

Analyse Data independence and Data dictionary.

Explain role of DBA.

Describe Data definition and manipulation languages.

A DBMS is a computer based system which manage the collection of data or collection of Files. The important word here is **manage** i.e. controlled use of resources, controlling its quality, coordinating shared use of a resource. The objective of the DBMS is to provide a convenient and effective method of defining, storing, and retrieving the information contained in the database. The DBMS interfaces with application programs, so that the data contained in the database can be used by multiple applications and users.

A DBMS is a central pool of data that can be shared by the users. The properties of DBMS are: defining user views. Access control backup and recovery, concurrency management, integrity constraints.

A major purpose of a database system is to provide users with an abstract view of the data. That is, the system hides certain details of how the data are stored and maintained. Thereby, data can be stored in complex data structures that permit efficient retrieval, yet users see a simplified and easy-to-use view of the data. The lowest level of abstraction, the physical level, describes how the data are actually stored and details the data structures. The next-higher level of abstraction, the logical level, describes what data are stored, and what relationships exist among those data. The highest level of abstraction, the view level, describes parts of the database that are relevant to each user; application programs used to access a database form part of the view level.

The overall structure of the database is called the database schema. The schema specifies data, data relationships, data semantics, and consistency constraints on the data.

History of DBMS

First-generation DBMS designed by Charles Bachman in the company General Electric in the early 1960s, referred to as the Data Storage Integrated (Integrated Data Store). Formed the basis for the network data model then by standardization Conference on Data System Languages (CODASYL). Bachman receive ACM Turing Award (Nobel award such in computer science) in 1973. And at the end of 1960, IBM developed management information system (Information Management System) DBMS. IMS formed from the data on the representation framework, called the data model hierarchy. In the same time, developed the system as a result of the Saber cooperation between the IBM with the United States airline. This system allows users to access data on the same computer network.

Then in 1970, Edgar Codd, the Research Laboratory in San Jose, proposed the model data relational. In 1980, became the model relational DBMS paradigm the most dominant. SQL query language developed for relational database project as part of IBM's System R. SQL standardization at the end of 1980, and SQL-92 adopted by the American National Standards Institute (ANSI) and International Standards Organization (ISO). Program used for parallel execution in the database is called a transaction. Users writing program, and is responsible for running the program simultaneously to the DBMS. In 1999, James Gray wins Turing Award for contributions to the management of transactions in DBMS.

At the end of 1980 and beginning of 1990, many areas of the database system developed. Research in the field of the database query language that includes powerful, comprehensive data model, and support the emphasis on analysis of data complex from all parts of the organization. Some vendors extend the system with the ability to store new data types such as image and text, and ability of complex queries. System-specific / special developed by many vendor to create a data warehouse, consolidate data from multiple base data. Phenomena the most interesting is the enterprise resource planning (ERP) and management resource planning (MRP), which adds substantially layer of feature-oriented applications. Package that includes covers Bean, Oracle, PeopleSoft, SAP, and Siebel. Packages to identify this set of tasks in general (eg., inventory management, financial analysis) and provide the application layer to the general handling purpose. Data stored in the DBMS relational, and applications layer can be adjusted to a different company. Furthermore, the DBMS enter the internet. At the time of the first generation of Web site store data exclusively in the file system operation, the current DBMS can used to store data that can be accessed through a Web browser. Query degenerate can form via the Web, and format the response using the markup language such as HTML for easier viewing in a browser. All vendors database to add this feature to their DMS. Management database consider the importance of data is on-line, and can be accessed through computer network. Current areas such as this realized in the database multimedia, interactive video, digital libraries, the project scientists, such as project mapping, earth observation system project NASA property, etc.

A collection of related part of data

- Representing/capturing the information about a real-world enterprise or part of an enterprise.

- Collected and maintained to serve specific data management needs of the enterprise.
- Activities of the enterprise are supported by the database and continually update the database.

Types of Database

- Deductive Databases: This types of databases are knowledge based, uses some deduction rules to draw some interface.
- Traditional Databases: This types of database are used for business data processing.
- Multimedia database: This stores pictures, video clips and sound messages.
- Geographical information system(GIS): This stores maps, weather data and satellite images etc.

Uses of DBMS

- it enables users to access and manipulate the database.
- it provides a building block in constructing data processing systems for applications requiring database access – MIS or systems for accounting, production and inventory control or customer support.
- it helps the DBA perform certain managerial duties.

The name 'database management system' was chosen recognizing that different names are in use and different types of systems exist. Substantial generalization is assumed in any DBMS of interest without using 'generalized.' 'Data is preferred over 'information' for the various reasons cited.

Functions of a Database Management System

- Database Definition
- Database creation (storing data in a defined database)
- Retrieval (query and reporting)
- Update(Changing the contents of the database)
- Programming User Facilities for system development)
- Database revision and restructuring

- Database integrity control
- Performance Monitoring

File Oriented Approach

File based systems are an early attempt to computerize the manual filing system. For example, a manual file can be set up to hold all the correspondence relating to a particular matter as a project, product, task, client or employee. In an organization there would be many such files which may be labeled and stored. The same could be done at homes where file relating to bank statements, receipts, tax payments, etc.,could be maintained.

For retrieval of information from these files the entries could be searched sequentially. Alternatively an indexing system could be used to locate information. This system works well if the number of items stored is small. However, a manual system crashes if the cross-referencing and processing of information is done in the files.

For example, in a university a number of students are enrolled who have the options of doing various courses. The university may have separate files for the personal details of the students, fees paid by them, the number and details of the courses taught, the number and details of each faulty member in various departments. Now if some queries are done on this, it would be cumbersome and time consuming to answer the questions in the file based system.

Limitations of File Based System

Separation and isolation of data: When the data is stored in separate files it becomes difficult to access. It becomes very complex to retrieve data from such files as large amount of data has to be searched.

Duplication of data: Due to de-centralized approach the file system leads to uncontrolled duplication of data wasting lots of storage space. It also costs time and money to reenter data. ex. The address information of students may have to be duplicated in bus list file data.

Inconsistent data: the data can become inconsistent if more than one person modifies the data concurrently, ex. If any student changes the residence and the change is notified to only his/her file and not to bus file.

Data dependence: in file based system it is extremely difficult to change the physical structure of data files and records as it may affect the programs. This feature is called data dependence.

Incompatible file formats: the programs written in COBOL language is quite different from programming in C language which makes the incompatible file formats, that means a file running on COBOL compatible computer cannot run on C compatible computer. And changing the format is time consuming and expensive.

Fixed queries: File based system are very much dependent on application programs. Any query or report needed by the organization has to be developed by the application programmer. Every time producing new report or queries is a tedious job, so number of queries are fixed.

Besides the above the maintenance of the file based system is difficult and there is no provision for security. Recovery is inadequate or non-existent.

DBMS Approach

1. Controlled Redundancy

- In the file processing approach, each user defines and implements the files needed and software applications to manipulate those files.

- Various files are likely to have different formats and programs may be written in different languages and same information may be duplicated in several files.

- Data redundancy leads to o wasted storage space, o duplication of effort (when multiple copies of a datum need to be updated), o a higher likelihood of the introduction of inconsistency.

- Database design stores each logical data item at one place to ensure consistency and saves storage.

- But sometimes, controlled redundancy is necessary to improve the performance.

- Database should have capability to control this redundancy & maintain consistency by specifying the checks during database design.

2. Restricting Unauthorized Access

- A DBMS provides a security and authorization subsystem, which is used by DBA to create user accounts and to specify restrictions on user accounts.

- File processing system provides password mechanism and very less security which is not sufficient to enforce security policies like DBMS.

3. Providing Persistent Storage for Program Objects

- Object oriented database systems are compatible with programming languages such as C++ and Java.

- A DBMS software automatically performs the conversion of a complex object which can be stored in object oriented DBMS, such an object is said to be persistent due to its survival after the termination of the program.

4. Providing Storage Structures for Efficient Query Processing

- The DBMS utilizes a variety of sophisticated techniques (view, indexes etc.) to store and retrieve the data efficiently that are utilized to improve the execution time of queries and updates.

- DBMS provides indexes and buffering for fast access of query result, the choice of index is part of physical database design and tuning.

- The query processing and optimization module is responsible for choosing an efficient query execution plan for each query submitted to the system.

5. Providing Backup & Recovery

- Data should be restored to a consistent state at the time system crash and changes being made

- If hardware or software fails in the middle of the update program, the recovery subsystem of DBMS ensures that update program is resumed at the point of failure.

6. Multiple user interfaces

- DBMS provides a variety of user interfaces for the users of varying level of technical knowledge.

- These includes query language for casual users, programming language interfaces for application programmers, forms and command codes for parametric users, menu driven interfaces and natural language interfaces for stand alone users etc.

7. Representing Complex Relationships among data

- A DBMS must have the capability to represent a variety of complex relationship among the data, to define new relationships as they arise, and to retrieve and update the related data easily and efficiently.

8. Enforcing Integrity Constraints

- The DBMS have certain integrity constraints that hold on data.
- These constraints are derived from the meaning of the data and of the miniworld.
- Some constraints can be specified to the DBMS at the time of defining data definitions and automatically enforced.
- Database does not allow violation of constraints at the time of updating the database.

9. Permitting Inference and Action Using Rules

- Deductive database systems provide capabilities for defining deduction rules for inferencing new information from the stored database facts.
- Triggers can be associated with tables.
- A trigger is a form of a rule activated by updates to the table, which results in performing some additional operations to some other tables, sending messages and so on.
- Stored procedure can also be used as a part of the overall database definition and are invoked appropriately when certain conditions are met.
- Active database provides more powerful functionality by providing the active rules that can automatically initiate actions when certain events and conditions occur.

Database Model

A data model in software engineering is an abstract model that describes how data are represented and accessed. Data models formally define data elements and relationships among data elements for a domain of interest. According to Hoberman (2009), "A data model is a way finding tool for both business and IT professionals, which uses a set of symbols and text to precisely explain a subset of real information to improve communication within the organization and thereby lead to a more flexible and stable application environment. There are basically five data models in DBMS:

1. Hierarchical model
2. Network model
3. Relational Model
4. Object/Relational Model
5. Object-Oriented Model

1. Hierarchical Model: The hierarchical data model organizes data in a tree structure. There is a hierarchy of parent and child data segments. This structure implies that a record can have repeating information, generally in the child data segments. Data in a series of records, which have a set of field values attached to it. It collects all the instances of a specific record together as a record type. These record types are the equivalent of tables in the relational model, and with the individual records being the equivalent of rows. To create links between these record types, the hierarchical model uses Parent Child Relationships. These are a 1:N mapping between record types. This is done by using trees, like set theory used in the relational model, "borrowed" from maths. For example, an organization might store information about an employee, such as name, employee number, department, salary. The organization might also store information about an employee's children, such as name and date of birth. The employee and children data forms a hierarchy, where the employee data represents the parent segment and the children data represents the child segment. If an employee has three children, then there would be three child segments associated with one employee segment. In a hierarchical database the parent-child relationship is one to many. This restricts a child segment to having only one parent segment. Hierarchical DBMSs were popular from the late 1960s, with the introduction of IBM's Information Management System (IMS) DBMS, through 1970's.

2. **Network Model:** The popularity of the network data model coincided with the popularity of the hierarchical data model. Some data were more naturally modeled with more than one parent per child. So, the network model permitted the modeling of many-to-many relationships in data. In 1971, the Conference on Data Systems Languages (CODASYL) formally defined the network model. The basic data modeling construct in the network model is the set construct. A set consists of an owner record type, a set name, and a member record type. A member record type can have

that role in more than one set, hence the multiparent concept is supported. An owner record type can also be a member or owner in another set. The data model is a simple network, and link and intersection record types (called junction records by IDMS) may exist, as well as sets between them. Thus, the complete network of relationships is represented by several pairwise sets; in each set some (one) record type is owner (at the tail of the network arrow) and one or more record types are members (at the head of the relationship arrow). Usually, a set defines a 1:M relationship, although 1:1 is permitted. The CODASYL network model is based on mathematical set theory.

3. **Relational Model:** (RDBMS - relational database management system) A database based on the relational model developed by E.F. Codd. A relational database allows the definition of data structures, storage and retrieval operations and integrity constraints. In such a database the data and relations between them are organised in tables. A table is a collection of records and each record in a table contains the same fields.

Properties of Relational Tables:
- Values Are Atomic
- Each Row is Unique
- Column Values Are of the Same Kind
- The Sequence of Columns is Insignificant
- The Sequence of Rows is Insignificant

Each Column Has a Unique Name Certain fields may be designated as keys, which means that searches for specific values of that field will use indexing to speed them up. Where fields in two different tables take values from the same set, a join operation can be performed to select related records in the two tables by matching values in those fields. Often, but not always, the fields will have the same name in both tables. For example, an "orders" table might contain (customer-ID, product-code) pairs and a "products" table might contain (product-code, price) pairs so to calculate a given customer's bill you would sum the prices of all products ordered by that customer by joining on the product-code fields of the two tables. This can be extended to joining multiple tables on multiple fields. Because these relationships are only specified at retreival time, relational databases are classed as dynamic database management system. The RELATIONAL database model is based on the Relational Algebra.

4. **Object/Relational Model:** Object/relational database management systems (ORDBMSs) add new object storage capabilities to the relational systems at the core of modern information systems. These new facilities integrate management of traditional fielded data, complex objects such as time-series and geospatial data and diverse binary media such as audio, video, images, and applets. By encapsulating methods with data structures, an ORDBMS server can execute comple x analytical and data manipulation operations to search and transform multimedia and other complex objects.

As an evolutionary technology, the object/relational (OR) approach has inherited the robust transaction- and performance-management features of it s relational ancestor and the flexibility of its object-oriented cousin. Database designers can work with familiar tabular structures and data definition languages (DDLs) while assimilating new object-management possibi lities. Query and procedural languages and call interfaces in ORDBMSs are familiar: SQL3, vendor procedural languages, and ODBC, JDBC, and proprie tary call interfaces are all extensions of RDBMS languages and interfaces. And the leading vendors are, of course, quite well known: IBM, Inform ix, and Oracle.

5. **Object-Oriented Model:** Object DBMSs add database functionality to object programming languages. They bring much more than persistent storage of programming language objects. Object DBMSs extend the semantics of the C++, Smalltalk and Java object programming languages to provide full-featured database programming capability, while retaining native language compatibility. A major benefit of this approach is the unification of the application and database development into a seamless data model and language environment. As a result, applications require less code, use more natural data modeling, and code bases are easier to maintain. Object developers can write complete database applications with a modest amount of additional effort.

According to Rao (1994), "The object-oriented database (OODB) paradigm is the combination of object-oriented programming language (OOPL) systems and persistent systems. The power of the OODB comes from the seamless treatment of both persistent data, as found in databases, and transient data, as found in executing programs." In contrast to a relational DBMS where a complex data structure must be flattened out to fit into tables or joined together from those tables to form the in-memory structure, object DBMSs have no performance overhead to store or retrieve a web or hierarchy of interrelated objects. This one-to-one mapping of object programming language objects to database objects has two benefits over other storage approaches: it provides higher performance management of objects, and it enables better management of the complex interrelationships between objects. This makes object DBMSs better suited to support applications such as financial portfolio risk analysis systems, telecommunications service applications, world wide web document structures, design and manufacturing systems, and hospital patient record systems, which have complex relationships between data.

Architecture of Database system: The logical architecture describes how data in the database is perceived by users. It is not concerned with how the data is handled and processed by the DBMS, but only with how it looks. The method of data storage on the underlying file system is not revealed, and the users can manipulate the data without worrying about where it is located or how it is actually stored. This results in the database having different levels of abstraction.

The majority of commercial Database Management Systems available today are based on the ANSI/SPARC generalised DBMS architecture, as proposed by the ANSI/SPARC Study Group on Data Base Management Systems. Hence this is also called as the ANSI/SPARC model. It divides the system into three levels of abstraction: the internal or physical level, the conceptual level, and the external or view level. The diagram below shows the logical architecture for a typical DBMS.

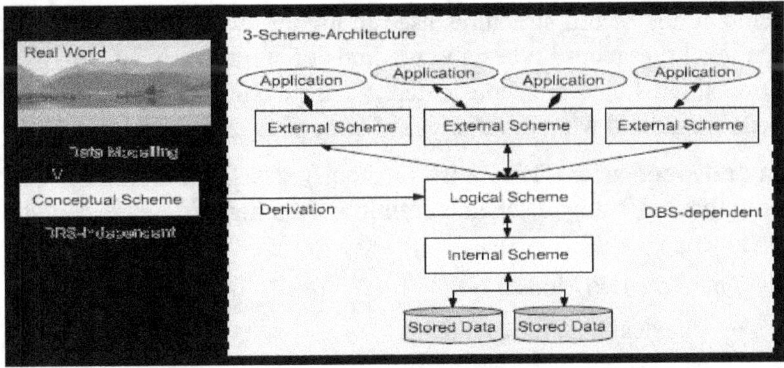

The External or View Level

The external or view level is the highest level of abstraction of database. It provides a window on the conceptual view, which allows the user to see only the data of interest to them. The user can be either an application program or an end user. There can be many external views as any number of external schema can be defined and they can overlap each other. It consists of the definition of logical records and relationships in the external view. It also contains the methods for deriving the objects such as entities, attributes and relationships in the external view from the Conceptual view.

The Conceptual Level or Global level

The conceptual level presents a logical view of the entire database as a unified whole. It allows the user to bring all the data in the database together and see it in a consistent manner. Hence, there is only one conceptual schema per database. The first stage in the design of a database is to define the conceptual view, and a DBMS provides a data definition language for this purpose. It describes all the records and relationships included in the database.

The data definition language used to create the conceptual level must not specify any physical storage considerations that should be handled by the physical level. It does not provide any storage or access details, but defines the information content only.

The Internal or Physical Level

The collection of files permanently stored on secondary storage devices is known as the physical database. The physical or internal level is the one closest to physical storage, and it provides a low-level description of the physical database, and an interface between the operating systems file system and the record structures used in higher levels of abstraction. It is at this level that record types and methods of storage are defined, as well as how stored fields are represented, what physical sequence the stored records are in, and what other physical structures exist.

Data Independence: The ability to modify a scheme definition in one level without affecting a scheme definition in a higher level is called data independence.

1. There are two kinds:
   - Physical data independence
   - The ability to modify the physical scheme without causing application programs to be rewritten
   - Modifications at this level are usually to improve performance
   - Logical data independence

- The ability to modify the conceptual scheme without causing application programs to be rewritten

- Usually done when logical structure of database is altered

2. Logical data independence is harder to achieve as the application programs are usually heavily dependent on the logical structure of the data. An analogy is made to abstract data types in programming languages.

Data Dictionary: A data dictionary stores information about the structure of the database. It is used heavily. Hence a good data dictionary should have a good design and efficient implementation. It is seen that when program becomes somewhat large in size, keeping track of all available names that are used and the purpose for which they are used becomes more and more difficult. After a significant time if the same programmer or another wants to modify the program, it becomes extremely difficult.

The problem becomes even more difficult when the number of data types that an organization has in its database increases. The data of an organization is a valuable corporate resource and therefore some kind of inventory and catalog of it must be maintained so as to assist in both the utilization and management of the resource. It is for this purpose data dictionary is emerging as a major tool. A dictionary provides definition of things. A dictionary tells you where to find them. A data dictionary contains information about data.

A comprehensive data dictionary would provide the definition of data items, how they fit into the data structure and how they relate to other entities in the database. In DBMS, the data dictionary stores the information concerning the external, conceptual and internal levels of the databases. It would combine the source of each data field value, i.e. from where the authenticate value is obtained. The updates regarding user identification with the time of each update is also recorded in the data dictionary.

An ideal data dictionary should include every thing that a DBA wants to know about the database.

- External, conceptual and internal data descriptions.

- Description of entities(record types), attributes(fields), as well as cross references, origin and meaning

- of data elements.

- Synonyms, authorisation and security codes.

- Which external schemas are used by which programs, who the users are, and what their authorisations are.

- Statistics about database and its usage including number of records, etc.

A data dictionary is implemented as a database so that users can query its contents.

Database Administrator: A **database administrator (DBA)** is a person responsible for the design, implementation, maintenance and repair of an organization's database. They are also known by the titles *Database Coordinator* or *Database Programmer*, and is closely related to the *Database Analyst, Database Modeler, Programmer Analyst*, and *Systems Manager*. The role includes the development and design of database strategies, monitoring and improving database performance and capacity, and planning for future expansion requirements. They may also plan, co-ordinate and implement security measures to safeguard the database.

The Database Administrator must be a manager, rather than a technician – seeking to meet the needs of people who use data. Since many users may share the same data resources, the DBA must be repared to mediate conflicting needs and objectives, sometimes imposing a compromise solution. Functions of Database Administration are as follows:

- Define, acquire and retire data according to the user needs.

- Provide tools to access and update the data and produce reports.

- Inform and assist users in planning and using data resources and database management tools.

- Maintain database integrity by protecting its existence, maintaining its quality and controlling access to private data.

- Monitor operations for efficient performance and integrity threats.

- The **database administrator** is a **person** having central control over data and programs accessing that data. Duties of the database administrator include:

  - **Scheme definition:** the creation of the original database scheme. This involves writing a set of definitions in a DDL (data storage and definition language), compiled by the DDL compiler into a set of tables stored in the data dictionary.

  - **Storage structure and access method definition:** writing a set of definitions translated by the data storage and definition language compiler.

- **Scheme and physical organization modification:** writing a set of definitions used by the DDL compiler to generate modifications to appropriate internal system tables (e.g. data dictionary). This is done rarely, but sometimes the database scheme or physical organization must be modified.

- **Granting of authorization for data access:** granting different types of authorization for data access to various users.

- **Integrity constraint specification:** generating integrity constraints. These are consulted by the database manager module whenever updates occur.

Database Manager: The database manager is a program module which provides the interface between the low-level data stored in the database and the application programs and queries submitted to the system. The database manager is a program module which provides the interface between the low-level data stored in the database and the application programs and queries submitted to the system. Databases typically require lots of storage space (gigabytes). This must be stored on disks. Data is moved between disk and main memory (MM) as needed. The goal of the database system is to simplify and facilitate access to data. Performance is important. Views provide simplification. So the database manager module is responsible for:

- Interaction with the file manager: Storing raw data on disk using the file system usually provided by a conventional operating system. The database manager must translate DML statements into low-level file system commands (for storing, retrieving and updating data in the database).

- Integrity enforcement: Checking that updates in the database do not violate consistency constraints (e.g. no bank account balance below $25)

- Security enforcement: Ensuring that users only have access to information they are permitted to see

- Backup and recovery: Detecting failures due to power failure, disk crash, software errors, etc., and restoring the database to its state before the failure

- Concurrency control: Preserving data consistency when there are concurrent users. Some small database systems may miss some of these features, resulting in simpler database managers. (For example, no concurrency is required on a PC running MS-DOS.) These features are necessary on larger systems.

Primary key: A primary key is a column (or columns) in a table that uniquely identifies the rows in that table. A primary key is a unique identifier of a record in a file. Every field in a data set other than the primary key is referred to as a non-key attribute. Some of the non-key attributes may be used to sort the file (or data set) to facilitate answering user queries. A foreign key is a field in a data set which is the primary key in a related data set, referred to as the "master" data set. There are two variants of the "foreign key" concept -- a foreign key can either be part of a composite primary key or simply a non-key attribute in a data set. That is, when a data set has a composite primary key (more than one field making up the primary key), then each individual element of that composite key will usually be the primary key in another related data set. Alternatively, a foreign key can simply be a non-key attribute in a data set which happens to be a primary key in a related data set.

Customers

Customer No	First Name	Last Name
1	Sally	Thompson
2	Sally	Henderson
3	Harry	Henderson
4	Sandra	Wellington

For example, in the table above, Customer No is the primary key.

The values placed in primary key columns must be unique for each row: no duplicates can be tolerated. In addition, nulls are not allowed in primary key columns.

The primary key of a relational table uniquely identifies each record in the table. It can either be a normal attribute that is guaranteed to be unique or it can be generated by the DBMS (such as a globally unique identifier, or GUID, in Microsoft SQL Server). Primary keys may consist of a single attribute or multiple attributes in combination.

Keys in Database Environments:

Key	Explanation
Primary key	Unique identifier of records in a data set.
Composite (concatenated) key	Two or more fields taken together serve as the primary key in the data set.
Non-key attribute	Any field that is not a primary key attribute.
Foreign key	Two variants: (1) an element of a composite key in a data set which is the primary key in a related data set, (2) a non-key attribute in a data set which is the primary key in a related data set.

Data Definition Language: The Data Definition Language (DDL) is used to create and destroy databases and database objects. These commands will primarily be used by database administrators during the setup and removal phases of a database project. Let's take a look at the structure and usage of four basic DDL commands:

The Data Definition Language (DDL) is used to create and destroy databases and database objects. These commands will primarily be used by database administrators during the setup and removal phases of a database project. Let's take a look at the structure and usage of four basic DDL commands:

Create: Installing a database management system (DBMS) on a computer allows you to create and manage many independent databases. For example, you may want to maintain a database of customer contacts for your sales department and a personnel database for your HR department. The CREATE command can be used to establish each of these databases on your platform. For example, the command:

CREATE DATABASE employees

creates an empty database named "employees" on your DBMS. After creating the database, your next step is to create tables that will contain data. Another variant of the CREATE command can be used for this purpose. Perhaps the most common CREATE command is the CREATE TABLE command. The typical usage is:

CREATE   [TEMPORARY]   TABLE   *[table   name]*   (*[column definitions]*) *[table parameters]*.

Column Definitions: A comma-separated list consisting of any of the following

- Column definition: *[column name] [data type] {NULL | NOT NULL} {column options}*

- Primary key definition: *PRIMARY KEY ([comma separated column list])*

- CONSTRAINTS: *{CONSTRAINT} [constraint definition]*

- RDBMS specific functionality

For example, the command to create a table named **personal_info** with a few sample columns would be:

CREATE TABLE **personal_info** (

id   INTEGER PRIMARY KEY,

first_name   CHAR(50) NULL,

last_name   CHAR(75) NOT NULL,

dateofbirth   DATE   NULL

);

Use: The USE command allows you to specify the database you wish to work with within your DBMS. For example, if we're currently working in the sales database and want to issue some commands that will affect the employees database, we would preface them with the following SQL command:

USE employees

It's important to always be conscious of the database you are working in before issuing SQL commands that manipulate data.

ALTER: Once you've created a table within a database, you may wish to modify the definition of it. The ALTER command allows you to make changes to the structure of a table without deleting and recreating it. Take a look at the following command:

ALTER *objecttype objectname parameters*.

For example:

ALTER TABLE personal_info

ADD salary money null

This example adds a new attribute to the personal_info table -- an employee's salary. The "money" argument specifies that an employee's salary will be stored using a dollars and cents format. Finally, the "null" keyword tells the database that it's OK for this field to contain no value for any given employee.

Drop: The final command of the Data Definition Language, DROP, allows us to remove entire database objects from our DBMS. For example, if we want to permanently remove the personal_info table that we created, we'd use the following general command :

DROP   *objecttype*   *objectname.*

For example:

DROP TABLE personal_info

Similarly, the command below would be used to remove the entire employees database:

DROP DATABASE employees

Use this command with care! Remember that the DROP command removes entire data structures from your database. If you want to remove individual records, use the DELETE command of the Data Manipulation Language.

Data Manipulation Language (DML): The Data Manipulation Language (DML) is used to retrieve, insert and modify database information. These commands will be used by all database users during the routine operation of the database. Let's take a brief look at the basic DML commands:

1. Data Manipulation is:

   - **retrieval** of information from the database
   - **insertion** of new information into the database
   - **deletion** of information in the database
   - **modification** of information in the database

2. A DML is a language which enables users to access and manipulate data.

   The goal is to provide efficient human interaction with the system.

3. There are two types of DML:

- **procedural**: the user specifies *what* data is needed and *how* to get it
- **nonprocedural**: the user only specifies *what* data is needed
- Easier for user
- May not generate code as efficient as that produced by procedural languages

4. A **query language** is a portion of a DML involving information retrieval only. The terms DML and query language are often used synonymously.

INSERT: The INSERT command in SQL is used to add records to an existing table. Returning to the personal_info example from the previous section, let's imagine that our HR department needs to add a new employee to their database. They could use a command similar to the one shown below:

insert into tablename

(column1name,column2name...columnxname)

values (value1,value2...valuex);

for example
INSERT INTO personal_info
values('bart','simpson',12345,$45000)

Note that there are four values specified for the record. These correspond to the table attributes in the order they were defined: first_name, last_name, employee_id, and salary.

SELECT: The SELECT command is the most commonly used command in SQL. It allows database users to retrieve the specific information they desire from an operational database. Let's take a look at a few examples, again using the personal_info table from our employees database. The general command is,

SELECT [ALL | DISTINCT] columnname1 [,columnname2]

FROM tablename1 [,tablename2]

[WHERE condition] [and|or condition...]

[GROUP BY column-list]

[HAVING "conditions]

[ORDER BY "column-list" [ASC | DESC]]

The command shown below retrieves all of the information contained within the personal_info table. Note that the asterisk is used as a wildcard in SQL. This literally means "Select everything from the personal_info table."

SELECT *
FROM personal_info

Alternatively, users may want to limit the attributes that are retrieved from the database. For example, the Human Resources department may require a list of the last names of all employees in the company. The following SQL command would retrieve only that information:

SELECT last_name
FROM personal_info

Finally, the WHERE clause can be used to limit the records that are retrieved to those that meet specified criteria. The CEO might be interested in reviewing the personnel records of all highly paid employees. The following command retrieves all of the data contained within personal_info for records that have a salary value greater than $50,000:

SELECT *

FROM personal_info

WHERE salary > $50000

UPDATE: The UPDATE command can be used to modify information contained within a table, either in bulk or individually. Each year, our company gives all employees a 3% cost-of-living increase in their salary. The following SQL command could be used to quickly apply this to all of the employees stored in the database:

update tablename

set columnname = newvalue [,columnxname = newvaluex...]

where columnname OPERATOR value [and|or columnnamex
OPERATOR valuex];

for example

UPDATE personal_info

SET salary = salary * 1.03

On the other hand, our new employee Bart Simpson has demonstrated performance above and beyond the call of duty. Management wishes to recognize his stellar accomplishments with a $5,000 raise. The WHERE clause could be used to single out Bart for this raise:

UPDATE personal_info

SET salary = salary + $5000

WHERE employee_id = 12345

DELETE: Finally, let's take a look at the DELETE command. You'll find that the syntax of this command is similar to that of the other DML commands.

Unfortunately, our latest corporate earnings report didn't quite meet expectations and poor Bart has been laid off. The DELETE command with a WHERE clause can be used to remove his record from the personal_info table:

delete from "tablename"

where columnname OPERATOR value [and|or

columnnamex OPERATOR valuex];

for example

DELETE FROM personal_info

WHERE employee_id = 12345

Exercises

Fill in the Blanks

1. The abbreviation DBMS stand for_______________.

2. A row or record in a database table called_____________.

3. The command to insert a record______________.
4. A DBMS is an interface between ______ and ______ requests.
5. One of the responsibilities of a ______ is to create database schema.
6. Primary key is ______ level constraint.

Answers

1. Database Management System. 2. Tuple
3. INSERT INTO
4. Physical database, user 5. DBA
6. Column

Questions

1. What is a database?
2. What is a key? what are different keys in database?
3. What is a primary key?
4. What is an attribute?
5. What is a join operation?
6. What is data definition language?
7. What are the features of SQL?
8. Write Role of DBA.
9. Describe Architecture of Database system.
10. Explain data dictionary.

Concepts of Networking with Internet and Network Security, E-Commerce

Objectives

At the end of this session, the learner will be able to:

Define Computer Networking and goals.

Explain ISO-OSI Model with function of different layers

Identify Internetworking concepts and devices.

Explain TCP/IP Model

Discuss Internet, WWW

Describe Network Security

Discuss E-commerce.

Introduction

A computer network is a network consisting of computers and communication devices like cables, modems etc through which users can communicate and share resources with each other.

So, computer network is a system in which users can share resources and information. This connection can be made through client/server or peer-to-peer method. these methods can be used to setup a network for home or business purpose. In the 1960s, the first operational computer network in the world the Advanced Research Projects Agency (ARPA) started funding the design of the Advanced Research Projects Agency Network (ARPANET) for the United States Department for defense. Thus the first computer network based on the design of ARPANET was launched in 1969.

A computer network can be a connection between two computers:

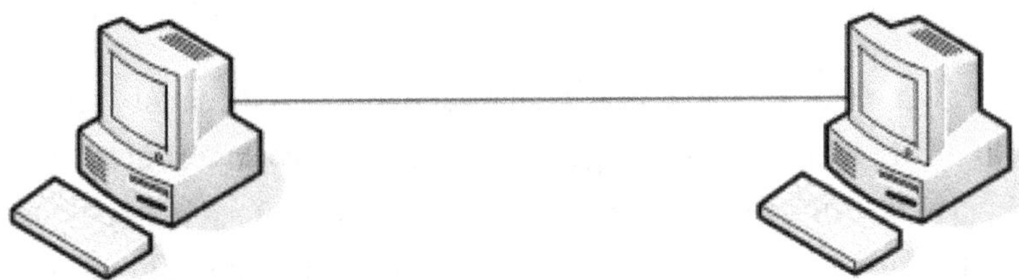

A computer network can also be a connection of more than two computers:

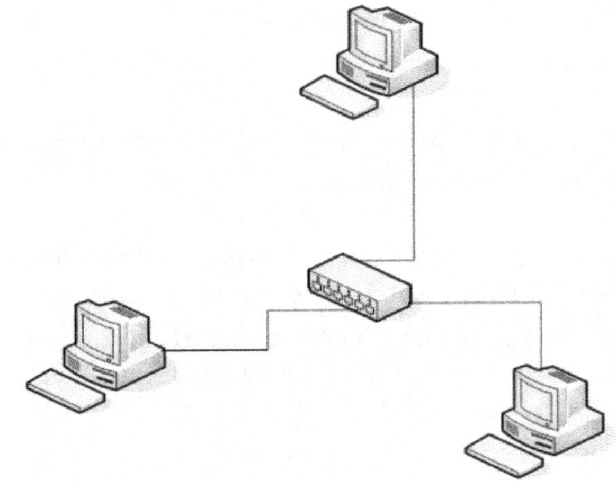

Purpose

Computer network has set several goals which help us to use this network.

Sharing hardware: Through this we can be able to share printers, modems, fax machines, scanners etc. by getting connected to the computer having attached this hardware components.

Sharing software: Users connected to a network may run application programms on remote computers like MS OFFICE

Sharing files, data, and information: Users can share files, data and important information from remote sites and worldwide which helps in saving time and money. user authentication can be easily done by securing the data and information by passwords .

Communication facilities: because of this facility user can communicate with each other via emails, chat rooms video conferencing etc. thus increasing the productivity.

Goals

Some of the basic goals that a computer network should satisfy are:

- Cost reduction by sharing hardware and software resources.
- Provide high reliability by having multiple sources of supply.
- Provide an efficient means of transport for large volumes of data among various locations (High throughput).
- Provide inter-process communication among users and processors.
- Reduction in delay driving data transport.
- Increase productivity by making it easier to share data among users.
- Repairs, upgrades, expansions, and changes to the network should be performed with minimal impact on the majority of network users.
- Standards and protocols should be supported to allow many types of equipment from vendors to share network (Interoperatability)
- Provide centralized/distributed management and allocation of network resources like host processors, transmission facilities etc.

ISO-OSI model

The International Organisation for Standardisation prepared a model of Open System Interconnection called as OSI model which divided the communication system into smaller divisions called layers. The layers in this system are so associated with each other that the layer between the two, provides services to the above layer and acquires services from the bottom one.

The International Organization for standardization started its work in 1978 and prepared an OSI model of network architecture which is now considered a primary model for inter-computer communications. An OSI is a reference model that has two major components: an abstract model of networking, called the Basic Reference Model or seven-layer model, and a set of specific protocols. The OSI model is a set of protocols that attempt to define and standardize the data communication process , we can say that it is a concept that describes how data communication should take place .

Although each layer of the OSI model provides its own set of functions, it is possible to group the layers into two distinct categories . The first four layers i.e. physical, data link, network and transport layer provides end-to end services needed for transfer of data between two systems. These layers provide protocols associated with communication.

The top three layers i.e. the application, presentation, and session layers provide the application services required for the exchange of information. That is they allow two application, each running on a different node of the network to interact with each other. Together they are data processing oriented.

OSI model

7. Application Layer

NNTP · SIP · SSI · DNS · FTP · Gopher · HTTP · NFS · NTP · SMPP · SMTP · DHCP · SNMP · Telnet · (more)

6. Presentation Layer

MIME · XDR · TLS · SSL

5. Session Layer

Named Pipes · NetBIOS · SAP · SIP · L2TP · PPTP

4. Transport Layer

TCP · UDP · SCTP · DCCP

3. Network Layer

IP · ICMP · IPsec · IGMP · IPX · AppleTalk

2. Data Link Layer

ARP · CSLIP · SLIP · Ethernet · Frame relay ·
ITU-T G.hn DLL · PPP

1. Physical Layer

RS-232 · RS-449 · V.35 · V.34 · I.430 · I.431 ·
T1 · E1 · POTS · SONET/SDH · OTN · DSL ·
802.11a/b/g/n PHY · 802.15.x PHY · ITU-T G.hn
PHY · Ethernet · USB · Bluetooth

OSI Model			
	Data unit	**Layer**	**Function**
Host layers	Data	7. Application	Network process to application
		6. Presentation	Data representation,encryption and decryption
		5. Session	Inter host communication
	Segments	4. Transport	End-to-end connections and reliability,Flow control
Media layers	Packet	3. Network	Path determination and logical addressing
	Frame	2. Data Link	Physical addressing
	Bit	1. Physical	Media, signal and binary transmission

1. **Application layer (layer 7):** This is the top layer of OSI model which defines the language and syntax that programs uses to communicate with other programs. Some examples of application layer implementations include Telnet, File Transfer Protocol (FTP), and Simple Mail Transfer Protocol (SMTP). One misunderstanding fact about this layer is that it probably itself does not provide the services but they are given by the protocol suite that it provides. For example, a program in a client workstation uses commands to request data from a program in a server. Common functions at this layer are, opening, closing,reading and writing files, transferring files and e-mail messages, executing

remote jobs and obtaining directory information about network resources etc.

2 **Presentation layer (layer 6):** The presentation layer performs code conversion and data reformatting (syntax translation). It is the translator of the network; it makes sure that the data is in correct form for the receiving application.

When data are transmitted between different types of computer system, the presentation layer negotiates and manages the way data are represented and encoded. For example, it provides a common denominator between ASCII and EBCDIC machines as well as different floating point and binary formats. Sun's XDR and OSI's ASN.1 are two protocols used for this purpose. This layer is also used to provide security features through encryption and decryption.

This layer is not associated with any one type of protocol stack. But uses some of the well-known standards for video including QuickTime and Motion Picture Experts Group (MPEG). QuickTime is an Apple Computer specification for video and audio, and MPEG is a standard for video compression and coding.

3. **Session layer (layer 5):** The session layer decides when to turn communication on and off between two computers. It provides the mechanism that controls the data exchange process and co-ordinates the communication between them. In short it manages and terminates communication session. Some examples of session layer protocols are AppleTalk's Zone Information Protocol (ZIP), and Decent Phase Session Control Protocol (SCP).

The session layer sets up and clears communication channels between two communicating computers. It determines one-way or two-way communication and manages dialogue between both parties. It makes sure that before sending the next request the previous one is fulfilled or not. It also marks the relevant parts of the data so that it can be recovered easily in case of connection failure. The session layer uses remote procedure call which may be either built in TCP or UDP. In this log in session uses TCP while during broadcasting UDP is used.

4. **Transport layer (layer 4):** The transport layer is responsible for overall end-to-end validity and integrity of the transmission i.e., it ensures that data is successfully sent and received between two computers. The data are broken down into manageable data packets and the information like the sequence no., address of

another host where the packet has to be reached, port no. etc. are added to it so that they can reach the destination safely. If a packet gets lost in the router somewhere in the enterprise internet, the transport layer will detect that. It ensures if a16MB file is sent then it should be received fully.

If the data is sent incorrectly then then this layer has the responsibility to ask for re-transmission of data. Specifically it provides a network- independent, reliable message-independent, reliable message- interchange to the top three application-oriented layers of the model. This layer acts as an interface between the top three and the bottom three layers of the model. Thus it provides session layer with the reliable message transfer service , and hides the process underlying it.

Important Features of Transport layer

- Breaks the message (from sessions layer) into smaller data packets, and appends appropriate header information.
- Responsible for communicating with the Session layer.

Important Features of TCP/UDP

- *TCP*: (Transport Control Protocol) TCP ensures that a packet has reached its intended destination by using an acknowledgment. If not, it re-transmits the lost messages. Hence, TCP is called a connection oriented protocol.
- *UDP (Universal Data gram Protocol)*: UDP simply transmits packets over the internet. It does not wait for an acknowledgment. It is the responsibility of upper layer protocols to ensure that the information had reached the intended partner(s). Hence, UDP is often called connection less protocol.
- TCP/IP widely used protocol for Transport/Network layers.
- Application programs that do not need connection-oriented protocol generally use UDP.

5. **Network layer (layer 3):** The network layer establishes the route between the sending and the receiving stations. The unit of data at the network layer is called a packet. It provides network routing flow and congestion function across computer networks interfaces. The physical address may change during hoping from one network to the other so, to maintain continuity logical are being used for transporting the packets. For IP networks, IP address is the logical address; and for Novell network, IPX address is the logical address, and so on.

The job of the network layer is to break the large sized data packets into smaller ones to they can reach the destination easily where they can be reassembled again to form original data packet. IP addresses are written as four dot-separated decimal numbers between 0 and 255, e.g., 129.79.16.40. The leading 1-3 bytes of the IP identify the network and the remaining bytes identifies the host on that network. The network layer is responsible for translating logical addresses into physical addresses. The main device found at the network layer is a router.

6. **Data link layer (layer 2):** The data link layer groups the bits present on the physical layer into frames. It is primarily responsible for error free delivery of data on a hop. The data link layer is split into two sub layers i.e., the logical link control(LLC) which Defines how data is transferred over the cable and provides data link service to the higher layers. And the other is media access control (MAC) which Controls media access by regulating the communicating nodes using pre-defined set of rules. (i.e. Token passing, Ethernet [CSMA/CD] all have MAC sub-layer protocol).

The data link layer handles the physical transfer, framing (the assembly of data in a single unit or block), flow control and error control functions (and retransmission in the event of an error) over a single transmission link; it is responsible for getting the data packaged and onto the network cable. The data link layer provides the network layer (layer 3) reliable information- transfer capabilities.

The main network device found at the data link layer is the bridge. This device works at the higher than the repeater and therefore is a more complex device. It has some understanding of the data it receives as to whether it needs to let the information pass, or can remove the information from the network. This means the amount of traffic on the medium can be reduced and therefore, the usable bandwidth can be increased.

7. **Physical layer (layer1):** The data unit on this layer are called bits. This layer defines the mechanical and electrical definition of the network medium (cable) and network hardware. This includes how data is impressed onto the cable and retrieved from it.

The physical layer is responsible for passing bits onto and receiving them from the connecting medium. This layer gives the data link layer its ability to transport a stream of serial data bits between two communicating systems; it conveys the bits that move along the cable.

The main network device found at physical layer is a repeater. The purpose of a repeater is simply to receive the digital signals, reform it, and re-transmit the signals. This has the effect of increasing the maximum length of a network, which would not be possible due to signal deterioration repeater, simply regenerates cleaner signal so it doesn't have to understand anything about the information it is transmitting and processing on to the repeater is non-existent.

An example of physical layer is rs-232.

Each layer with the exception of physical layer, adds information to the data as it moves from application layer down to physical layer. The extra information is called header. The physical layer does not append a header to information because it is only concerned with sending and receiving of information.

OSI model reference table layer	Functions	Protocols	Network components
Application User Interface	• Used for applications specifically written to run over the network • Allows access to network services that support applications; • Directly represents the services that directly support user applications • Handles network access, flow control and error recovery • Example apps are file transfer, e-mail, NetBIOS-based applications	DNS; FTP; TFTP; BOOTP; SNMP;RLOGIN; SMTP; MIME; NFS; FINGER; TELNET; NCP; APPC; AFP; SMB	**Gateway**
Presentation **Translation**	• Translates from application to network format and vice-versa • All different formats from all sources are made into a common uniform format that the rest of the OSI model can understand • Responsible for protocol conversion, character conversion, data encryption / decryption, expanding graphics commands, data compression		**Gateway Redirector**

Table contd...

	• Sets standards for different systems to provide seamless communication from multiple protocol stacks • Not always implemented in a network protocol		
Session **Syncs and** **Sessions**	• Establishes, maintains and ends sessions across the network • Responsible for name recognition (identification) so only the designated parties can participate in the session • Provides synchronization services by planning check points in the data stream => if session fails, only data after the most recent checkpoint need be transmitted • Manages who can transmit data at a certain time and for how long • Examples are interactive login and file transfer connections, the session would connect and re-connect if there was an interruption; recognize names in sessions and register names in history	NetBIOS Names Pipes Mail Slots RPC	**Gateway**
Transport **Packets;** **Flow control** **& Error-** **handling**	• Additional connection below the session layer • Manages the flow control of data between parties across the network • Divides streams of data into chunks or packets; the transport layer of the receiving computer reassembles the message from packets • A train is a good analogy => the data is divided into identical units • Provides error-checking to guarantee error-free data delivery, with on losses or duplication	TCP, ARP, RARP; SPX NWLink NetBIOS NetBEUI ATP	**Gateway** **Advanced** **Cable Tester** **Brouter**

Table contd…

	• Provides acknowledgment of successful transmissions; requests re transmission if some packets don't arrive error-free • Provides flow control and error-handling		
Network Addressing; Routing	• Translates logical network address and names to their physical address (e.g. computer name ==> MAC address) • Responsible for • addressing • determining routes for sending • managing network problems such as packet switching, data congestion and routing • If router can't send data frame as large as the source computer sends, the network layer compensates by breaking the data into smaller units. At the receiving end, the network layer reassembles the data • Think of this layer stamping the addresses on each train car	IP; ARP; RARP, ICMP; RIP; OSFP; IGMP; IPX NWLink NetBEUI OSI DDP DECnet	**Brouter** **Router** **Frame Relay Device** **ATM Switch** **Advanced Cable Tester**
Data Link **Data frames to bits**	• Turns packets into raw bits 100101 and at the receiving end turns bits into packets. • Handles data frames between the Network and Physical layers • The receiving end packages raw data from the Physical layer into data frames for delivery to the Network layer • Responsible for error-free transfer of frames to other computer via the Physical Layer • This layer defines the methods used to transmit and receive data	Logical Link Control error correction and flow control manages link control and defines SAPs 802.1 OSI Model 802.2 Logical Link Control Media Access Control communicates	**Bridge** **Switch** **ISDN Router** **Intelligent Hub** **NIC** **Advanced Cable Tester**

Table contd...

	on the network. It consists of the wiring, the devices use to connect the NIC to the wiring, the signaling involved to transmit / receive data and the ability to detect signaling errors on the network media	with the adapter card controls the type of media being used: 802.3 CSMA/CD (Ethernet) 802.4 Token Bus (ARCnet) 802.5 Token Ring 802.12 Demand Priority	
Physical Hardware; Raw bit stream	• Transmits raw bit stream over physical cable • Defines cables, cards, and physical aspects • Defines NIC attachments to hardware, how cable is attached to NIC • Defines techniques to transfer bit stream to cable	IEEE 802 IEEE 802.2 ISO 2110 ISDN	**Repeater** **Multiplexer** **Hubs** **Passive** **Active** **TDR** **Oscilloscope** **Amplifier**

TCP/IP model

TCP/IP stands for Transmission Control Protocol / Internet Protocol. It is a protocol suite used by most communication software. TCP/IP is a robust and proven technology that was first tested in the early 1980's on ARPANET, the U.S. Military's Advanced Research Project Agency network, and the worlds first packet-switched network. TCP/IP was designed as an open protocol that would enable all types of computers to transmit data to each other via a common communication language.

TCP/IP is a layered protocol similar to the ones used in all major networking architectures, including IBM's SNA, Windows NETBIOS, Apple's AppleTalk, Novell's NetWare and Digital's DECnet. Layering means that after an application initiates the communications, the message(data) to be transmitted is passed through the no. of stages or layers until it actually moves out onto the wire. The data are packaged with the different header at each layer. At the receiving end the corresponding programs unpack the data, moving it "back up the stack" to the receiving application.

TCP/IP is composed of two major parts i.e. TCP(Transmission Control Protocol) at the transport layer and IP(Internet Protocol) at the network layer. TCP is a connection oriented protocol that passes its data to IP, which is a connectionless one. TCP sets up a connection at both ends and guarantees reliable delivery of the full message sent. TCP tests for error detection and request tranmission if necessary, because IP does not.

An alternative protocol to TCP within the TCP/IP suite is UDP(User Datagram Protocol),which does not guarantee delivery. Like IP, it is also connectionless, but very useful for real-time voice and video, where it doesn't matter if a packet is lost.

Internet Protocol Suite
Application Layer
BGP · DHCP · DNS · FTP · HTTP · IMAP · IRC · LDAP · MGCP · NNTP · NTP · POP · RIP · RPC · RTP · SIP · SMTP · SNMP · SSH · Telnet · TLS/SSL · XMPP ·   (more)
Transport Layer
TCP · UDP · DCCP · SCTP · RSVP · ECN ·   (more)
Internet Layer
IP (IPv4, IPv6) · ICMP · ICMPv6 · IGMP · IPsec ·   (more)
Link Layer
ARP/InARP · NDP · OSPF · Tunnels (L2TP) · PPP · Media Access Control (Ethernet, DSL, ISDN, FDDI) · (more)
This box: view · talk · edit

7	Application
6	Presentation
5	Session

Application

4	Transport

(Host-to-Host) Transport

3	Network

Internet

2	Data Link

Network Interface

1	Physical

(Hardware)

OSI Model   **TCP/IP Model**

The TCP/IP model instead of consisting of seven layers consist of only four layers:

1. **Application Layer (layer 4):** The top layer of the protocol stack is the application layer. It refers to the programs that initiate communication in the first place. TCP/IP includes several application layer protocols for mail, file transfer, remote access, authentication and name resolution. These protocols are embodied in programs that operate at the top layer just as the custom-made or packaged client server application would. There are many Application Layer protocols and new protocols are always being developed.

The most widely used application layer protocol are those used for the exchange of user information, some of them are:

- ***The HyperText Transfer Protocol(HTTP):*** It is used to transfer files that make up the web pages of the World Wide Web.

- ***The File Transfer Protocol(FTP):*** It is used for interactive file transfer.

- ***The Simple Mail Transfer Protocol (SMTP):*** It is used for transfer 0f mail messages and attachments.

- ***Telnet:*** It is a terminal emulation protocol, and is used for remote login to network hosts.

Other Application Layer protocols that help in the management of TCP/IP networks are:

- *The Domain Name System(DNS)*, which is used to resolve a host name to an IP address.

- *The Simple Network Management protocol (SNMP)*, *which* is used between network management consoles and network devices (routers, bridges and intelligent hubs) to collect and exchange network management information.

  Examples of Application Layer Interfaces for TCP/IP applications are Windows Sockets and NetBIOS.

  Windows Sockets provides a standard application programming interface (API) under the Microsoft Windows operating system. NetBIOS is an industry standard interface for accessing protocol services such as sessions, datagrams, and name resolution.

2. **Transport Layer (layer 3):** The Transport Layer (also known as host-to-host Transport Layer) is responsible for providing the Application Layer with session and datagram communication services.

   TCP/IP does not contain Presentation and Session layers, the services are performed if required, but they are not part of the formal TCP/IP stack. For example, Layer 6 (Presentation Layer) is where data conversion (ASCII to EBCDIC, floating point to binary, etc.)and encryption /decryption is performed. Layer 5 is the Session Layer, which is performed in layer 4 in TCP/IP. Thus we jump from layer 7 of OSI to layer 4 of TCP/IP.

   From Application of Transport Layer, the application delivers its data to the communication system by passing the data stream of data bytes to the transport layer along with the socket of the destination machine.

   The core protocols of the Transport Layer are TCP and UDP

   TCP: TCP provides a one-to-one, connection oriented, reliable communication service. TCP is responsible for the establishment of a TCP connection, the sequencing and acknowledgment of packet sent, and the recovery of packets lost during transmission.

UDP: UDP provides a one-to-one or one-to-many, connectionless, unreliable communications service. UDP is used when the amount of data to be transferred is small (such that the data would fit into a single packet), when the overhead of establishing a TCP connection is not desired, or when the applications or upper layer protocols provide reliable delivery.

The Transport Layer encompasses the responsibilities of the OSI Transport Layer and some of the responsibilities of the OSI Session Layer.

3. **Network Layer/Internet layer (layer 2):** The Internet layer handles the transfer of information across multiple networks through the use of gateway and routers. The Internet layer corresponds to the part of OSI Network Layer that is concerned with the transfer of packets between machines that are connected to different networks. It deals with the routing of packets across these networks as well as with the control of congestion. A key aspect of the Internet layer is the definition of globally unique addresses for machines that are attached to the internet.

The Internet layer provides a single service namely, best-effort connectionless packet transfer. IP packets are exchanged between routers without a connection setup; the packets are routed independently and so they may traverse different paths. For this reason IP packets are also called datagrams. The connectionless approach makes the system robust; that is, if failures occur in the network, the packets are routed across the point of failure; hence there is no need to setup connections. The gateway that interconnect the intermediate networks may discard packets when congestion occurs. The responsibility for recovery from these losses is passed onto transport layer.

The core protocols of the Internet Layer are IP, ARP, ICMP, and IGMP.

- **The Internet Protocol (IP)** is a routable protocol responsible for IP addressing and the fragmentation and reassembly of packets.
- **The Address Resolution Protocol (ARP)** is responsible for the resolution of Internet Layer address to the Network Interface Layer address, such as a hardware address.

- **The Internet Control Message Protocol (ICMP)** is responsible for providing diagnostic functions and reporting errors of conditions regarding the delivery of IP packets.
- **The Internet Group Management Protocol (IGMP)** is responsible for the management of IP multicast groups. The Internet Layer is analogous to the Network Layer of the OSI model.

4. **Link/Physical Layer (layer 1):** The Link/ Physical Layer (also called the Network Access Layer) is responsible for placing TCP/IP packets on the network medium and receiving TCP/IP packets of the network medium. TCP/IP was designed to be independent of the network access method, frame format and medium. In this way TCP/IP can be used to connect different network types. This includes LAN technologies such that Ethernet or Token Ring and WAN technologies such as X.25 or Frame Relay. Independence from any specific network technology gives TCP/IP the ability to be adapted to new technologies such that Asynchronous Transfer Mode (ATM).

The Network Interface Layer encompasses the Data Link and Physical layers of the OSI Model. Note, that the Internet Layer does not take the advantage of sequencing and acknowledgment services that may be present in the Data Link Layer. An unreliable Network Interface Layer is assumed, and reliable communications through session establishment and sequencing and acknowledgment of packets is the responsibility of the Transport Layer.

Introduction to Internet

The Internet is a global system of interconnected computer networks that use the standard Internet Protocol Suite (TCP/IP) to serve billions of users worldwide.

The Internet is a global network of networks.

- People and organizations connect into the Internet so they can access its massive store of shared information.
- The Internet is an inherently participatory medium. Anybody can publish information or create new services.
- The Internet is a cooperative endeavor -- no organization is *in charge* of the net.

The Internet employs a set of standardized protocols which allow for the sharing of resources among different kinds of computers that communicate with each other on the network. These standards, sometimes referred to as the Internet Protocol Suite, are the rules that developers adhere to when creating new functions for the Internet. The Internet thrives and develops as its many users find new ways to create, display and retrieve the information that constitutes the Internet.

History and Development of Internet: When ARPANET and NSFNET were interconnected the number of networks, machines and users grew exponentially, many regional network joined up and connections were made across many countries.

The internet is said to have been officially born around 1982 when the different networks (BITNET, EARN, etc.) agreed on using the TCP/IP protocol as a standard for their interconnections making it a network of networks and overcoming some of the previous cacophony of standards, protocols increasing its coverage.

The word Internet was coined from the words "interconnection" and "network". Now Internet is the world's largest computer network. It is considered to be networks of the networks, and is scattered all over the world. The computers connected to the internet may communicate with each other through fiber optic cables, telephone lines, satellite links and other media.

The development of internet is coordinated by a non-profit organization called the Internet Society (ISOC). The Internet Architecture Board (IAB), plans long term trends and keeps the record of the RFC(Request for Comments) documents on various technical solutions and protocols used in internet. The development is also steered by the IETF (Internet Engineering Task Force), which has several sub-groups for handling various problems and planning new standards etc..

The rapid growth of internet may also be due to several important factors:

- Easy-to-use software – graphical browsers
- Improved telecommunications connections
- Rapid spread of automatic data processing, including electronic mail, bank transfers, etc.

The major information services provided by the Internet are (with the protocol within parenthesis): electronic mail(SMTP), remote file copy(FTP), remote login terminal connections(TELNET),menu-based file access(GOPHER), wide area information servers(WAIS, Z39.50), the world wide web (HTTP), and the packet internet groper(PING).

How Can We Connect to the Internet?

Computer

- Connection - Phone Line, Cable, DSL, Wireless,
- Modem
- Network Software - TCP/IP
- Application Software - Web Browser, Email, ...
- Internet Service Provider (ISP)

What Can We Do on the Internet?

- Send and receive *email* messages.
- Download free software with FTP (File Transfer Protocol).
- Post your opinion to a Usenet newsgroup.
- Yack it up on IRC (Internet Relay Chat).
- Surf the *World Wide Web*.
- and much, much more.
- There is *no charge* for most services.

World Wide Web: It is an example of an Information Protocol/Service that can be used to send and receive information over the Internet. WWW is an internet navigation tool that helps you to find and retrieve information links to other WWW pages. The WWW is a distributed hypermedia environment consisting of documents from around the world. The documents are linked using a system known as hypertext, where elements of one document may be linked to the specific elements of another document. The documents may be located on any computer connected to Internet. The word document is not limited to text but may include video, graphics, database and a host of other tools.

A British engineer and computer scientist Sir Tim Berners-Lee, now the Director of the World Wide Web Consortium, wrote a proposal in March 1989 for what would eventually become the World Wide Web. At in CERN, Switzerland, Berners-Lee and Belgian computer scientist Robert Cailliau proposed in 1990 to use "Hyper Text [...] to link and access information of various kinds as a web of nodes in which the user can browse at will",and publicly introduced the project in December.

"The World-Wide Web (W3) was developed to be a pool of human knowledge, and human culture, which would allow collaborators in remote sites to share their ideas and all aspects of a common project".

The World Wide Web is described as a "wide area hypermedia information initiative among to give universal access to large volume of documents". World Wide Web provides users on computer networks with a consistent means to access a variety of media in a simplified fashion. A popular software program to search the Web is called Mosaic, the Web project has modified the way people view and create information. It has created the first global hypermedia network.

The World Wide Web model follows client/server software design. A service that uses client/server design requires two pieces of software to work: Client Software, which you use to request information, and Server Software, which is an Information Provider.

It supports

- Multimedia Information (text, movies, pictures, sounds, programs.......).
- Hypertext Information (information that contains links to other information resources).
- Graphic User Interface (so, users can point and click to request information instead of typing in text commands).

The server software for World Wide Web is called an HTTP sever(or informally a Web server). Examples are Mac HTTP, CERN HTTP, and NCSA HTTP. The client software for World Wide Web is called a Web browser. Examples are, Netscape Navigator and Internet Explorer.

Network Security

Network security or Computer security is the process of preventing and detecting unauthorized use of your computer. Prevention measures help you to stop unauthorized users (also known as "intruders") from accessing any part of your computer system.

It can be defined as technological and managerial procedures applied to computer and network systems to ensure the availability, integrity, and confidentiality of the information managed by the computer. It implies the protection of Integrity, Availability and Confidentiality of the Computer Assets and services from associated Threats and Vulnerabilities. Protection of networks and their services from unauthorized modification, destruction, disclosure and the provision of assurance that the network will perform its critical functions correctly and that there will be any harmful side effects. The major point of weakness in a computer system are hardware, software and data. However other components may also be targeted.

Hacking is a serious problem and a consistent one for which no permanent solution has been derived. Computer hacking is also referred to as "intrusion" which may be defined as an attempt to break into or misuse a computer system. It may be done by sending prank messages from the users e-mail system. Hackers can exploit software bugs, system configuration bugs, Internet browsers and operating systems, password access, insecure modems, cookies, denial of service, attacks on Internet Domain Name System, Attacks against routers, viruses and trojans.

To overcome this type of vulnerabilities, an authentication of electronic record by a subscriber by means of Digital Signature was used. In this a private key is used to create a digital signature whereas a public key is used to verify it. They both are unique for each subscriber and together form a functioning key pair.

Once authenticated, a firewall enforces access policies such as what services are allowed to be accessed by the network users. Though effective to prevent unauthorized access, this component may fail to check potentially harmful content such as computer worms or Trojans being transmitted over the network. Anti-virus software or an intrusion prevention system (IPS) help detect and inhibit the action of such malware. An anomaly-based intrusion detection system may also monitor the network and traffic for unexpected (i.e. suspicious) content or behavior and other anomalies to protect resources, e.g. from denial of service attacks or an employee accessing files at strange times. Individual events occurring on the network may be logged for audit purposes and for later high level analysis.

To overcome this type of vulnerabilities we can take some preventive measures as:

- Regular security audits are a must for all organizations.
- The audits can be both internal and external.
- Based on the audits adequate measures and system have to be adopted by organization. This is mainly done through adopting a security policies.
- Security policies has certain standards to protect the confidentiality and integrity. This includes:
- Physical security

- Personnel security
- Access controls
- Security technology
- Security response and recovery.

E-commerce

The buying and selling of products and services by businesses and consumers through an electronic medium, without using any paper documents. E-commerce is widely considered as buying and selling of products on Internet but, any transaction that is completed solely through electronic measures is termed as e-commerce.

E-commerce has many advantages for E-consumers. By using internet facility prior to buying one can know the range, quality and price of the object desired to purchase. Online world allows things like customer aggregation and auction to be done in ways that are impossible in the physical world. Price and product comparison have been made easier by development of "shopping bots". Websites like, Mysimon.com and Dealpilot.com enable buyers quickly to compare products, prices and availability.

E-commerce Evolution: In the early 1960's, computers were increasingly used to disseminate information across geographical space. Through telegraphs, telephones, telex etc. were still the relied upon options nevertheless the big corporations opted for Electronic Data Interchange(EDI). It refers to the process by which goods are ordered, shipped, and tracked computer to computer using standardised protocol. EDI permits the " electronic settlement and reconciliation of the flow of goods and services between companies and consumers". EDI saves money because the computer, and not an office staf, submits and processes orders, claims, and other routine tasks.

In late 1970's, the American National Standard Institute(ANSI) authorized a committee called the Accredited Standards Committee(ASC) X-12 to develop a standard between trading partners. The standard was called ANSI X-12.

Under the aegis of United Nations, organisations from different sectors collaborated and developed an internationally approved standard structure for transmitting information between different trading partners, called the United Nations Electronic Data Interchange for Administration, Commerce and Transport(UN/EDIFACT) in 1986.

In 1990, Tim Berners-Lee invented the World Wide Web browser transformed an academic telecommunication network into a worldwide every man everyday communication system called internet/WWW. Commercial enterprise on the Internet was strictly prohibited until 1991.[1] Although the Internet became popular worldwide around 1994 when the first internet online shopping started, it took about five years to introduce security protocols and DSL allowing continual connection to the Internet. By the end of 2000, many European and American business companies offered their services through the World Wide Web. Since then people began to associate a word "e-commerce" with the ability of purchasing various goods through the Internet using secure protocols and electronic payment services.

Types of E-commerce model: E-commerce is subdivided into three categories: business to business or B2B (Cisco), business to consumer or B2C (Amazon), consumer to business or C2B and consumer to consumer or C2C (eBay). also called electronic commerce.

	Business	**Consumer**
Business	B2B www.vendome.niit.com	B2C www.indiatimes.com
Consumer	C2B www.makemytrip.com	C2C www.ebay.in

E-commerce Model Matrix

These models represent "online" commercial transactions and are comparable to their "offline" counterparts. In other words all these online models have adopted the functionalities of "brick and mortar" companies and are being identified as "click and mortar" companies. Clicks have replaced the bricks for faster, efficient and effective commercial transactions. For ex. One can purchase a Dell computers or a server by visiting the site: www.dell.co.in and clicking on the desired computer and server configuration.

Exercises

Fill in the Blanks

1. Software programs which provide access to files on the WWW called__________.

2. Commerce which is based on transactions using computers connected by telecommunication network ________________ -

3. By encryption of a text we mean________________.

4. An authentication of an electronic record by tying it uniquely to a key only a sender knows _________.

5. _________ is an electronic device that separates or isolates a network segment from the main network while maintaining the connection between networks.

6. A network architecture in which each workstation (or PC) within the network has equivalent responsibilities and capabilities is normally known as______.

Answers

1.Browser 2.Electronic Commerce 3. scrambling it to preserve its security 4. A digital signature 5.Firewall 6. a peer-to-peer network.

Questions

1. What Is TCP/IP Model? How Is It Different From ISO-OSI Model?
2. Define the terms network and Internet.
3. With the help of diagram explain ISO-OSI model.
4. Explain Hyperlink.
5. Explain Firewall.
6. Describe Network Security
7. Explain Computer Networking.
8. Describe Types of E-commerce.
9. List networking devices.
10. What is the role of modem in Internet?

List of Experiments

1. Study and Practice of Internal External DOS commands

In MS-DOS there are two types of commands. An Internal command, which is a command embedded into the command.com file, and an external command, which is not embedded into command.com and therefore requires a separate file to be used.

A command that is stored in the system memory and loaded from the command.com. Below are examples of internal commands in MS-DOS currently listed in the Computer Hope database.

Assoc	For	Rd	Unlock
Atmadm	Goto	Ren	Ver
Break	If	Rename	Verify
Call	LH	Rmdir	Vol
CD	Loadhigh	Set	
Chdir	Lock	Setlocal	
Cls	Md	Shift	
Color	Mkdir	Start	
Copy	Move	Switches	
Ctty	Path	Time	
Date	Pause	Title	
Del	Popd	Type	
Dir	Prompt		
Drivparm	Pushd		
Echo			
Endlocal			
Erase			
Exit			

DIR

This command gives a listing of most of the files and directories on a disk (Hard disk and floppy disk). In DOS 3.3 and below, there are only 2 known switches:

/W - gives the directory listing wide across your screen without times, dates, and sizes listed

/P   -   pauses the output of the DIR command if there are more files
than can be listed on your screen at once

C:/DIR,

TYPE

This command will dump the contents of a text file to your screen.
Example: C: /type bill.txt

A MS-DOS command that is not included in command.com. External
commands are commonly external either because they require large
requirements or are not commonly used commands. Below are examples of
MS-DOS external commands currently listed in the Computer Hope database.

Append	Fasthelp	Pathping	Taskkill
Arp	Fc	Ping	Telnet
Assign	Fdisk	Power	Tracert
At	Find	Print	Tree
Attrib	Format	Reg	Undelete
Backup	FTP	Route	Unformat
Cacls	Gpupdate	Runas	Xcopy
Chcp	Graftabl	Scandisk	
Chkdsk	Help	Scanreg	
Chkntfs	Hostname	Setver	
Choice	Ipconfig	Sfc	
Cipher	Label	Share	
Comp	Loadfix	Shutdown	
Compact	logoff	Smartdrv	
Convert	Mem	Sort	
Debug	Mode	Subst	
Defrag	More	Sys	
Delpart	Msav	Systeminfo	
Deltree	Msbackup		
Diskcomp	Mscdex		
Diskcopy	Mscdexnt		
Doskey	Mwbackup		
Dosshell	Msd		
Dumpchk	Nbtstat		
Edit	Net		
Edlin	Netsh		
Expand	Netstat		
Extract	Nlsfunc		
	Nslookup		

2. **Study and Practice of MS Windows – Folder Related Operations, My-Computer**

Window explorer, Control Panel,

Windows Explorer is a file manager application that is included with releases of the Microsoft Windows operating system from Windows 95 onwards. It provides a graphical user interface for accessing the file systems. It is also the component of the operating system that presents many user interface items on the monitor such as the taskbar and desktop. Controlling the computer is possible without Windows Explorer running (for example, the File | Run command in Task Manager on NT-derived versions of Windows will function without it, as will commands typed in a command prompt window). It is sometimes referred to as the Windows Shell, explorer.exe, or simply "Explorer".

The Control Panel is a part of the Microsoft Windows graphical user interface which allows users to view and manipulate basic system settings and controls via applets, such as adding hardware, adding and removing software, controlling user accounts, and changing accessibility options. Additional applets can be provided by third party software.

The Control Panel has been an inherent part of the Microsoft Windows operating system since its first release (Windows 1.0), with many of the current applets being added in later versions. Beginning with Windows 95, the Control Panel is implemented as a special folder, i.e. the folder does not physically exist, but only contains shortcuts to various applets such as Add or Remove Programs and Internet Options. Physically, these applets are stored as .cpl files. For example, the Add or Remove Programs applet is stored under the name appwiz.cpl in the SYSTEM32 folder.

In recent versions of Windows, the Control Panel has two views, Classic View and Category View, and it is possible to switch between these through an option that appears on the left side of the window.

Many of the individual Control Panel applets can be accessed in other ways. For instance, Display Properties can be accessed by right-clicking on an empty area of the desktop and choosing Properties.

The classic view consists of shortcuts to the various control panel applets, usually without any description (other than the name). The categories are seen if the user use "Details" view.

The category view consists of categories, which when clicked on display the control panel applets related to the category. In Windows Vista, the category displays links to the most commonly used applets below the name of the category.

3. **Study and practice of Basic linux Commands – ls, cp, mv, rm, chmod, kill, ps etc**

mkdir - make directories

Usage

mkdir [OPTION] DIRECTORY

Options

Create the DIRECTORY(ies), if they do not already exist.

 Mandatory arguments to long options are mandatory for short options too.

- m, mode=MODE set permission mode (as in chmod), not rwxrwxrwx - umask

- p, parents no error if existing, make parent directories as needed

- v, verbose print a message for each created directory

- help display this help and exit

- version output version information and exit

cd - change directories

Use cd to change directories. Type cd followed by the name of a directory to access that directory.Keep in mind that you are always in a directory and can navigate to directories hierarchically above or below.

mv- change the name of a directory

Type mv followed by the current name of a directory and the new name of the directory.

 Ex: mv testdir newnamedir

pwd - **print** working directory

will show you the full path to the directory you are currently in. This is very handy to use, especially when performing some of the other commands on this page

rmdir - Remove an existing directory

rm -r

Removes directories and files within the directories recursively.

chown - change file owner and group

Usage

chown [OPTION] OWNER[:[GROUP]] FILE

chown [OPTION] :GROUP FILE

chown [OPTION] --reference=RFILE FILE

Options

Change the owner and/or group of each FILE to OWNER and/or GROUP. With --reference, change the owner and group of each FILE to those of RFILE.

- c, changes like verbose but report only when a change is made
- dereference affect the referent of each symbolic link, rather than the symbolic link itself
- h, no-dereference affect each symbolic link instead of any referenced file (useful only on systems that can   change the ownership of a symlink)
- from=CURRENT_OWNER:CURRENT_GROUP

   change the owner and/or group of each file only if its current owner and/or group match those specified here. Either may be omitted, in which case a match is not required for the omitted attribute.

- no-preserve-root do not treat `/' specially (the default)
- preserve-root fail to operate recursively on `/'
- f, -silent, -quiet suppress most error messages
- reference=RFILE use RFILE's owner and group rather than the specifying OWNER:GROUP values
- R, -recursive operate on files and directories recursively
- v, -verbose output a diagnostic for every file processed

The following options modify how a hierarchy is traversed when the -R option is also specified. If more than one is specified, only the final one takes effect.

- H if a command line argument is a symbolic link to a directory, traverse it

- L traverse every symbolic link to a directory encountered

- P do not traverse any symbolic links (default)

chmod - change file access permissions

Usage

chmod [-r] permissions filenames

r Change the permission on files that are in the subdirectories of the directory that you are currently in permission Specifies the rights that are being granted. Below is the different rights that you can grant in an alpha numeric format filenames File or directory that you are associating the rights with Permissions

u - User who owns the file.

g - Group that owns the file.

o - Other.

a - All.

r - Read the file.

w - Write or edit the file.

x - Execute or run the file as a program.

Numeric Permissions

CHMOD can also to attributed by using Numeric Permissions:

400 read by owner

040 read by group

004 read by anybody (other)

200 write by owner

020 write by group

002 write by anybody

100 execute by owner

010 execute by group

001 execute by anybody

ls - Short listing of directory contents

-a   list hidden files

-d   list the name of the current directory

-F   show directories with a trailing '/'

        executable files with a trailing '*'

-g   show group ownership of file in long listing

-i   print the inode number of each file

-l   long listing giving details about files and directories

-R   list all subdirectories encountered

-t   sort by time modified instead of name

cp - Copy files

cp myfile yourfile

Copy the files "myfile" to the file "yourfile" in the current working directory. This command will create the file "yourfile" if it doesn't exist. It will normally overwrite it without warning if it exists.

cp -i myfile yourfile

With the "-i" option, if the file "yourfile" exists, you will be prompted before it is overwritten.

cp -i /data/myfile

Copy the file "/data/myfile" to the current working directory and name it "myfile". Prompt before overwriting the file.

cp -dpr srcdir destdir

Copy all files from the directory "srcdir" to the directory "destdir" preserving links (-poption), file attributes (-p option), and copy recursively (-r option). With these options, a directory and all it contents can be copied to another dir

ln - Creates a symbolic link to a file.

ln -s test symlink

Creates a symbolic link named symlink that points to the file test Typing "ls -i test symlink" will show the two files are different with different inodes. Typing "ls -l test symlink" will show that symlink points to the file test.

locate - A fast database driven file locator.

slocate -u

This command builds the slocate database. It will take several minutes to complete this command. This command must be used before searching for files, however cron runs this command periodically on most systems.locate whereis Lists all files whose names contain the string "whereis". directory.

more - Allows file contents or piped output to be sent to the screen one page at a time

less - Opposite of the more command

cat - Sends file contents to standard output. This is a way to list the contents of short files to the screen. It works well with piping.

whereis - Report all known instances of a command

wc - Print byte, word, and line counts

bg

bg jobs Places the current job (or, by using the alternative form, the specified jobs) in the background, suspending its execution so that a new user prompt appears immediately. Use the jobs command to discover the identities of background jobs.

cal month year - Prints a calendar for the specified month of the specified year.

cat files - Prints the contents of the specified files.

clear - Clears the terminal screen.

cmp file1 file2 - Compares two files, reporting all discrepancies. Similar to the diff command, though the output format differs.

diff file1 file2 - Compares two files, reporting all discrepancies. Similar to the cmp command, though the output format differs.

dmesg - Prints the messages resulting from the most recent system boot.

fg

fg jobs - Brings the current job (or the specified jobs) to the foreground.

file files - Determines and prints a description of the type of each specified file.

find path -name pattern -print

Searches the specified path for files with names matching the specified pattern (usually enclosed in single quotes) and prints their names. The find command has many other arguments and functions; see the online documentation.

finger users - Prints descriptions of the specified users.

free - Displays the amount of used and free system memory.

ftp hostname

Opens an FTP connection to the specified host, allowing files to be transferred. The FTP program provides subcommands for accomplishing file transfers; see the online documentation.

head files - Prints the first several lines of each specified file.

ispell files - Checks the spelling of the contents of the specified files.

kill process_ids

kill - signal process_ids

kill -1

Kills the specified processes, sends the specified processes the specified signal (given as a number or name), or prints a list of available signals.

killall program

killall - signal program

Kills all processes that are instances of the specified program or sends the specified signal to all processes that are instances of the specified program.

mail - Launches a simple <u>mail client</u> that permits sending and receiving email messages.

man title

man section title - Prints the specified man page.

ping host - Sends an echo request via TCP/IP to the specified host. A response confirms that the host is operational.

reboot - Reboots the <u>system</u> (requires root privileges).

shutdown minutes

shutdown -r minutes

Shuts down the system after the specified number of minutes elapses (requires root privileges). The -r option causes the system to be rebooted once it has shut down.

sleep time - Causes the command interpreter to pause for the specified number of seconds.

sort files - Sorts the specified files. The command has many useful arguments; see the online documentation.

split file - Splits a file into several smaller files. The command has many arguments; see the online documentation

sync - Completes all pending input/output operations (requires root privileges).

telnet host - Opens a login session on the specified host.

top - Prints a display of system processes that's continually updated until the user presses the q key.

traceroute host - Uses echo requests to determine and print a network path to the host.

uptime - Prints the system uptime.

w - Prints the current system users.

wall - Prints a message to each user except those who've disabled message reception. Type Ctrl-D to end the message.

4. Creation and editing of Text files using MS- word.

How to use MSWORD

Switch on your computer and wait until a whole lot of picture symbols appear with a Start button on the bottom left of the screen. Use the left button on the mouse to click on the Start button. Then click on programmes and then double-click on the MSWORD programme. Some computers have a MSWORD symbol that will come up when your computer is on and you do not have to go to start – simply double click the left button of the mouse on the symbol.

The Microsoft word programme will appear on the screen.

There will be a blank screen called Document 1. Every thing you type is called a document. Above the blank screen there are various terms and signs you should know about.

- The first line has a list of titles called commands - File, Edit, View, etc

- The second and third lines are called the toolbar and have different blocks that you can use to give quicker commands to the computer.

- The fourth line [if there is one] shows your page margins – it is called the ruler.

The File title

Click on this and a box with different sections will appear. This is your file organiser and you use the first section:

- To start a new document (click on new) You can use the block with a folder on it on the toolbar to do this more quickly. Use your mouse to click on it.)

- To open an old document (click on open) and then click on the name of the document you want to open

- To close a document. The computer will ask you if you want to save it before you close it and then you click on Yes or No.

The next section is to do with saving documents.

If you press save, the document will be saved under its heading in the general folder called My Documents. You can do this with the block on the toolbar showing stiffy disk. Click on it with your mouse.

Save As allows you to save a document under a new name in the folder of your choice. When you click on Save as, a new box will open on screen. First go to the Save In square. It should say My Documents. In the block below yellow folders will appear if you have made them. (See Step 2 in Using MSWORD as an Office) Click on the folder you want to save the document in. Click on Open. Then check that you like the name of the document. If you like it press save. If you don't like it delete the file name and type a new name. Then click save.

If your document is an update of an old document but you want to save it as a new version click on Version in the Save box under file. Type in your comments and click Save. (I don't use this much as I just give the document a new date and use Save As to save it under a new name.)

The next section is to do with how the document looks (Page Set Up) and Print Preview and to print documents.

Page set up allows you to change the margins of the page so that you can get more (or less) typing on a page. If you click on Paper Size it allows you to change the page into Portrait (normal A4) or Landscape (sideways A4)

Print preview allows you to see what the document will look like on a printed page. You can also to this by using the block on the toolbar with a page and magnifying glass on it.

Print allows you to print the document if your computer is connected to a printer. You can also print quickly by using the block with a printer on your toolbar.

The next section allows you to Send your document either to another computer via email or to a fax machine. Your computer has to be set up for this. You can also email your document by using the block on the bottom toolbar with an envelope on it. Properties allows you to store information about your document.

The next section is a list of the last four documents you worked on. Clicking on the right file name is a quick way of opening the any of these documents.

The last section says Exit. If you click on this the MSWORD programme will shut down and you can return to Windows. If you have forgotten to save any documents the computer will ask you if you want to Save. Click on Yes or No. You can also exit or close down MSWORD by clicking on the X in the last square on the top right hand side of the screen.

The Edit title

This section allows you to change or edit your work.

The most useful tools in the list are Cut, Copy and Paste.

Cut: this allows you to delete a section but not to throw it away completely in case you need it later. Use your mouse and drag it over the section you want to delete. Then go to Edit. Click Cut. If you want to use it again you can add it in later or move it to another section. You use the Paste command to move the section to a new place. Take your cursor to where you want to place the section. Click on Edit. Click Paste and the cut section will be pasted or put in this new place. We call this Cutting and Pasting.

You can also Copy a section of your work and use it again. Highlight the section with your mouse. Click on edit. Click on Copy. Then take your cursor to the new place you want to put it. Click on Edit. Click Paste and the section will be repeated.

If you want to do it quickly, you can use the scissors symbol on your toolbar to cut, the two pages next to it to copy and the clipboard next to that, to paste.

5. Creation and operating of spreadsheet using MS-Excel.

Spreadsheets are made up of

- columns

- rows

- and their intersections are called cells

In each cell there may be the following types of data

- text (labels)

- number data (constants)

- formulas (mathematical equations that do all the work)

In a spreadsheet the COLUMN is defined as the vertical space that is going up and down the window. Letters are used to designate each COLUMN'S location.

In a spreadsheet the ROW is defined as the horizontal space that is going across the window. Numbers are used to designate each ROW'S location.

In a spreadsheet the CELL is defined as the space where a specified row and column intersect. Each CELL is assigned a name according to its COLUMN letter and ROW number.

6. Creation and editing power-point slides using MS- power point

Start PowerPoint by either of two methods:

1. Go to the Start menu. Choose Programs and then click on Microsoft PowerPoint.

2. Double-click the icon of any PowerPoint document. When you double-click a PowerPoint document, PowerPoint opens with the document already loaded.

A PowerPoint presentation consists of slides that can contain text, graphics, charts, and other data types. When you start PowerPoint, you can start with a blank presentation, or you can begin from a template or use the AutoContent Wizard.

The AutoContent Wizard is series of step-by-step instructions designed to assist you. The Template button accesses slide templates to help create a consistent, professional look for your slide presentation.

Choose Blank Presentation if you want to start with a clean slate. This method is recommended because it provides the most flexibility and lets you focus on content first rather than appearance.

After you choose Blank Presentation, select the layout of your slides from the New Slide dialog box. Choose from slides with titles and bullets, titles only, titles and clip art, and other options. For example, choose the Title Slide and click OK.

Save a Power Point Presentation

Changes you make to a document are not saved to disk until you issue a Save command. Saving is quick and easy, and you should save often to minimize the loss of your work. PowerPoint has two save commands, Save and Save As, that work similarly. Both commands are on the File menu.

Save

When you save a new presentation for the first time, PowerPoint displays a dialog box similar to the Open dialog box. Select the disk in which to save the presentation and specify a name for the file. When you save an existing document that you have been editing, the newly saved version replaces the older version.

Save As

This command displays a dialog box where you can choose a document name and destination folder or disk. Use the Save As command whenever you want to save a copy of the current document with a different name or in a different folder or disk. The newly saved copy becomes the active document

A presentation is normally saved as ³name.ppt² file type. However, PowerPoint Show with the extension of ³name.pps² is also a useful file type so that your file is able to run regardless of OS. You can also create your own template and save it as ³pot² file.

7. Creation and manipulation of database table using

SQL in MS-Access.

Microsoft Office Access, previously known as Microsoft Access, is a pseudo-relational database management system from Microsoft that combines the relational Microsoft Jet Database Engine with a graphical user interface and software-development tools. It is a member of the Microsoft Office suite of applications, included in the Professional and higher editions or sold separately. In mid-May 2010, the current version Microsoft Office Access 2010 was released by Microsoft in Office 2010; Microsoft Access 2007 was the prior version. Access stores data in its own format based on the Access Jet Database Engine. It can also import or link directly to data stored in other applications and databases[1]

Software developers and data architects can use Microsoft Access to develop application software, and "power users" can use it to build simple applications.[citation needed] Like other Office applications, Access is supported by Visual Basic for Applications, an object-oriented programming language that can reference a variety of objects including DAO (Data Access Objects), ActiveX Data Objects, and many other ActiveX components. Visual objects used in forms and reports expose their methods and properties in the VBA programming environment, and VBA code modules may declare and call Windows operating-system functions.

To use data definition statements, follow these steps:

1. Create a new query in a Access database.

2. On the **Query** menu, point to **SQL Specific**, and then click **Data Definition**.

   Note In Access 2007, click **Data Definition** in the **Query Type** group on the **Design** tab.

3. Enter your data definition statement in the **Data Definition Query** window, and then run the query by clicking **Run** on the **Query** menu.

QL DML and DDL

SQL can be divided into two parts: The Data Manipulation Language (DML) and the Data Definition Language (DDL).

The query and update commands form the DML part of SQL:

- SELECT - extracts data from a database
- UPDATE - updates data in a database
- DELETE - deletes data from a database

- INSERT INTO - inserts new data into a database

The DDL part of SQL permits database tables to be created or deleted. It also define indexes (keys), specify links between tables, and impose constraints between tables. The most important DDL statements in SQL are:

- CREATE DATABASE - creates a new database
- ALTER DATABASE - modifies a database
- CREATE TABLE - creates a new table
- ALTER TABLE - modifies a table
- DROP TABLE - deletes a table
- CREATE INDEX - creates an index (search key)
- DROP INDEX - deletes an index

8. WAP to illustrate Arithmetic expressions

```cpp
#include <iostream.h>
#include <conio.h>

void main()
{
clrscr();
int x;
float sinterest,principal,rate,time;
for(x=4;x>=0;x--)
{
cout << "Enter the principal, rate & time : " << endl;
cin>>principal>>rate>>time;
sinterest=(principal*rate*time)/100;
cout << "Principal = $" << principal << endl;
cout << "Rate = " << rate << "%" << endl;
cout << "Time = " << time << " years" << endl;
cout << "Simple Interest = $" << sinterest << endl;
}
```

```cpp
getch();

}
```

9. WAP to illustrate Arrays

```cpp
#include <iostream.h>

#include <conio.h>


void main()

{

clrscr();

int array[10],t;

for(int x=0;x<10;x++)

{

cout << "Enter Integer No. " << x+1 << " : " <<
endl;

cin>>array[x];

}

for (x=0;x<10;x++)

{

for(int y=0;y<9;y++)

{

if(array[y]>array[y+1])

{

t=array[y];

array[y]=array[y+1];

array[y+1]=t;

}

}

}

cout << "Array in ascending order is : ";

for (x=0;x<10;x++)
```

```cpp
cout << endl << array[x];
getch();
}
```

10. WAP to illustrate functions.

```cpp
#include <iostream>
int addition (int a, int b)
{
   int r;
   r=a+b;
   return (r);
}


int main ()
{
   int z;
   z = addition (5,3);
   cout << "The result is " << z;
   return 0;
}
```

11. WAP to illustrate constructor & Destructor.

```cpp
class String
{

public:

String() //constructor with no arguments
    :str(NULL),
    size(0)
{
```

```
}


String(int size) //constructor with one argument
    :str(NULL),
    size(size)


{

    str = new char[size];
}



~String() //destructor
{
    delete [] str;
};

private:

    char *str;


    int size;


}
```

12. WAP to illustrate Object and classes.

```
Class classname
{
   acess specifier:
   data member;
   member functions;
```

```
    acess specifier:
    data member;
    member functions;
};
```

Creation of object

```
class exforsys
{
    private:
    int x,y;
    public:
    void sum()
    {

        .........

          .........

    }
};


main()
{
    exforsys e1;
    ..............

    ..............

}
```

13. WAP to illustrate Operator overloading

```
#include <iostream.h>
class Exforsys
{
private:
int x;
int y;
```

```cpp
public:
Exforsys()                              //Constructor
{ x=0; y=0; }


void    getvalue(   )   //Member    Function    for
Inputting                                      Values

{
cout << "\n Enter value for x: ";
cin >> x;
cout << "\n Enter value for y: ";
cin>> y;
}


void  displayvalue(  )              //Member   Function
forOutputting Values
{
cout <<"value of x is: " << x <<"; value of y is:
"<<y
}
Exforsys operator +(Exforsys);
};


Exforsys Exforsys :: operator + (Exforsys e2)
//Binary  operator  overloading  for  +  operator
defined
{
int x1 = x+ e2.x;
int y1 = y+e2.y;
return Exforsys(x1,y1);
}
```

```cpp
void main( )

{
Exforsys e1,e2,e3;                //Objects e1, e2,
e3 created
cout<<\n"Enter value for Object e1:";

e1.getvalue( );

cout<<\n"Enter value for Object e2:";

e2.getvalue( );

e3= e1+ e2;                        //Binary Overloaded
operator used
cout<< "\nValue of e1 is:"<<e1.displayvalue();

cout<< "\nValue of e2 is:"<<e2.displayvalue();

cout<< "\nValue of e3 is:"<<e3.displayvalue();

}
```

14. WAP to illustrate Function overloading.

```cpp
#include <iostream>
using namespace std;

class arith {
public:
    void calc(int num1)

{
cout<<"Square of a given number: " <<num1*num1 <<
endl;
}

    void calc(int num1, int num2 )

{
cout<<"Product of two whole numbers: " <<num1*num
2 <<endl;
}
};


int main() //begin of main function
```

```cpp
{
    arith a;
    a.calc(5);
    a.calc(6,7);
}
```

15. WAP to illustrate Derived classes & Inheritance.

```cpp
#include <iostream>

class CRectangle {
    int width, height;
  public:
    void set_values (int, int);
    int area () {return (width * height);}
    friend CRectangle duplicate (CRectangle);
};

void CRectangle::set_values (int a, int b) {
  width = a;
  height = b;
}

CRectangle duplicate (CRectangle rectparam)
{
  CRectangle rectres;
  rectres.width = rectparam.width*2;
  rectres.height = rectparam.height*2;
  return (rectres);
}
int main () {
  CRectangle rect, rectb;
  rect.set_values (2,3);
  rectb = duplicate (rect);
  cout << rectb.area();
  return 0;
}
```

Inheritance Example:

```cpp
Class exforsys
{
public:
exforsys(void) { x=0; }
void f(int n1)
{
x= n1*5;
}

void output(void) { cout<<x; }

private:
int x;
};

class sample: public exforsys
{
public:
sample(void) { s1=0; }

void f1(int n1)
{
s1=n1*10;
}

void output(void)
{
exforsys::output();
cout << s1;
}

private:
int s1;
};
```

```
int main(void)
{
sample s;
s.f(10);
s.output();
s.f1(20);
s.output();
}
```

The output of the above program is

```
50
200
```